Rousseau Between Nature and Culture

Culture & Conflict

Edited by
Isabel Capeloa Gil and Catherine Nesci

Editorial Board
Arjun Appadurai · Claudia Benthien · Elisabeth Bronfen · Joyce Goggin
Lawrence Grossberg · Andreas Huyssen · Ansgar Nünning · Naomi Segal
Márcio Seligmann-Silva · António Sousa Ribeiro · Roberto Vecchi
Samuel Weber · Liliane Weissberg · Christoph Wulf

Volume 8

Rousseau Between Nature and Culture

Philosophy, Literature, and Politics

Edited by
Anne Deneys-Tunney and Yves Charles Zarka

In collaboration with
Karen Santos da Silva

DE GRUYTER

ISBN 978-3-11-076457-4
e-ISBN (PDF) 978-3-11-045718-6
e-ISBN (EPUB) 978-3-11-045667-7
ISSN 2194-7104

Library of Congress Cataloging-in-Publication Data
A CIP catalog record for this book has been applied for at the Library of Congress.

Bibliographic information published by the Deutsche Nationalbibliothek
The Deutsche Nationalbibliothek lists this publication in the Deutsche Nationalbibliografie;
detailed bibliographic data are available on the Internet at http://dnb.dnb.de.

© 2021 Walter de Gruyter GmbH, Berlin/Boston
This volume is text- and page-identical with the hardback published in 2016.
Cover image: © Stephen Tunney
Printing and binding: CPI books GmbH, Leck

♾ Printed on acid-free paper
Printed in Germany

www.degruyter.com

Table of Contents

Editions and Abbreviations —— VII

Anne Deneys-Tunney, Yves Charles Zarka
Introduction —— 1

I Technology: Between Nature and Anti-Nature

Pierre Guenancia
Rousseau, Lévi-Strauss's "Master" —— 11

Philip Knee
Rousseau and the Authority of Nature —— 27

Stéphane Lojkine
Nature as Blind Space —— 45

Anne Deneys-Tunney
Rousseau and Technology: The Invention of a New Ecological Paradigm —— 57

Masano Yamashita
Rousseau and "The Mechanical Life" —— 67

II Politics and Ethics: Beyond the Nature/Culture Polarity

Paul Audi
Rousseau's Ethical Freedom —— 85

Pasquale Pasquino
Remarks on Rousseau's Dictatorship: Between Machiavelli and Carl Schmitt —— 101

Simon Critchley
Politics and Religion in the Social Contract —— 111

Mira Morgenstern
Alienation and Freedom: Rousseau and Transcending Nature/Culture Dualism —— 119

Yves Charles Zarka
Rousseau and the Sovereignty of the People —— 137

III The Philosophical Novel: Culture as Nature's Supplement

Christophe Martin
Nature and Supplementation in *Julie ou La Nouvelle Héloïse* —— 153

Lucien Nouis
Recomposing the Diffracted Text: Rousseau and the Metaphor of the Book of Nature —— 167

Tanguy L'Aminot
Nature, Culture, and the Social Contract: Emile's point of view —— 179

Contributors —— 197

Index —— 201

Editions and Abbreviations

Unless otherwise indicated, the references to Rousseau's works and correspondence are from the following standard editions and will be indicated right after references or quotations in the body of the chapters, rather than in footnotes.
Rousseau, Jean-Jacques. *Œuvres complètes*. Gen. Eds. Bernard Gagnebin and Marcel Raymond. 5 vols. Paris: Gallimard, "Bibliothèque de la Pléiade," 1959–1995.
The title will be abridged throughout as *OC* followed by the volume number and the pagination in Arabic numerals.
Rousseau, Jean-Jacques. *The Collected Writings of Rousseau*. Gen. Eds. Roger D. Masters and Christopher Kelly. 13 vols. Hanover: UP of New England, 1990–2010.
The title will be abridged throughout as *CW* followed by the volume number and the pagination in Arabic numerals.
Correspondance complète de Jean-Jacques Rousseau. Ed. Ralph A. Leigh. 52 vols. Geneva: Institut et Musée Voltaire; Madison: U of Wisconsin P; Oxford: Voltaire Foundation, 1965–1998.
The title will be abridged throughout as *CC* followed by the volume number and the pagination in Arabic numerals.
In addition, the following acronyms will be used to refer to Rousseau's works:

C: for *Les Confessions (OC 1); The Confessions and Correspondence, Including the Letters to Malesherbes (CW 5)*.
CS: for *Du Contrat Social (OC 3); Social Contract (CW 4)*.
D: for *Rousseau Juge de Jean Jaques (OC 1); Rousseau, Judge of Jean-Jacques: Dialogues (CW 1)*.
DSA: for *Discours sur les sciences et les arts (OC 3); Discourse on the Sciences and Arts (CW 2)*.
E: for *Émile, ou De l'éducation (OC 4) ; Emile or On Education (CW 13)*.
EOL: for *Essai sur l'origine des langues (OC 5); Essay on the Origin of Languages (CW 7)*.
Julie: for *Julie, ou La Nouvelle Héloïse (OC 2); Julie or the New Heloise (CW 6)*.
LA: for *Lettre à d'Alembert (OC 5); Letter to d'Alembert (CW 10)*.
LF: for *Lettre à M. de Franquières (OC 4); Letter to Franquières (CW 8)*.
LM : for *Lettres morales (OC 4)*.
R: for *Les Rêveries du promeneur solitaire (OC 1); The Reveries of the Solitary Walker (CW 8)*.
SD: for *Discours sur l'origine et les fondements de l'inégalité parmi les hommes [Second discours] (OC 3); Discourse on the Origins of Inequality [Second Discourse] (CW 3)*.

When citations and paginations refer to both editions, references to the English editions will follow the pagination in *OC* and will be given in brackets, such as: *Second Discourse* (*OC* 3: 122 [*CW* 3: 12]), or (*SD* 122 [12]).

Anne Deneys-Tunney,
Yves Charles Zarka
Introduction

> Like the statue of Glaucus, which time, sea, and storms had
> so disfigured that it looked less like a God than a wild Beast,
> the human soul, altered in the bosom of society by a
> thousand continually renewed causes, by the acquisition
> of a mass of knowledge and errors, by changes that
> occurred in the constitution of Bodies, and by the
> continual impact of the passions, has, so to speak,
> changed its appearance to the point of being nearly
> unrecognizable; and, instead of a being acting always
> by fixed and invariable Principles, instead of that
> Heavenly and majestic simplicity with which its
> Authors had endowed it, one no longer finds anything
> except the deformed contrast of passion which
> believes it reasons and understanding in delirium.
> (Rousseau, Preface,
> *Second Discourse* (122 [12]))

It is of course no accident that we begin the volume with this quotation. It underscores what is most at stake in the relationship between nature and culture, not only in Rousseau's thought, which is to be expected, but for this day and age as well. Indeed, it contains Rousseau's characteristic imprint about loss, degradation, confusion, even the degeneration from natural man to cultural man. But if we put aside this value judgment – though we would have to, in many respects, counterbalance it with what Rousseau says elsewhere – this metaphor of Glaucus's statue, whose meaning will subsequently be developed in the preface to the *Discourse on the Origins of Inequality* (or *Second Discourse*), says what is most essential about the contemporary confusion regarding the relationship between nature and culture. We will return to this further down.

The relationship between nature and culture is today one of the major concerns at the heart of the humanities and social sciences. If thinking this rapport as a simple duality no longer seems substantiated in light of the effects of human action over nature, the earth's vulnerability, and the status of other living species, particularly animals, how are we to redefine this relationship?

The originality of this project consists in a return to Jean-Jacques Rousseau's work in order to find, if not answers, at least some enlightening interpretations and directions likely to guide today's research. This project is thus twofold: a historical examination of Rousseau's works and ideas, and an illustration of the ways in which these texts and ideas shed light on contemporary problems within the humanities and social sciences.

Rousseau has indeed placed the relationship between nature and culture at the center of his philosophical thought (*Discourse on the Origins of Inequality, Essay on the Origin of Languages, The Social Contract*, etc.) as well as of his literary texts *(Emile, Reveries of The Solitary Walker,* etc.*).* In contrast to Enlightenment optimism, in which his thought nevertheless participated, Rousseau has shown that the development of culture and of technical progress – the appropriation of the earth, the disappearance of simple ways of life (such as that of the Hottentots living on hunting and fishing), and the social inequalities that have resulted from such changes – should not be considered from the unilateral perspective of a narrative of human progress, featuring subjects seeking rights and freedom throughout history. Rousseau saw the destructive aspects of men's actions and desires when they become unilateral, having no other concern than the satisfaction of *amour-propre* (self-love): such unilateralism conceals a disfiguration, even a destruction of the nature within and outside of us. This lesson is extremely important, for does such a diagnosis not resonate with the one we have come to make, nowadays, on the destruction of nature by man-made factors and environmental disasters?

Does this mean that the paradigm of nature has been lost? Does it mean that man himself is lost by way of the impossibility to go backwards, back to the time of a now lost "pure" nature? The answer to these questions can only be no, because Rousseau also developed a positive outlook on culture. As regards to politics, shouldn't the social contract help man transition from a savage form of freedom – close to instinct – to a moral and civil freedom that raises human beings to the level of responsibility? Doesn't Emile provide the way to an education guided by nature? It is clear that in both his philosophical and his literary works, Rousseau's answers are far from unequivocal. Our belief is that we still have much to learn from Rousseau. The considerable importance granted to him by Claude Lévi-Strauss on the one hand, and Jacques Derrida on the other, despite their considerable differences, testifies to how topical Rousseau remains in contemporary thought.

As we will see, the totality of Rousseau's œuvre helps us think through the complex relationships between nature and culture. Nature is both a universal substratum, and the foundation from which (and at times against which) culture establishes itself. Modern culture, says Rousseau, has separated or emancipated itself from this foundation, and has degenerated into a society of luxury, inequality, and moral corruption. Furthermore, Rousseau's work strives to restructure nature, within the political, moral, and anthropological context of social man. Rousseau's genius is to have first defined the principles of this restructuring: on the level of pedagogy in *Emile*; on the level of anthropology in the *Second Discourse*; at the political level in *The Social Contract*; at the level of autobiography in *The Confessions*; at the aesthetic level in *Letter to d'Alembert*.

In this day and age, when references to nature seem to vanish while the notion of culture is multiplying so as to become uncertain, a return to Rousseau seems to us a necessity in order to arrive at a different understanding of the relationship between nature and culture. The implicit position in all of the texts gathered in this volume is to show that such a return to the work of the Genevan philosopher provides parts of a response and may also help understand our current situation. Rousseau is without a doubt the eighteenth-century philosopher who is closest to us, our contemporary in a manner of speaking. He had seen the dark side of the Enlightenment, but he had also shown the paths leading out of it. Can man find within himself the resources capable of overcoming the decadence, the sickness, the corruption, and the inequalities that he has himself created? Such was for Rousseau the central problem. It is also ours.

Let us return to the preface of the *Second Discourse* and examine what it says, especially in relation to our own situation today. Four points can be made.

First, natural, social, and political history has changed humans, as much in the constitution of their bodies as in their behaviors and thoughts, such that we can no longer know what in them comes from nature and what comes from culture. All considerations on natural man, or on what is natural within man, can only be the fruit of conjecture: "for it is no light undertaking to separate what is original from what is artificial in the present Nature of man, and to know correctly a state which no longer exists, which perhaps never existed, which probably never will exist [...]" (*SD* 123 [13]). There is not a single aspect of individual or social life today that one can call purely natural. There is nothing archaic within us, nothing so obviously biological or organic that has not been modified by culture; birth, growth, death, but also sexuality, parenting, illness and health, food, etc., are an inseparable mix of nature and culture. Might we believe that experiments could find a solution out of this maze? Illusion: neither the greatest philosophers nor the most powerful sovereigns could do it, says Rousseau, to which we could add, nor could the physical, chemical, or biological sciences, since the cultural has changed the organic, and continues to do so.

Is that to say that the paradigm of nature, and particularly of human nature, is definitely lost? In some ways the answer is yes, but in others no. Indeed, pure nature, Rousseau said so himself, has perhaps never existed, and never will. Even if we could conceive of a natural man before a cultural one, one must completely lose hope of finding him again. However we may want to turn back time, we can only progress forward. Thinking that we are returning to a point of origin, we in fact just drift further and further from it. Pure nature is no longer, and it can only exist in our thought. But does this mean that examining nature, and more specifically human nature, is a vain approach? Must we today acknowledge the obsoleteness of the Rousseauian project of returning to natural man in order to elucidate today's human condition and understand the differences that emerged in cultures, in mores, in the conditions (of inequality), and so on?

Such a question leads us to make another point. What is Rousseau's objective? This is his answer: "This same study of original man, of his true needs, and of the fundamental principles of his duties, is also the only good means one could use to remove those crowds of difficulties which present themselves concerning the origin of moral inequality, the true foundations of the Body politic, the reciprocal rights of its members, and a thousand similar questions as important as they are ill explained." (*SD* 15 [126]) In other words, if we were to lose any and all possibilities to discern what a human being is (or a natural man), independently from the differences introduced by history and the development of culture, we would no longer have the slightest criteria to distinguish, in today's existence, what is good from what is bad, what is legitimate from what is not, what is just from what is unjust. We would be forced to accept what is, the historical present as we are experiencing it, to consider fact as right, and thus to validate what is. In what name could we judge that inequality, oppression, violence, and predation, are unacceptable? What would this value judgment be based on? On the equality of men, you might answer? But from where does one draw this equality? Where does one actually observe it? Nowhere! And yet this equality is what leads us to believe that inequality and oppression are unacceptable. One is therefore forced to say something about human nature (that is, about man as man). That is the meaning of Rousseau's position: "It is easy to see that one must seek in these successive changes of the human constitution the first origin of the differences distinguishing men – who, by common avowal, are naturally as equal among themselves as were the animals of each species [...]" (12 [123]). To conceive of human nature is, indeed for Rousseau, to conceive of man before any cultural modification, but it also and more essentially means for him, and for us, that we must attempt to determine the principles and the norms according to which we could judge what makes our current condition. Kant, who was, if there were any, a great reader of Rousseau, understood the necessity for a normative foundation for the moral, juridical and political dimensions of our existence.

"Leaving aside therefore all scientific books which teach us only to see men as they have made themselves, and meditating on the first and simplest operations of the human Soul, I believe I perceive in it two principles anterior to reason, of which one interests us ardently in our well-being and our self-preservation, and the other inspires in us a natural repugnance to see any sensitive Being perish or suffer, principally those like ourselves." (*SD* 14–15 [125–126]) Love of the self (and not *amour-propre*) and pity are the simplest operations of human nature, and they predate the constitution of diversity at all levels: of peoples, customs, governments, and cultures. But what assurance do we have that those two mechanisms are common to humanity in its entirety? How do we know that they do not belong to a specific culture? Quite simply from the fact that these mechanisms have no cultural dimensions, they are pre-cultural, or better, infra-cultural; they are not even predicated on sociability. Furthermore, they do not only characterize human nature, but also animals. This is a serious indication that they cannot be produced by culture: if every living being did not have within it a principle of self-preservation, we cannot conceive how not only man, but all living species in general, would not quickly become extinct. As for pity, it is not a complex emotion requiring thought, but rather a spontaneous attitude that allows us to feel within us, and not as a purely exterior event, what happens to another being, independently from whether or not it belongs to the human species: "It is very certain, therefore, that pity is a natural feeling which, moderating in each individual the activity of love of oneself, contributes to the mutual preservation of the entire species." (37 [157]) Here again, this is hardly an aptitude unique to humans: it can also be found in animals, as both reason and experience shows us.

When searching for the nature of man, we must look to other qualities, which, for Rousseau, are the concepts of perfectibility and freedom. But here again, these qualities are hardly arbitrary: they are the minimal resources necessary to understand the becoming of the human species, and especially the diversity of languages, cultures, and social structures.

"But as [animals] share something of our Nature through the sensitivity with which they are endowed, one will judge that they too ought to participate in natural right, and that man is subject to some sort of duties toward them" (*SD* 15 [16]). Humans share with animals a sensitive nature as well as the two mechanisms mentioned above. As a result, there is no radical rupture between human and animal. True, humans will emancipate themselves from their animal condition, and circumstances will bring them to develop faculties, passions, and aptitudes that we do not see in animals. However, that does not mean that humans no longer have a community with them: man's sensitive nature is what not only brings him closer to animals, but further awakens the idea that he has an obligation towards them. Here Rousseau asserts the irreducible entrenchment of humans in the living world, and the responsibility that they have with respect to it.

One can also see that, while Rousseau pushes the confusion with regard to the relationship between nature and culture to its furthest limit, such that it is impossible to decide on any point between what is natural and what is artificial, he nevertheless shows that it is possible to think about nature as being below culture, by a mechanism of the mind that is by no means a game, but that corresponds to the needs of our reason: that of discovering the normative principles according to which we will be able to judge our condition today. It would naturally be possible to reject this allusion to a minimal form of nature, below culture, below cultures we should say, but if we do, we have to assume the consequences until the end, and resign ourselves to what is, without critical resources, alternatives, without other possibilities.

Jacques Derrida's last chapter in *Writing and Difference*, "Structure, Sign, and Play in the Discourse of the Human Sciences," is very rich for us. This text helps to think critically through the duality or structure of nature/culture, from Rousseau to contemporary thought. It is first the very notion of structure that is put into question, with its corollary, the invariant center. Even if at the beginning of the chapter, Derrida challenges the notion of structure itself without reference to Rousseau or to the opposition between nature and culture, he eventually does both: "The function of this center was not only to orient, balance, and organize the structure – one cannot in fact conceive of an unorganized structure – but above all to make sure that the organizing principle of the structure would limit what we might call the *play* of the structure. By orienting and organizing the coherence of the system, the center of a structure permits the play of its elements inside the total form." (Derrida 1981: 278–279) The center is incarnated in Rousseau by nature, or the origin, an invariant center that is defined in its difference or supplementarity in relationship to its other, culture, that is, everything that comes after it or constitutes a deviation from it. This center being immutable, Rousseau always speaks in the singular about the "state of nature," even if Rousseau immediately subjects it to a process of deviation, or a shift in meaning, since it moves from being a historical state that came before culture, to an immanent and universal presence. In the Preface to the *Discourse on the Origin of Inequality* we thus move from a diachronic or historical model, to a self-presence, what Rousseau calls "the voice of nature" in the definition of the structure nature/culture. Derrida comments on the plasticity of the notion of center when we reflect upon the notion of structure, as a center that is both immutable ("it is the point at which the substitution of contents, elements, or terms is no longer possible" [279]) and also from which history, in its subsequent developments, will garner meaning:

[...] on the basis of what we call the center (and which, because it can be either inside or outside, can also indifferently be called the origin or end, *archē* or *telos*), repetitions, substitutions, transformations, and permutations are always *taken* from a history of meaning [*sens*] – that is, in a word, a history – whose origin may always be reawakened or whose end may always be anticipated in the form of presence. (279)

Nature will thus be the name given in Rousseau to presence: "the names [...] have always designated an invariable presence [...]" (279). To this opposition between nature and culture in the discourses of modern anthropology, Derrida dedicates a long passage that ends with the idea that the incest taboo is at the intersection of structure's two poles: nature and culture. The prohibition of incest is both universal and therefore natural, and at the same time the foundation of instituted culture. Derrida remarks that "Lévi-Strauss simultaneously has experienced the necessity of utilizing this opposition and the impossibility of accepting it" (283). Similarly, we will see Rousseau both place this opposition at the heart of his system, and move it constantly by a series of natural catastrophes and intermediary states that attest to the fact that culture has always been present at the heart of nature, and inversely, that the traces or palimpsests of nature are always present, inhabit culture. Derrida writes of the "scandal" at which Lévi-Strauss arrives, scandal or challenge on which Rousseau also stumbles: "Lévi-Strauss, who has begun by giving credence to these concepts, encounters what he calls a *scandal*, that is to say, something which no longer tolerates the nature/culture opposition he has accepted, something which *simultaneously* seems to require the predicates of nature and of culture" (283).

In this book, we will see how and why Rousseau, before Lévi-Strauss, founded this opposition in order to simultaneously deconstruct it. Rousseau starts by writing that he has set aside "all of the facts," both to allow the structure of the nature/culture opposition to be perfectly readable, and also to say that this opposition is the product of a certain type of discourse, a philosophical discourse, at the intersection of history and anthropology, and all of the plays and deviations that this conjuncture will bring about. If nature has become for Rousseau nothing but a barely audible voice at the heart of our societies, he has made himself its incarnation. He utters it, or it speaks in him. Against the preceding metaphysical discourse, Rousseau founds the opposition between nature and culture, while at the same time questioning and deconstructing it. The goal of this book is to explore how.

Translated by Karen Santos Da Silva

Work Cited

Derrida, Jacques. "Structure, Sign, and Play in the Discourse of the Human Sciences." *Writing and Difference*. Trans. Alan Bass. London: Routledge and Kegan Paul, 1981. 278–293.

Rousseau, Jean-Jacques. *Œuvres complètes*. Gen. Eds. Bernard Gagnebin and Marcel Raymond. 5 vols. Paris: Gallimard, "Bibliothèque de la Pléiade," 1959–1995.

Rousseau, Jean-Jacques. *The Collected Writings of Rousseau*. Gen. Eds. Roger D. Masters and Christopher Kelly. 13 vols. Hanover: UP of New England, 1990–2010.

Rousseau, Jean-Jacques. *Discours sur l'origine et les fondements de l'inégalité parmi les hommes*. Ed. Jean Starobinski. *Œuvres complètes*, vol. 3. 1964. [SD]

Rousseau, Jean-Jacques. *Discourse on the Origins of Inequality (Second Discourse), Polemic, and Political Economy*. Eds. Roger D. Masters and Christopher Kelly. Trans. Judith R. Bush et al. *Collected Writings*, vol. 3. 1992. [SD]

I **Technology: Between Nature and Anti-Nature**

Pierre Guenancia
Rousseau, Lévi-Strauss's "Master"

Claude Lévi-Strauss is "Rousseau's modern disciple," so designated by Jacques Derrida (1967) in his famous essay "La violence de la lettre: de Lévi-Strauss à Rousseau" (154). Indeed, Rousseau is the only philosopher both constantly present and quoted in Lévi-Strauss' work, and also the only one to be repeatedly praised.[1] This despite the fact that philosophy itself is for the most part criticized, and Lévi-Strauss seems concerned with distancing himself from it, leaving it behind, so as to enter the reliable path of anthropological and ethnological science. For in addition to his personal inclination for him, Rousseau is also for Lévi-Strauss the one who, having turned away from a philosophy trapped by the ego and its pseudo certainty, opened the royal path to social science, in the same way that Marx and Durkheim, Saussure and Freud did, by seeking what structuralism wanted to accomplish: "reveal to consciousness *an object other than itself*," as Lévi-Strauss writes in the finale of *The Naked Man*:

> What structuralism tries to accomplish in the wake of Rousseau, Marx, Durkheim, Saussure and Freud, is to reveal to consciousness an *object other than itself*; and therefore to put it in the same position with regard to human phenomena as that of the natural and physical sciences, and which, as they have demonstrated, alone allows knowledge to develop.[2]

In Lévi-Strauss's famous 1962 lecture,[3] Jean-Jacques Rousseau is considered the "founder of the human sciences" and not as a philosopher belonging to the family of philosophers. One wonders whether Lévi-Strauss does not see in Rousseau's fate an analogy to his own fate as a philosopher who rejected academic philosophy to create a new science, an anthropology. The true science of man asks that the observer directs his gaze in the distance, that he does not, at least in the beginning, seek to know himself, according to the most ancient saying in philosophy: if one wants to study man, one must look from afar. This is the

---

[1] See the vibrant homage that Lévi-Strauss gives of Rousseau in a Rousseauist style that is completely unusual to him: "Rousseau, our master, our brother [...] to whom every page of this book could have been dedicated, had the homage been worthy of his great memory" (*TT* 1955: 421).
[2] *L'homme nu* (1971: 563); *The Naked Man* (1981: 629). See also *Tristes Tropiques:* "Following Rousseau [...] Marx taught that social science is no more constructed at the level of events than physics is built from sense data" (49). All translations are by the translator of the article unless otherwise indicated.
[3] Included in chapter II of *Anthropologie structurale deux* (*AS II* 1973: 45–et seq.).

famous sentence from *Essay on the Origin of Languages* that Lévi-Strauss adopts as the defining idea of his own enterprise.[4] Rousseau plays as it were the role of the totem animal in the tribe that has constituted itself through this reference and in this lineage. The presence of Rousseau in Lévi-Strauss's work is more in the margins, in the commentary that the work offers of itself, rather than at its center, in the properly scientific part of the work, even if Lévi-Strauss seizes the moment while studying a myth to pay tribute to the "profound and unjustly criticized views" of *The Discourse on the Origins of Inequality*.[5] If Rousseau plays in a sense the role of a totem animal in Lévi-Strauss's work, it is because he has the totem's double function: that of being an ancestor, and that of being a protector. Ancestor, because he is the founder of the human sciences; protector, because Lévi-Strauss sometimes uses his elementary and rustic philosophy – more a patch-job than a systematic construction – as an antidote or a lightning rod against contemporary philosophy, against Sartrean existentialism, born out of the Cartesian cogito whose death Rousseau sounded the knell by deposing the "I" from its sovereign position.

In this essay, we return to and comment on Rousseau's dual function as precursor and protector, which refers back to two distinct moments in Lévi-Strauss's work: one that corresponds to the writing of *Tristes Tropiques* (1955), and the other that corresponds to a variety of texts written in a single year, 1962, in which the aim of Rousseau's thought is explicitly opposed to that of Sartre's. These texts are *The Savage Mind – La Pensée sauvage*, the last chapter of which is a refutation of Sartre's *Critique of Dialectical Reason* – and *Totemism – Le Totémisme aujourd'hui*, in the final pages of which Lévi-Strauss has a lengthy reference first to Bergson and then to Rousseau, the latter because of having better understood the essence of totemism before the ethnologists who studied it. It is therefore not only Rousseau and Lévi-Strauss that are present in this project, but also and obliquely Sartre, the three thinkers thus positioned in a triangle that is not historical, but structural, i.e. it can be looked at from all angles. My argument is that the opposition between Lévi-Strauss and Sartre (the totem animal of the philosopher's tribe out of which Lévi-Strauss soon escaped) in part explains how Rousseau is not only for Lévi-Strauss the one who made a scientific anthropology possible by turning its back on dominant philosophy, but also the one whose thought helps us, today even more than during his time, criticize and reject the most engrained presuppositions of our civilization: its sense

---

4 "When one wishes to study men, one has to look close by; but in order to study man, one has to learn to cast one's eyes far off; first one has to observe the differences in order to discover the properties." (Rousseau, *Essai sur l'origine des langues* 1970: 89; 1998: 305).
5 *Du miel aux cendres* [*From Honey to Ashes*], *Mythologiques [2]* (1966: 260).

of superiority over those cultures diminished to the rank of primitive cultures, people without a history, societies without writing. Reversing these disparaging denominations, Lévi-Strauss takes it upon himself to challenge European civilization and show that societies without history ("cold") intend it to be so; that writing is linked to power; and that primitive thought is not a primitive mentality, but a savage mind whose logic Rousseau – through his reflections on botany, music, and on the origins of language – had brilliantly glimpsed before anyone else. Against all forms of dualism, Rousseau is capable, according to Lévi-Strauss, of elevating us to a unified vision, differentiating but not ranking, man and men, nature and culture, self and other.[6]

First, we will follow the thoughts about Rousseau in *Tristes Tropiques* that refer to the problem of the foundation of societies, as well as to the problem of history and of writing (1955: 137), seeking these "almost imperceptible stages of man's beginnings" out of which Rousseau sought to create a thought-experience in the *Second Discourse*, and for which Lévi-Strauss went "to the ends of the earth" (339). Second, we will examine what theoretical elements Lévi-Strauss lifts from Rousseau, "founder of the human sciences," in order to oppose them to the philosophical cogito that Sartre has extended to apply to the historical universe and which, for Lévi-Strauss, is based on man's dominion over nature (Descartes), on a dog-eat-dog world (Hobbes), and on the violence of history (Sartre).

1 Rousseau, "the most ethnographic of philosophers"

On two occasions, towards the end of *Tristes Tropiques* (*TT* 336, 421), Lévi-Strauss pays homage to Rousseau based on the following: first of all, he is the first philosopher to have understood the fundamental and originating nature of consent in society; second, he shows the necessity of the process that goes from "the ruins left behind by *The Discourse on the Origins of Inequality* (the "first treatise on general anthropology," Lévi-Strauss writes in *Totemism* 146) to the broad construction that is *The Social Contract*" (*TT* 421). References to Rousseau lead to three points of convergence between the two texts, which allow Lévi-Strauss to perform an anthropological revival of Rousseau.

---

6 "Lévi-Strauss understands better than anyone the ambiguity of his own moral universe, in many ways comparable to Rousseau's ambiguity," Aron writes fittingly in *Histoire et politique* (1985: 476).

1.1 The state of nature

Contrary to the current image of this concept, Rousseau did not idealize the state of nature. He did not uphold the good savage as a pure form of humanity to foil social man's corruption. He sought to reveal, through a method of sociological variation – before its time – rather than through deduction, "the unshakable foundation of human society" (*TT* 422). Rousseau, having understood that this foundation could not be found in our civilized societies that are, among all societies, the furthest from such an origin, constructed a pure model of human society, easier to observe in primitive societies than in our own, in the same way that the permanent forms of human thought, the constants of the human mind, are more perceptible in the activities of savage thinking than in those of domesticated or scientific thought. "The study of these savages leads to something other than the revelation of a Utopian state of nature or the discovery of the perfect society in the depths of the forest; it helps to build a *theoretical model* of human society, which does not correspond to any observable reality, but with the aid of which we may succeed in distinguishing between [in Rousseau's words] 'what is primordial and what is artificial in man's present state [...]'" (*TT* 423).[7] What Lévi-Strauss finds in Rousseau is his quest, ethnological in nature but transcendental in ambition, to find the difference between the originary and the artificial, the given and the constructed, or more generally, between what is immanent to society (or to thought) and what transcends it. Given that the state of nature is a theoretical model and not an historical era, it is important to find its traces wherever there are societies, in the same way that one should recognize in certain forms of rational or domesticated thought the activities of a savage mind that are immanent to the activities of the human mind such as it is.

Rousseau is the only philosopher who, during the Enlightenment, confronted the idea (or the myth) of progress and of history with the opposing idea of the decadence or degradation of complex social forms. These forms are themselves opposed to the simple and permanent form of a society that comes from nature as it were, and allows us to glimpse, in vivo, the principle that separates life in the state of nature from social life.[8] At the other end of the world among the

---

[7] See also: "Marx was the first to systematically use the method of models in the social sciences. All of *Capital*, for example, is a model constructed in a laboratory that the author manipulates in order to then confront the results with observable facts." (*De près et de loin*, 151–152)
[8] "Natural man is neither anterior nor exterior to society. It is up to us to rediscover his form, which is immanent to the social state outside of which the human condition is inconceivable." (*TT* 423)

Nambikwara, Lévi-Strauss, after Rousseau, went to experience first-hand a concrete transition from nature to culture, and witnessed as it were the "almost imperceptible progress of beginnings" in a nuclear form of social and political organization, which will only decline following the increase of its own power and the proliferation of ties of enslavement among men. Rousseau had sought out, in the new and original form of the State, a reliable machine of production ("cold") shielded from the accidents that lead to the dissolution of the social body in the atomism of particular interests, a kind of machine capable of pushing back against history ("hot"). What Lévi-Strauss finds in these societies on the margins of world history, at the ends of the earth, are immemorial forms of power that rely on consent and unanimity. These closed, precarious societies, whose limits are invisible, are rudimentary as concerns culture, but more human than any of those that we know.

1.2 "Primitive democracy" (The foundation of power)

The ethnographic quest fills the gap between the ruins of the *Second Discourse* and the expansive construct of *The Social Contract*, texts that Lévi-Strauss does not consider to be in opposition. What the Nambikwara tribe, considered an elementary social structure, taught Lévi-Strauss regarding the origin and function of power, is that the foundation of social life, and even more so for societies considered primitive, is consent: "Consent is at the basis of power, and it is also consent that maintains its legitimacy" (TT 331). With this necessary condition, social man separates from nature, and it is a true rupture, much like the one that the prohibition of incest establishes within the order of exchanges. The role of chief in these societies has nothing to do with the figure of the father. The social structure isn't derived from the structure of the family. There must be a founding act for a man to be chosen as the one to exert power over the others, much in the same way that there must be an absolute ban on incest for there to be any exchange or any true form of social life. "At the origin of the most rudimentary forms of power, we have discovered a decisive approach that introduces a new element as concerns biological relationships: this approach is consent. Consent is both at the heart of, and the limit to, power" (TT 336).

Lévi-Strauss thus relies on Rousseau to counter an evolutionary sociology and obtain the principle that is immanent to all social life that brings together societies otherwise far-removed from each other in time and space, whatever the degree of complexity they have reached. In Rousseau's mind (preferring to be a man of a paradox rather than a man of prejudice), Lévi-Strauss sees in these primitive societies, and even in their most rudimentary forms, the purest political model, a democracy truer than ours (though proud of it we may be). In his *Inaugural Lesson to the College de France* (1960), Lévi-Strauss returns to this aspect of primitive societies that incarnate more clearly than ours the social contract given to us by Rousseau in his pure theoretical model, that of "a political life founded on consent, allowing no other decision than those made unanimously, seemingly conceived to exclude the driving force behind a collective life based on differential relationships between power and opposition, majority and minority, exploiters and exploited" (*AS2* 40).[9] But this founding act does not occur once and for all at the solemn moment when men assemble and produce a pact of association, "a moral and collective body," as Rousseau calls it in his famous chapter on the social pact (*The Social Contract* Book i, chap. vi). Or rather: this "body" is reproduced in every instant of social life, without which this social life could not be maintained for an instant. Lévi-Strauss in *Tristes Tropiques* says to have experienced this kind of continuous creation of society in the tribes and groups with which he spent time and in which tyrants do not stay chiefs for long. Instead, chiefs continually exercise their power by relying on the consent of their subjects in a much more direct and visible way than in our societies. But Lévi-Strauss, in interpreting and recovering Rousseau's thought, blunts the edge of the political philosophy contained in *The Social Contract* by presenting consent, or the rule of unanimity, as a fact arrived at through sociological observation and not as the test to which all forms of social organization should be submitted to in order to determine their legitimacy – and thus by turning the contract into a structure that is barely more explicit than potlatch: "Potlach is in other words nothing but a continued social contract. Rousseau's social contract determines the social order once and for all. Potlach determines it incessantly" (Davy 1922: 148–149). This is why Lévi-Strauss sees in the notion of contract (as opposed to that of a state of nature) a primitive social fact rather than a concept produced by reason independently of any historical or ethnographical consideration. Wouldn't such a reading (see the following quotation) reduce, or even abolish, the crucial difference for Rousseau – as for Kant – between the *is* and the *ought?*

> Rousseau and his contemporaries displayed profound sociological intuition in grasping the fact that cultural attitudes and features such as "the contract" and "consent" are not sec-

---

[9] Much later, Lévi-Strauss will return to the same idea, using the same terms: "Rousseau, in *The Social Contract* [...] formulated the most profound idea – as well as the idea the most apt to being generalized, in other words, verified on a large number of societies – of what could be the political organization, and even the theoretical conditions of any possible political organization." (*Entretiens avec Claude Lévi-Strauss* 1961: 42–43).

ondary creations [...]: they are the basic material of social life, and it is impossible to imagine any form of political organization in which they would not be present. (*TT* 337)

By thus making Rousseau into the most ethnographic of the philosophers, Lévi-Strauss who is himself the most philosophic of the ethnographers, proceeds to harness the philosophical heritage of the philosopher for the profit of ethnography and sociology, of which, above being among the great philosophers of modern political thought, he is the founder.

1.3 The problem of history

Cold societies are those that always maintain themselves at the same temperature – low, because they do not undergo those changes that revolutionize societies that live in history, or rather in the future. Of these societies, we can say that all of their effort aims to persevere in their being, or to maintain the same state of being, integrating events and historical accidents in a temporality marked by the recurrence of events. Decadence for these societies would be entering into a process that would distance them from mechanical equilibrium and thermal constancy. Other societies, ours in fact, are tormented by the "voracious need for change that is the particularity of our civilization" (*PS* 312). For them, decadence would be to remain the same indefinitely. Admittedly, the former do not ignore history (how could they?), and the latter do not ignore the institutions that maintain identity despite change. But we are dealing with tendencies here, and moreover, of the self-image that each has of itself. Yet if we are to believe Lévi-Strauss, these images are radically different: in the eyes of primitive people, any change is a degradation of their being, whereas for us immobility is synonymous with stagnation, and thus with decadence. It is therefore not history as a discipline and mode of storing the past that separates cold societies from hot ones, but the idea of becoming itself.

Out of what is perceived as a deficiency or a weakness, by Sartre for example in *Critique of Dialectical Reason* (to which Lévi-Strauss particularly seems to be responding), Lévi-Strauss as a worthy descendant of Rousseau will make a positive trait. He will in fact turn it into the sign of the savage mind's greater explanatory capacity, capable of both integrating history into mythology – diachrony with synchrony – but also of refusing to make historicity the distinctive mark of the human, or of praxis to use Sartre's words. Lévi-Strauss's radical critique of the Sartrean enterprise in the last chapter of *The Savage Mind*, clearly reveals what Lévi-Strauss, from the outset of his work, sought to establish beyond the prejudices inherent in our own civilization: the rationality of so-called primitive societies, both in terms of their social organization, and in terms of the philosophy that emanates from it. Instead of considering that these people without a history lacked a dimension that, according to us, is constitutive of humanity, he wanted to show that the timeless nature of the savage mind, likely inseparable from the permanence of their social institutions, was not the product of a pre-logical mentality at the level of their thinking, nor of under-development at the level of history, but was the expression of their choice of myth over history, of a closed society over an open one. Conversely, history appears to Lévi-Strauss, in particular in the usage that Sartre makes of it, as a myth, the one to which we are perhaps the most attached because it reflects back to us, through the image of a transcendental humanity en route towards its *telos*, that of our personal becoming as continual change. This is why Lévi-Strauss has insisted on the rules, structures, and the rigorous logic of exchanges of the social organization of people without history, in contrast with the majority of his contemporaries. They, like Sartre, on the contrary underscore the role of violence in history, beginning with the struggle of all against all, all the way to class warfare (without even mentioning war), without which it seems humanity would have stagnated, as is the case, we believe, of men living in "cold" societies.

In the majority of his texts, Lévi-Strauss links history and inequality (of power, of wealth) according to a Rousseauist scheme of which he is fully conscious. Disorder and entropy are concomitant with progress; in other words, what culture produces as order (the relationships between men and things: wealth, technology, the arts, etc.), society – the relationship between men – disperses in the form of inequality, oppression and exploitation. Primitive societies are exempt from the suffering of our societies subject to history and entropy, because of the one characteristic invariably present in their social organization: the unanimity and consent of all of the members of their societies, or, in Rousseauist terms, the supremacy of the general will over individual will (without even mentioning sects or political parties, which are even more damaging to the exercise and respect of the general will than are individual interests): "All the while being in history, these societies seem to have elaborated or retained a particular kind of wisdom that has encouraged them to resist desperately any form of modification of their structure that might allow history to burst in on them." (*AS II* 40)

Thus historical development introduced inequality among men (for Lévi-Strauss, the historical condition of man seems at times to be the secular equivalent of original sin, the fall, or decadence…). The social organization of primitive people, founded on unanimity and consent, or in other words, on the social contract, limits the effects of this disorder and cools down the cauldron of history. For it is in the societies that he has studied and visited (see the moving narration of his stay with the Nambikwara in *Tristes Tropiques*) that Lévi-Strauss sees in action the social contract that Rousseau had established as the theoretical model of a machine made to produce and especially maintain equality among men. Against historical chaos, it is the political order of a people that forms a coherent whole and of which individual members think themselves members rather than considering themselves as private individuals separate from the others.

But this "communal I" that is manifest in each and every one by the feeling of being oneself in the other (to use Hegel's words this time) appears in Lévi-Strauss as much more emotional and sentimental than rational and juridical, which is the way Rousseau endeavors to present it.

In this way, in a text published in 1954 on anthropology,[10] Lévi-Strauss, expressing himself with touching openness and simplicity, states that by negatively defining primitive societies (*not* civilized, *without* writing, *not* technological), one forgets their positive reality that consists in the presence, at a much higher degree, of "personal relations" and "concrete relationships between individuals." Conversely (for primitive societies always take on the role of a critical test for our societies' thinking, as a kind of counter-model to ours, much like Rousseau's descriptions of savages): "Our relations with the other are no longer [...] founded on this global experience, this concrete perception of one subject by another," just like the relationship we have to our past, which Lévi-Strauss returns to in a remarkable chapter in *The Savage Mind*, is "no longer [through] an oral tradition that implies lived contact with people – storytellers, priests, wise men, or elders – but through books crammed into libraries" (*AS* I, 400–401). Technical progress and the emergence of the historical consciousness that makes it possible come at the cost, it seems, of the degradation of social and human ties that have become increasingly abstract and inauthentic. In response and contrast to the creation of order through culture (which we might more aptly call technology), is the image of societies carried away by disorder (inequalities, injustices, and the oppression of some by others).

1.4 Conclusion to the first section

Lévi-Strauss trivializes the *model of the social contract*. He sees in consent, unanimity, and solidarity among members, the basic forms of social existence, present in a purer form among the savages than they are in our societies, where they also

---

10 *Anthropologie structurale*, ch. xvii (1958: 400 [ff.]).

play a fundamental role in the context of the state.[11] Lévi-Strauss lends the contract the meaning of a sociological experience, revealing it to be not a deliberate creation of those who, by this act of commitment of one to all, suddenly become citizens of a state, but as a distinctive element (or a primitive element) of social life – which is an extension of the dichotomy between nature and culture at the heart of the enterprise of *Elementary Structures of Kinship* (1949). But like the relationships of exchange and matrimony studied in the context of marriages among parallel or cross cousins, the contract that unites individuals in primitive societies does not lead to a concerted decision among the members of society. It is on the contrary, the social structure (visible to the naked eye in primitive societies) that dictates its own form of social relationships destined to maintain it in its constant state, as a factor of the homeostasis of the social body.[12]

The political philosophy that Lévi-Strauss lays out in the final pages of *Tristes Tropiques* in which he pays homage to Rousseau, seems directly derived from a Rousseauist analysis of the causes of inequality among men, and the conditions of possibility of any social order. Derrida duly noted the presence for Lévi-Strauss "like for Rousseau, [of] the theme of a necessary or rather fatal degradation as the very form of progress" (1967: 194), "a fatal accident that would be none other than history itself" (195). Derrida evokes this "dream of [a] full and immediate presence closing history" (168) that would be common to them, and would explain the deep attachment that Lévi-Strauss had towards Rousseau (and that he never refuted). At the foundation of this far-reaching gaze, aimed at exotic social forms, one can likely find a profound disagreement with the society and civilization in which they are born.[13] "Each ethnographic career finds its principle in 'confessions,' be they written or untold," Lévi-Strauss famously wrote (*AS II* 48). Where Rousseau saw a sinister accident force humanity down the path of property and inequality among men, Lévi-Strauss sees the catastrophe of the discovery of the new world which led to the squashing of all non-western cultures. Lévi-Strauss transposed the Rousseauist question of the origin of

---

[11] Let us recall the work of Mauss in *The Gift* as well as of Davy's *La Foi jurée* presented as part of "a body of research that we have been pursuing for some time, M. Davy and myself, on archaic forms of the contract" (*The Gift* 5).

[12] "Society, placed outside and above history, would be able to exhibit once again that regular and almost crystalline structure which the best-preserved of primitive societies teach us is not antagonistic to the human condition"; anthropology would find its highest justification and could not seek to preserve this teaching "if in the most remote places of the earth, men had not obstinately resisted history, and had not remained as living testimonials of that which we want to preserve" (*AS II* 40–42).

[13] See in *Tristes Tropiques*, the beginning of chapter 38.

inequality to the level of cultures. Following the example of the *Second Discourse*, he sought to show in *Tristes Tropiques* and in the rest of his work that it was absurd and criminal to establish a hierarchy among cultures or societies whose internal logic ethnology helped us understand. Against a historical or historicizing vision that tends to organize things along a line that represents the progress of civilizations, he seeks to show the nature of the problems needing to be resolved by societies that differ from each other only in the methods that they allow themselves: "Our position amounts to saying that men have always and everywhere had the same task, identified the same objective, and that in the course of their becoming, only the means have differed" (*TT* 424).

This inequality of cultures has thus allowed a comparison between them from the sole vantage point of the balance among the goals they have set and the means they employ to reach them. From this perspective (that which Lévi-Strauss arrived through Rousseauist mediation), it is not clear that our western civilizations succeed that much better than the other ones, which ours have named primitive or backward. Lévi-Strauss can then fully assume as his own, in the middle of the twentieth century, the assessment that Rousseau had made two centuries earlier:

> Rousseau was probably right to think that it would have been better, for our happiness, that humanity hold a "golden mean between the indolence of the primitive state and the petulant activity of our amour-propre"; that this state was the "best for man" and that to leave it there had to be some "unhappy chance" in which one can recognize this doubly exceptional phenomenon – because it is unique, and because it is belated – that consisted in the advent of mechanical civilization. (*TT* 423)

2 Rousseau, founder of the human sciences: "the end of the *cogito*"

2.1 Anthropological doubt

In the manner of Rousseau, Lévi-Strauss poses as a precondition to any true understanding a double refusal: a refusal to identify the other with oneself, and the refusal to identify oneself to oneself. For it is clear that the goal of anthropology, whether it be structural or not, which is of course to understand men in their diversity, involves looking at these differences as an expression of shared properties. Rousseau often compares his method of observation and experimentation to that of chemistry; it is not at all evident that, according to him, a science of man is not just like physics or chemistry, rather than being a "human science." One must, or one should, in this area also structure experiments that leave the least possible room for the scientist – then we would see a reversal in what we thought was the order of things. The most distant differences (absurd beliefs that mix distinctive categories, repugnant practices such as cannibalism), that shame this upside-down world that the world of savages appears to be, would now appear as different manifestations of properties shared by both savages and civilized. Conversely, what seems to be analogous in both would be linked back to different origins. It is therefore not, like in metaphysical doubt, the difference of what seems exterior to myself that finds itself charged and indicted, it is on the contrary the experimenter's self that is undone, dissolved and then decomposed as a result of an alterity that presents itself as such and leads him to doubt his own identity.

It is in this way that Lévi-Strauss can say that at the heart of any ethnological vocation, one finds confessions. He could ask himself, along with Rousseau on the threshold of his *Rêveries:* "But I, detached from them and from everything, what am I?"[14] But this search for knowledge of oneself will happen far away, as far away as possible, not to verify the self's resistance to geographical variations (the way Descartes tests the identity of the spirit – a single thing that thinks – by changing the things around it), but so that it deteriorates and thus discovers itself as it is and not as it seemed to be before this experience of depersonalization (Lévi-Strauss narrates this experience in *Tristes Tropiques* 245): "The 'anthropological doubt' does not only consist of knowing that one knows nothing, but of resolutely exposing what one thought one knew – and one's very ignorance – to the insults and denials directed at one's most cherished ideas and habits by those best able to challenge them" (*AS II* 37).

In anthropological doubt, and not in metaphysical doubt, the self disappears, absorbed by the discovery that must precede the study of one's object. The observer, according to Lévi-Strauss, is his own instrument of observation (*AS II* 48). But as for me, who am I? Descartes asks ceaselessly in the second meditation, at each moment that he considers a particular object (the body, the soul, the piece of wax). The question that motivates and sustains ethnological inquiries instead asks itself: what is really that which is other to me? Is it another version of myself, or a self entirely other to me?

The situation of the ethnologist is therefore symmetrical but inverted to that of the philosopher who doubts. The relationship between his self and others, a relationship that *is* his object, which he abstracts from the totality in which they find themselves trapped together, is this not the true object of the changes that

---

14 *Les Rêveries du promeneur solitaire*, première promenade (*OC* 1: 995 [*CW* 8: 3]).

methodically happen under his eyes, at the end of which he will no longer recognize the one he was before? It is this double movement in opposing directions that Lévi-Strauss calls, in his Geneva conference of 1962, Rousseau's paradox, by which he means that "in all of his work, the systematic need to identify with the other goes hand in hand with an obstinate refusal to identify with the self" (*AS II* 47), and further: "in truth, I am not 'me,' but the weakest, the most humble of 'others'" (51). In the last page of *Tristes Tropiques*, Lévi-Strauss formulates this remark in Pascalian terms: "The self isn't only hateful: it has no place between an 'us' and a 'nothing'" (*TT* 448).

2.2 The self and the other

Conversely, the relationship (though it is not represented as such) that he had with his own world, with his culture, and even maybe with his cognitive categories, will no longer be what it once was before having been invalidated by the ethnological experience of distance, giving way to the one he now imagines. In thinking about this irreversibility, Lévi-Strauss said in his response to Roger Caillois that the ethnologist was the man who had returned from among the dead and could no longer be in his world with the same massive and unquestioned bond of one who had never left it: "He will never again feel at home anywhere" (*TT* 47). The situation here is more complex than in the case of metaphysical doubt, for the relationship of the self to others is compounded by the relationship of others to the self, which it is incumbent upon the ethnologist to formulate, or at the very least to take into consideration for them. But it is only under this condition (seeing oneself from the point of view of the other) that understanding can modify the self:

> Under the name of savage thinking, I designate the system of postulates and axioms on which to base a code that allows us to represent the other with the least amount of ourselves, and reciprocally. [...] Ultimately, "the savage mind" is, in my intent, nothing but the meeting place, the effect of an effort at understanding, *me* putting myself in *their* place, *them* put in *my* place by me.[15]

Isn't it in very similar terms that Rousseau evokes the function of pity in the *Second Discourse*? For it is not only the emotional disposition that all sensible beings share, it is also and inextricably a mode of knowing whose extreme generality (feeling here is the opposite of a distinctive perception) is linked to the nature of its object: the other, not only the other man, my fellow man, but also the an-

---

[15] Entretien *Esprit* (1963), reprinted in *Esprit* (2004): 175.

imal, "the most other of all others," Lévi-Strauss will go so far as to say in his 1962 conference (*AS II* 51). This tendency to assimilation or confusion that is also part of the savage mind, the man at this moment of the *Second Discourse* is incapable of having only because the great rifts (those unfortunate accidents) have not yet occurred between nature and culture; between sensibility and understanding; between myself and other men; between all humans and the totality of sentient beings; between our society and other societies; and even more so between mine and yours. Savages are not more inclined to pity than those who are civilized, far from it, but only in the moral sense of the word, which is already a degraded meaning, for pity is not compassion but identification (and is this not how the savage mind proceeds, by identifying all beings, all things, and relating them to each other in a vast system of combinations that leaves out nothing?). If the *cogito* consisted in distinguishing the self from what is not-self, pity consists in identifying the self from what is not-self.

Two philosophies come from this radical opposition: "a philosophy of originary identification to all others," which is, according to Lévi-Strauss, Rousseau's, and which is opposed to that of Hobbes and of Sartrean existentialism based on the war of one against all, and thus, on the most radical distinction between the self and the other (all others).[16] In this philosophy whose starting point is the *cogito*, man is part of a distinct realm from which animals are excluded, nature is now nothing but an object of domination at the hands of technology, and men and other societies (savages, primitives) are considered sub-human because they lack what we have (history, writing, science, and power). It is a humanism that Lévi-Strauss never ceased to criticize and denounce because it seems to him, from its very inception (from the *cogito*), based on *amour-propre* and corrupted by it. The last chapter of *The Savage Mind* proceeds to the destruction of this "transcendental humanism" (*PS* 347) whose last avatar Lévi-Strauss sees in the *Critique of Dialectical Reason* by Sartre, in its shift from the I to the We that leaves man's superiority over the world intact, that consecrates, by defending "History" and human historicity, the separation between man and nature, western man and... others.[17] It is again Rousseau that Lévi-Strauss summons here, against Sartrean praxis, as a kind of historicized mutant of the Cartesian *cogito*, much like in the two other texts of this same year, 1962. After having once again quoted the famous sentence from Rousseau's *Essay on the Origin of Languages* that opens the anthropological field and closes the era of Cartesian metaphysics, Lévi-Strauss crosses, as easily as did Rousseau in his *Second Discourse*, the vast spaces between eras, the gap that separated

---

16 *Le Totémisme aujourd'hui* (2009: 149).
17 See my article "Des fourmis et des hommes: le débat entre Lévi-Strauss et Sartre."

nature from culture in *Elementary Structures of Kinship*, asking the natural sciences to "reintegrate culture in nature and, ultimately, life in the totality of its physical-chemical conditions" (*PS* 327).[18] On this point, Lévi-Strauss could have easily made Rousseau the precursor of such a profession of materialist faith.

Translated by Karen Santos Da Silva

Works Cited

Aron, Raymond. *Histoire et politique*. Paris: Julliard, 1985.
Davy, Georges. *La Foi jurée. Etude sociologique du problème du contrat*. New York: Arno Press, 1922.
Derrida, Jacques. *De la grammatologie*. Paris: Minuit, 1967.
Guenancia, Pierre. "Des fourmis et des hommes: le débat entre Lévi-Strauss et Sartre." *Claude Lévi-Strauss et ses contemporains*. Eds. Pierre Guenancia, Jean-Pierre Sylvestre, and François Dosse. Paris: PUF, 2012. 37–59.
Lévi-Strauss, Claude. *Tristes Tropiques*. Paris: Plon, 1955. Quoted as *TT*.
Lévi-Strauss, Claude. *Mythologiques [4]/L'Homme nu*. Paris: Plon, 1971.
Lévi-Strauss, Claude. *Anthropologie structurale*. 2 vols. Paris: Plon, 1958. Quoted as *AS*.
Lévi-Strauss, Claude. *Anthropologie structurale Deux*. Paris: Plon, 1973. Quoted as *AS II*.
Lévi-Strauss, Claude. *Mythologiques [2]/Du Miel aux cendres*. Paris: Plon, 1966.
Lévi-Strauss, Claude. *The Naked Man. Mythologiques*. Vol. 4. Chicago: U of Chicago P, 1981.
Lévi-Strauss, Claude. *La Pensée sauvage*. Paris: Plon, 1962. Quoted as *PS*.
Lévi-Strauss, Claude. *Le Totémisme aujourd'hui*. 1962. Paris: PUF, 2009.
Lévi-Strauss, Claude. *Tristes Tropiques*. Paris: Plon, 1955.
Lévi-Strauss, Claude. "Autour de la *Pensée Sauvage*. Réponses à quelques questions." *Esprit* (1963). Rpt. 2004.
Lévi-Strauss, Claude, and Didier Eribon. *De près et de loin*. Paris: O. Jacob, 1988.
Lévi-Strauss, Claude, and Georges Charbonnier. *Entretiens avec Claude Lévi-Strauss*. Paris: Plon, Julliard, 1961.
Mauss, Marcel. *The Gift: The Form and Reason for Exchange in Archaic Societies*. Trans. W.D. Halls. New York: Norton, 1990.
Rousseau, Jean-Jacques. *Essai sur l'origine des langues*. Ed. Charles Porset. Bordeaux: Ducros, 1968.
Rousseau, Jean-Jacques. *Essay on the Origin of Language and Writings Related to Music*. Trans. and ed. John T. Scott. Hanover: UP of New England, 1998.
Rousseau, Jean-Jacques. *Œuvres complètes*. Gen. Eds. Bernard Gagnebin and Marcel Raymond. 5 vols. Paris: Gallimard, "Bibliothèque de la Pléiade," 1959–1995.

---

18 We learn, in the note accompanying this broad program, or this "brutal thesis," that "the opposition between nature and culture, on which we had long insisted, seems today only to have methodological value."

Philip Knee
Rousseau and the Authority of Nature

In one of the canonical texts of the French Enlightenment, the *Lettres philosophiques*, Voltaire ridicules Pascal's *Pensées:* Man is not defined by his corrupt nature, but by his projects in the world, even if they are partial, inconstant, and relative.[1] His vocation is to aim for happiness, counting on the contributions of knowledge, wealth-production and the exchange of free speech; the way to happiness is made of lights that cross and correct each other, forming what could be called crisscrossing beams of *enlightenment*. For Pascal, however, Man exhausts and loses himself without ever catching anything: hunting after wealth, seduction, knowledge and diversion cannot be a source of meaning, something we soon realize with the arrival of sickness or death. Only love of God and submission to that Whole of which man is a part can truly provide meaning. It is that Whole that enlightens the world with the divine *light* that enfolds Man, and is given to him if he only consents to abandon himself to it in love. By affirming the natural capacity of men to order their common life, governing their passions and forging appropriate social institutions, the horizon forged by the *Philosophes* revives what the Augustinian tradition sees as a form of *Pelagianism*. Against the relinquishment of wills, and in the name of a legitimate egoism that can be directed by reason, confidence in *sweet commerce* and *well-understood interest* gradually asserts itself.[2]

If Rousseau's position in this context is so significant, it is because he refuses both Pascal's theologism and the *Philosophes*'s reasoning irreligion. His critique of revealed religion and intolerance makes him truly part of the Enlightenment; yet he also echoes Pascal's critique of rationalism and skepticism and his attempt to locate authority on the level of the heart. In explicitly attacking the "lights of the century" for their hypocrisy (*OC* 3: 9, 11) and the "baneful lights of civil man" for the corruption they conceal (*OC* 3: 170), he is evidently looking for *other lights*.[3] He repeatedly warns against the idea of progress, and in place of the theological narrative he substitutes a narrative of replacement – that of the formation of societies and the loss of the state of nature – which gives a different

---

1 Voltaire, "Vingt-cinquième lettre. Sur les *Pensées* de M. Pascal," *Lettres philosophiques*.
2 Particularly in Montesquieu, *De l'esprit des lois*, Livres XX et XXI; Helvétius, *De l'esprit*.
3 For this often-neglected aspect of Rousseau's thought, which makes him a man of the Enlightenment at war with the Enlightenment, see Hulliung's 1998 book and Garrard's 2003 book. Rousseau's *Discours sur l'origine et les fondements de l'inégalité parmi les hommes* is quoted as *SD*.

account of the Fall of Man. With a historical fable which puts the Holy Texts aside even as it echoes them, Rousseau offers a different intelligibility of what Man has become over time, so that his perfectible existence appears as an issue for the will, not simply an expectation or a hope (*SD, OC* 3: 132).

In his letter to Voltaire about the Lisbon earthquake of 1755, where he feels obliged to account for evil in history (*OC* 4: 1059–1075), Rousseau adopts the traditional vision of a God who is all-powerful and good, excluding the possibility that He could be the source of the catastrophe Himself; nor does he explain it (at least not solely) as one of the accidents of nature. The origin of suffering is the way men react to the circumstances of their existence: it is they who constructed the buildings that buried them, and they who – wanting to save their belongings at any price – exposed themselves to danger when the earth shook. Men are not evil, however, in the sense that their nature is fallen as a result of sin; they have become corrupt in social life, and the consequences of the disaster are to be understood in the light of that corruption. They do not choose evil, as sinners choose to turn away from God; but they are no less the bearers of evil, and responsible for it. How can one be a bearer of evil without choosing it, and without *being* evil? In striving to provide an answer, the narrative of the *Discours sur l'inégalité* defines a new type of authority, that of Nature lost.

The answer is an interaction between contingent circumstances of the physical situation in which men found themselves (their proximity over a restricted territory), the development of the species (growth in numbers, capacity to improve themselves) and psychological traits proceeding from that development. Individuals do not control all these factors – in some respects they are controlled by them – but they are nonetheless agents of change, and up to a certain point they can react to it and orientate it.[4] Originally, they are independent, animated only by self-love and pity; but the increase in their relationships transforms these sentiments into passions, above all by their desire to distinguish themselves from other men and to exist in those other men's eyes. This desire engenders self-esteem (*amour-propre*), which is the spring of inequality, since it means being more esteemed than others; the desire also proceeds from a multiplication of relationships, which is an incitement to distinction. Hence the procession of passions: envy, jealousy and pride – and thence, gradually, an inclination to harm others, which did not exist in the beginning. These passions deepen inequality, and the resulting social institutions exacerbate it in their turn. So men act by misusing their faculties in circumstances which lend themselves to inequality, and by orienting their perfectibility in such a way that they come

---

4 Rousseau, *Lettre à Philopolis* (*OC* 3: 232).

to be dominated by their *amour-propre* – which is not natural, but tends to *become* natural inasmuch as Man, incapable of going back, has to manage the *second nature* thus acquired. For Rousseau it is at this stage that the Enlightenment *Philosophes*, blind to the history which has generated men as corrupt as they have become, characterize them as beings of *interest* and strive in vain to rationalize their clashing egoisms.

Rousseau's explanation, then, resembles that of sin, since men degrade the freedom they possess; but it is different because of certain positive dimensions brought in by socialization. When collective life gradually takes form its sweetness is enjoyed; Rousseau evokes a Golden Age of humanity, which he locates between the solitude of the natural man and the corruption of social life (*SD*, *OC* 3: 170–171). In fact it is only with the development of *dependence* that *amour-propre* produces its negative effects, which implies that they can be moderated. In addition, Rousseau does not exhort his reader to condemn those who are in the grip of this corrupting process, but to sympathize with them, and he puts the accent on their status as victims. Famous episodes in the *Confessions* illustrate this, such as the *stolen ribbon* or the *faults* of Madame de Warens. Circumstances can lead the relationship with oneself astray, and make an individual act badly whilst his heart remains pure.[5] In difficult social conditions, under the influence of peers who consider themselves enlightened and who urge that reason should be one's sole guide, a weak will may let itself falter and individual interest gain the upper hand. Then individuals behave badly without being evil; the voice of Nature becomes inaudible in them, without disappearing, however.

The grip of this new authority on eighteenth-century minds is partly explained by the fact that it concerns individuals' intimate experience. True, since at least Augustine's *Confessions*, the Christian tradition has turned the attention of the faithful towards their inner life; but its value has lain in the divine Will which is revealed there, God being (as Augustine puts it) "more inward to me, than my most inward part."[6] But now this inwardness becomes autonomous as a source of norms, and its value is diffused by readers' identification with the characters Rousseau portrays in his fictional works, or even with Rousseau himself as he tells the story of his life. *La Nouvelle Héloïse* and autobiographical texts contribute to this displacement of authority, inviting readers to follow the inclination of their emotions, and thus transform first their inner disposition, then their opinions, and finally their behavior. Fascinated by the desires, torments and passions they read about, readers detach their feelings from the meaning

---

5 Rousseau, *Confessions* (*OC* 1: 84–87, 198–199). Title abridged *C*.
6 Augustine, *The Confessions* (1952: 37).

the biblical account conferred on them, and accord them a legitimacy from the simple fact that they are experienced. Acquiring a sort of sacredness, the individual conscience claims responsibility for its own capacity to judge for itself what is true, good, and beautiful in the name of its uniqueness. This cult of inwardness is not unconnected with the postures of revolt and defiance that develop at the end of the century, as this proximity with oneself gives rise to a psychological assurance that can arouse criticism of the political authority. In Rousseau, the voluntarism of *The Social Contract* is articulated with an increased value given to the personal domain of feelings, reflecting on a model of communion between men – a *transparency of hearts* which has the features of an "ideal" or "enchanted world"[7] – one which individuals think they have in their grasp.

As Rousseau describes this new authority of Nature in the two main domains his work deals with – individual morality and the collective will – his ambivalent relationship with the Enlightenment project, far from being resolved, persists and sharpens: first, because the inner voice is also the voice of God; second, because the political imagination requires dissimulation.

1 Moral conscience or divine instinct

How can we be assured that the voice of Nature in Man speaks what is true and good? Rousseau declines to demonstrate this, as such a demonstration in his view would go beyond our understanding. Faced with the quarrels which entangled the "miserable reasoners" in this respect, he prefers to note that the inner voice "sets things down for itself"; that the rationalism and materialism of the *Philosophes* make people insensitive to that voice, and stifle the pleasures it procures.[8] He does however specify its metaphysical status, defining it both as the voice of Nature in Man, and as that of God murmuring in his ear; and he stands by this position, affirming his opposition to two intolerances: that of "atheist fanaticism" and of "pious fanaticism" (C 567).[9]

Like the majority of the *Philosophes* who adopt an empiricist approach, Rousseau rejects the Cartesian innateness of ideas; but he substitutes another innateness which restores divine order as the source of morality. It has sometimes been suggested that Rousseau combined the thinking of Descartes and Locke; but we should rather say that he modifies both, placing the accent on inner feel-

---

7 Rousseau, *Rousseau juge de Jean-Jacques. Dialogues* (OC 1: 668, 672).
8 Rousseau, *Émile ou de l'éducation* (E, OC 4: 600).
9 On this point, see also the *Lettre à C. de Beaumont* (OC 4: 1006–1007).

ing. In the savage state, Man "gives himself over to the sole feeling of his present existence" (*SD* 164) and his other affections must be understood on this basis: he feels pleasure at whatever tends to preserve his existence, and pain at whatever tends to destroy it. So here it is not a question of a *thinking substance*, for at his origin Man does not think; he develops his faculties by his perfectibility, and rather than *knowing*, he *feels* his existence. Whilst this feeling is not an idea, however, Rousseau does not reduce it, as Locke does, to sense experience. In his *Profession de foi*, the *vicaire Savoyard* observes through self-examination that he has a proper feeling of his existence which is not reducible to his sensations (*E* 570 [ff.]). Feeling is animated by the senses, but it has a moral scope as it is formed by a double relationship: to oneself, and to others. If it is indeed a pleasure, it is a reasonable pleasure which demonstrates an order. When the feeling of self is spiritualized and becomes a love of that order, the *true self* is born, endowed with a conscience which is present virtually in the primitive feeling. Here, then, Rousseau distances himself from Locke, and from the French *Philosophes* like Diderot and Helvétius who were inspired by him, and who draw sensualism towards materialism. He opposes them with a spiritualism whose point of departure is close to Locke's analyses of sense experience, but which lays out a sort of *metaphysics of feeling* animated by reference to the transcendent.

The moral scope thus accorded to feeling by Rousseau can be explained by the influence – direct or indirect – of Malebranche.[10] Though a Cartesian in many respects, Malebranche modifies the Cartesian conception of self-knowledge, employing precisely the term *conscience** which is almost absent in Descartes: to know oneself is not to have a clear, distinct idea of the self, comparable to the idea of a triangle; it is to have a *feeling of one's existence* or a *conscience*.[11] Malebranche makes this idea the basis of Man's relationship to God and morality, incorporating it in the narrative of sin. Following the Fall, Man became incapable of loving God by his reason – that is, by a clear view of the mind which would be assured that what it sees is good; he can only love God by a *present pleasure*. And God took account of this, giving feeble Man the capacity to love Him by an *inner delectation* or a feeling. Thus Man is capable of loving moral truths by making his heart sensitive to those truths, rather than by reasoning about them. He relates to the good by a sort of instinct analogous to the one

---

10 Here we are indebted to Émile Bréhier's essay.
11 *Translator's note: "conscience" and "consciousness" are the same word in French. While Descartes is also "the philosopher of consciousness" (see following note), the translation "conscience" has been preferred in light of what follows.
Despite his reputation for being the philosopher of conscience, Descartes uses neither the Latin *conscientia* in the *Méditations* nor the French term *conscience* in the *Discours de la méthode*.

that, at the very lowest level of his moral life, attaches him to his body. Man cannot reach an apprehension of morality by the conduct of his reason, for with sin the order of the world in its complexity has become inaccessible to him. That is why God made him to love virtue through feeling, which binds him to the universal good by a "holy concupiscence."[12]

Malebranche's explanation is helpful in terms of seeing both what Rousseau drew from it – the foundation of morality in feeling – and what he left aside – the explanation through sin. These two points make it possible to define what Rousseau means by the authority of Nature. In Malebranche's perspective, feeling is a sort of compensation for the effects of sin, which cloud men's faculty of knowledge; and even if the function of feeling is salutary it is the indication of their evil nature, the sign of their pride. In Rousseau the resort to feeling marks a break with that tradition, as it has its source in Man's nature, which is good. It is not God who allows Man to do good after the fall, and in spite of it; sin does not come into Rousseau's explanation, which says that God placed love of the good, and the feeling that corresponds to that good, in Man *from his origin*. So Rousseau can replace the Christian narrative of the Fall with a quite different story: that of socialization, starting with Man animated by the pure feelings of self-love and pity.

The nature demonstrated by conscience is not *natural goodness* in a strong sense; as, contrary to what is often suggested, natural Man in the *Discours sur l'inégalité* is not *morally good*. He is without wickedness in that he is *pre-moral*; his self-love makes him fear pain and death, and seek wellbeing; his pity makes him care about his species, and inflict no unnecessary suffering. The impulse of conscience is then born from the articulation of these two natural feelings, and shows the way to a new sociability. The universality of these feelings can be seen by the "first movements" of the heart, which lead one to help the oppressed, to admire clemency and generosity, to take pleasure in the happiness of others when one carries out an act of charity – and on the other hand, to feel remorse when one has acted badly in secret.[13] Conscience is thus infallible in terms of its honesty when it is solicited; but it is weak, as it is in danger of being covered over by the effects of socialization and by artificial feelings, which derive from *amour-propre*. The feeling which leads Man to love the good is innate, but it is not always actualized, or present to his mind, as his conscience becomes darkened and has to recover itself.

---

12 Malebranche, *Méditations chrétiennes* (1928: xiv, 272–281).
13 Rousseau, *Lettres morales* (*OC* 4: 1108–1111).

The common usage of the term *conscience*, particularly in the Thomist tradition, is much more intellectual than Rousseau's. According to this usage, the rules imprinted in Man, which allow him to determine what is right for him, are accessible by reason *in their generality*, and he has to resort to conscience to apply them to *particular cases*. It is thus a faculty that enables the practical translation of the general rules of natural law extracted by reason. For Rousseau, such an approach overestimates the connection between what reason indicates to men and their behavior, as they can perfectly well reason correctly about the rules they ought to give themselves without applying them. Among those who see the good, the will is not necessarily led to embrace it; they can be lucid but insensitive, intelligent but cold; some of them can contemplate virtue without being moved and without acting, like the philosopher mentioned in the *Discours sur l'inégalité:* while a man's throat is being cut outside his window, he only has to argue with himself a little to prevent Nature, rising up within him in revolt, from identifying with the man who is being murdered (*SD* 156). In the socialized man who has developed his reason, therefore, reason must be combined with feeling so that he is led to *adhere* to what reason illuminates as being true. Because conscience is not only a *practical reason* but also a *feeling*, men are *struck* by the moral obviousness of right behavior, and hence *love* the order it brings into being.

While the moral inclination thus finds its moving force in feeling, it does not mean that reason plays no role in virtuous conduct. Reason is only sound if the heart is upright; left to itself, the heart does not *see* what it ought to love. Depending on the expected readership, and the intentions of his texts, Rousseau sometimes emphasizes one requirement, sometimes the other; sometimes their distinctness and sometimes their complementariness; but fundamentally he maintains their articulation. Without rational enlightenment (and even sometimes *with* such enlightenment), feeling can be reduced to prejudice, can be nothing but received opinion or caprice; and without the guide of conscience reason can make use of egotistical reckonings, become abstract, or even sink into skepticism, content with vainly dissolving all beliefs.

This authority, then, is based neither on being torn away from the senses by sovereign reason, nor on submission to religion; it is neither Cartesian nor Pascalian, nor is it akin to the skeptical consent to uncertainty we find in Montaigne. Rousseau reproaches Montaigne for ignoring the naturalness demonstrated by conscience and for giving way to a facile relativism (*E* 598–599). This reproach is a caricature of Montaigne's position, which does not simply substitute diversity of customs for traditional authority but also introduces the authority of a "director within";[14] but this conscience is not a *celestial voice* which indicates the path to goodness, it is forged in the uncertain exercise of judgment on customs. Yet the only thing Rousseau retains from the *Essais* is their questioning of the natural, and he only sees it as an experience terrified by diversity, which risks imprisoning men in confusion when faced with norms that contradict one another. For him the moral life requires men to be delivered from the dangers resulting from this skeptical reason which is tossed about on all sides. Their representations, no doubt, always come to them from the outside (their education, their habits), but their moral evaluation of them has its source in their hearts. It is to the heart that they must turn to find their guide; and to be persuaded of this they have to be able to count on the distinction between *natural feelings* and *acquired perceptions*, going beyond the impression of chaos Montaigne condemns them to. So there is truly a *skeptical moment* in Rousseau, when he makes his critique of the pretensions of philosophy or theology to explain the universe; but he hastens to get away from this "state, too violent for the human mind." Since Man "prefers to be mistaken rather than believe nothing" (*E* 568) he has to be encouraged to believe what corresponds to his good. From this results a certain dogmatism of feeling, for the feeling invoked by Rousseau is not the result of particular research caught in the diversity of customs; it is the indisputable voice of Nature itself.

To ensure this authority Rousseau brings together two realities which, *a priori*, are distinct: an instinct that leads Man without reflection, and which alone can alleviate the insufficiency of his reason, and a transcendence which raises him above his immediate desires or what can justly be called his *animal instincts*. Hence the expression *divine instinct*, used in a famous passage in the *Profession de foi du vicaire savoyard* (*E* 600), which demonstrates a will to combine the Christian moral heritage with Enlightenment sensualism. The reference to the interiority of conscience echoes Pascal's *heart* as the point where divine grace enters Man, but Rousseau's position is also anti-Pascalian as it rules out the authority of *positive religions*, notably the revealed truth of Christianity (*E* 606–635).[15] Its place is taken by the individual's conscience, by which men please – or fail to please – God. Those who do not recognize the Christian God can thus behave *instinctively* with uprightness; in support Rousseau invokes the case of savages who do not offend God, even though they do not know Him. The danger comes rather from the *Philosophes*, whose reasonings about God,

---

14 Montaigne, *Essais* (1992: iii, 2, 807).
15 He gives an equally careful explanation of this thesis in his *Lettre à M. de Franquières*, who had expressed his doubts in religious matters (*OC* 4: 1138–1139).

and materialist speculations about chance, are exactly what risks undermining this natural uprightness.

In the name of this religion of Nature, Rousseau is thus content to express his emotion on reading the gospels and his admiration for their moral message. Should this conception of an authority situated outside tradition be connected with his upbringing in the Protestant Reform Church in Geneva? If men owe no "account to anyone for the manner in which they serve God,"[16] didn't the Reformation make an explicit rule out of what is the universal essence of the Christian faith? Rousseau's quarrel with the pastors of Geneva in 1764 makes this issue clear, as he proposes that he is himself more faithful to the spirit of the Reformation than those who are supposed to represent it. According to him, the Geneva church had become as hierarchical and punctilious as the Catholic Church; his critique echoes that of governments found in the *Contrat social*: just as governments tend naturally towards usurpation, the general tendency of churches leads them to intolerance and fanaticism, and the Calvinists of Geneva are no exception. While the only dogma their doctrine does not tolerate is intolerance, they have become intolerant themselves "without even knowing why."[17] Perhaps; but doesn't unity among the faithful have to be ensured by a church, ask the pastors? Rousseau replies that the only unity the Reformed should claim is the diversity in their ways of thinking (*LDM* 717). But given that hypothesis, can such a religion be passed on? Doesn't a minimal common doctrine have to be defined by some rules which at least permit the formation of children? Rousseau allows that, but the fundamental points needed for teaching do not involve imposing what has to be believed. Does that mean that the doubts aroused by resorting to individual conscience should themselves find a place in religion, with no authority of last instance to decide? Rousseau seems to go as far as to allow a religion that is uncertain of its doctrinal content, and thus exposes himself to a final objection: in the case where no truth is passed on, but only a requirement of tolerance, how can it be claimed that the religion of tolerance is itself the truest?

In the last analysis, the authority of Nature seems to assign men a single task in order to reform themselves morally: not to philosophize or theologize, but to turn towards themselves, so that conscience can make itself heard. Is that enough to ensure that the feeling one experiences is really a manifestation of Nature; that it is in harmony with sound reason, and not slipping towards sophisms? Rousseau admits that the inner voice remains a fragile, vulnerable au-

---

16 *Lettre à Voltaire* (*OC* 4: 1072). Title abbreviated as *LV*.
17 Rousseau, *Lettres écrites de la montagne* (*OC* 3: 716, footnote). Title abbreviated as *LDM*.

thority; that it can turn out to be nothing but a "prejudice," and that speaking of "proof by feeling" is somewhat delicate (*LV* 1071). For in dismissing rationalism, skepticism and theology one after the other, this authority identifies the inner space where we are to place our confidence and our effort, but offers no guarantee. Should we require more of it? We can understand why Rousseau's critics, philosophers as much as theologians, would be puzzled and hostile; in claiming to rely both on God and Nature, while casting suspicion on reason, he seems to make everything depend on his Self and a sort of *heroism of inner feeling*.[18] According to some, his ego-centered metaphysic results after all in a compromise with traditional theological authority; for others, it ruins all authority and engenders *indifference*.

2 The political will or the directed imagination

Just as Rousseau associates individual conscience with the divine order, his political thought also fosters an ambivalence. This is partly explained by a concern for prudence; forging a collective will according to the norms indicated by Nature cannot ignore the entrenched beliefs of those whom one is addressing, particularly in the context of the emerging Enlightenment, with their *new gods*, reason and individual liberty. The paradox of the *Discours sur les sciences et les arts* – incomprehensible to the *Philosophes*[19] – as well as the uncertainty which characterizes progress in the *Discours sur l'inégalité*, bear witness to this concern. It is also demonstrated by the *mise en scène* which governs the *Profession de foi du vicaire savoyard:* while carrying out his critique of positive religions, the *vicaire* nonetheless advises against "professing another religion than the one in which one was born"; and in drawing up his religion of conscience and its inner God, he still recommends that his young interlocutor "return to the religion of [his] fathers" (*E* 631). Everything shows that Rousseau was particularly sensitive to the classical problem of consent to the opinions of the city and the veiling of political discourse, whereas his own discourse on popular sovereignty nevertheless places him in the forefront of the Enlightenment.

The common interpretation of the *Contrat social*, which sees it only as the realization of the program in the *Discours sur l'inégalité* by an institutional order ensuring men their liberty, tends to leave aside an essential requirement

---

[18] Jacques Maritain speaks of a "Pelagianism of interiority" to clarify the relationship between Pelagianism and Protestantism in Rousseau (1925: 25).
[19] Particularly when Rousseau deplores the weakening of religion by modern philosophy (*DSA, OC* 3: 27–29).

of Rousseau's politics: that of acting upon men from within, on the level of their desires and hopes, without resort to reasoning or constraint. In the *Contrat social* individuals do not really associate with one another by a contract; each one contracts with himself, committing to a Whole, which is a projection of his will. By this projection a *general will* is created; that is, the will of each inasmuch as it is identified with the Whole. For this identification to take place, each one must develop a certain image of himself, by which his intimate feeling extends beyond him and becomes a feeling of belonging to a group; the idea of the contract is in the end only the means of making the birth of that feeling intelligible. The authority of Nature is neither a calculation of interests nor a rational arrangement of needs. Its political content supposes making a collective way of seeing and wanting one's interest emerge, the love one bears oneself being extended to other members of the group.

The issue is as much affective and cultural as it is political; more than a state, it is an imaginary universe which has to be constructed; more than rules for a collectivity to function, it is the psychological conditions of happiness adapted to each community which have to be put in place. These imaginary mediations are often neglected by the *Philosophes* in the name of reason.[20] But just as the individual cannot count on reason alone to choose the good, as we saw earlier, the citizen can quite well recognize a rule of justice when it is shown to him, without seeing why he should submit to it; and the moralist's preaching is no more sufficient than the presentation of rational arguments to convince him. Only the images conveyed by myths and fables have the power to direct passions and guide practices. This is why the real legislators are the poets and prophets, who know how to stir souls and who incline hearts to love the common good, which is itself endowed with no power of attraction. If men are to work towards the common good, a public will has to be created artificially using a set of beliefs, so that each man sees his own good in the context of the common good. Patriotic and religious symbols, persuasion, institutions that reflect the historical particularities of each people, all have to be set in motion so that meeting points emerge between interests which did not exist on the level of primary nature – a nature which as it were has to be *duplicated* by the imagination in order to reach Nature.

This is the meaning of the hidden exercise of authority in a large part of Rousseau's œuvre – particularly in the *Lettre à d'Alembert*, his writings on Corsica and Poland, and the letters on the organization of Clarens in the *Nouvelle*

---

[20] "A great deal of art must be employed to prevent social man from being quite artificial", Rousseau writes (*E* 640).

Héloïse where the manipulation of the domestics by Wolmar and Julie consists above all in forging an imaginary arrangement.²¹ The Legislator's *secret* action in the *Contrat social* nonetheless constitutes the most concentrated illustration of what is required to translate the authority of Nature in the political field.²² Its intervention is necessary because the people's *general will* – the only source of legitimacy, as it is always upright – does not always *see* the good it seeks; it needs enlightenment if its quest for the good is to produce laws which are appropriate for it. Therefore it must be helped to constitute itself, in advance of laws, on the level of beliefs:

> [It is] the most important [law] of all [which is engraved] in the hearts of citizens, which makes the veritable constitution of the state; which gains new strengths every day; which when other laws become old or die revives or replaces them, maintains a people in the spirit of its institution, and imperceptibly substitutes the force of habit for that of authority. I speak of manners, of customs, and above all of opinion; a field unknown to our politicians, but on which the success of all the others depends: a field with which the great legislator is occupied in secret, while he appears to confine himself to particular regulations which are only the arch of the vault – whose unshakeable keystone is formed by manners which come to birth more slowly. (*CS* 394)

In assuming this task the Legislator does not take the place of the *general will*, whose externalization in the Sovereign indeed remains *sovereign*. But it is not enough; the contract cannot be established on the basis of nothing. As we saw with morality, political authority raises the problem of what makes it possible; it requires us to think about the ambiguity of will and that which envelops it; and this need for a received wisdom is not compatible with a transparent constitution of the *general will*. This is why Rousseau's political voluntarism has to be articulated with religion in the foundation of cities: unable to "employ either force or reasoning, it is a necessity [for the Legislator] to resort to an authority of another order" and put his words in the mouths of the gods; hence to make the *general will* see "objects as they are, sometimes as they must appear to it, to show it the right path it seeks" (*CS* 383, 380).²³

---

21 Rousseau, *Julie* (*OC* 2, particularly iv, 10). On the systematic use of duplicity in these texts (to which one must add the tutor's hidden authority in *Émile*), see my book *Penser l'appartenance*, ch. ii, 3.
22 Rousseau, *Du contrat social* (*CS*, ii, ch. 6–7).
23 "Never did a people survive, nor ever will survive, without religion," Rousseau writes in *Du contrat social*, first version (*OC* 3: 336), as witness his development concerning *civil religion* in *Contrat social* (iv, chap. 8).

Since liberty consists in living under the authority of laws, in such a way that the people ratify those laws and recognize themselves in them, the people must be trained not to see them as dependent on the power of other men, and this is achieved by a ruse: the people must see the laws as having a divine origin, for consenting to them on that basis makes men free. Rousseau might say that consenting in this way is the *rational* means of realizing the sought-for *natural* end: obedience to oneself. But it is not a rational act in the sense of a deliberated act, guided by reason, since men consent to what they believe to be divine commandments, when the laws have in fact a human origin. This concealed or impersonal dependence produces no ill effects, as social man finds in it the taste for his natural independence; but the experience of the citizen is not really that of independence, since it depends on those who have fashioned his imagination.

Nature, then, can only exercise its authority in social life by means of this fabrication of beliefs; but are they true? Let us say that their truth is in abeyance and their necessity is ethical. As Julie says of the Supreme Being, if it did not exist it would still be good for Man to be occupied with it, in order to be "more the master of himself; stronger, happier, wiser" (*Julie* 359). These beliefs are in the nature of a *wager* or an *imaginary projection*, since they are at once eminently fragile (believing in a thing whose existence is uncertain because that existence *depends* on belief) and necessary (the *common self* in the city requires a shared imagination). In fact Rousseau's question is above all this: on what conditions are these necessary beliefs possible? And one of those conditions marks his distance from the *Philosophes:* one should stop claiming to illuminate everything in the name of criticizing superstitions and illegitimate powers, and consent to make a certain illusion the condition of liberty.

This does not mean that the political order is essentially imaginary for Rousseau, as it is for Pascal, for example. For Pascal the political world proceeds from a desire which no finite object can satisfy, and ceaselessly solicits the imagination so that it produces objects of substitution (*Pensées* 828, 1963: 606). Justice therefore draws its foundation only from the imagination, although the political world is not *unreal* according to Pascal: the imagination produces an ensemble of *signs* of happiness to which desire attaches, believing that it recognizes what it seeks; the imagination sets these signs in a hierarchy, confers value on them, and these illusions contribute effectively to the forging of social links. But since this imaginary world proceeds only from concupiscence, the question as to what is the best regime is secondary; the only legitimacy of political regimes is to substitute a symbolic order for force, making it look like a justice founded in nature.

If religion is an indispensable motivating force for the imaginary order in Rousseau, it does not however define, as in Pascal, the ultimate end of the city. The imaginary dimension does not empty politics of all value in the name of the supernatural, as it is possible to intervene according to a Nature which transcends power-relationships. In the terms of the *Discours sur l'inégalité*, the vocation of the political order is to oppose *moral inequality*, that is, the dependence in which the mass of men is placed, taken in by the false contract of the powerful (*SD, OC* 3: 176–178); and there are inequalities authorized by Nature, those to which the heart consents without hardship, which cooperate "in like proportion with physical inequality," such as "differences in age, health, bodily strength, qualities of the mind and soul" (193–194). Nature indicates that Man must therefore submit to certain dependences and tear himself away from others – slavery, for example – to ensure his liberty. Even so, it is not enough for a dependence to be naturally good for it to work towards liberty. As we have seen, it must be *lived* in a certain manner, avoiding certain effects of the feeling of dependence aroused by *amour-propre* in a corrupted society; and it is in this respect that it is necessary to work on citizens from within.

What is the proper discourse for conducting this political education of the imagination? Once again Pascal shows the way, for even as he denounces the imposture of the political imagination he recognizes its necessity, as long as men live in sin. Wishing to overcome their subjection to the imagination would be failing to understand the necessity of the illusion; undertaking a denunciation which is more dangerous for civil peace than the pursuit of the *cloaked concupiscence* which is the political order. Such is the folly of those Pascal calls the *semi-learned*, who criticize the imperfect justice of men in the name of an unattainable natural justice. The *learned* on the other hand understand that imaginary politics is the condition of peace; and that if justice is recognized by the people as imaginary, obedience will dissolve, taking peace and the political order with it (*Pensées* 90, 1963: 510).

It is in this Pascalian spirit that anti-Enlightenment thinkers reproached the *Philosophes* of the eighteenth century for being *semi-learned*;[24] and following the use made of the *Contrat social* during the Revolution, this criticism was evidently aimed at Rousseau. But we have seen that, while he does not dissolve all political ambitions as Pascal does, his politics is far from being merely a requirement for *a priori* natural justice which turns the existing order upside down. It explores the different levels of discourse which enable the formation of consciences: natural feelings, the virtue of the Ancients, the morality of the gospels; ac-

---

[24] For Chateaubriand, for example, the Christian thinkers of the seventeenth century had already foreseen all the *liberal* ideas of the eighteenth century, but knew that they should remain veiled so that they did not lead to destructive consequences (*Génie du christianisme*, 1978: 826–830).

cording to what Montesquieu calls the *general spirit* of each people; and this political art thus places the ruse at the service of Nature. Rousseau is no less oriented towards a political future to be constructed, and he recognizes in Man an agent who is capable, up to a certain point, of thought and action. His politics therefore make what could be called the *voluntarist wager of modernity*, while showing important reservations about the self-legislating capacity of individuals and societies.

Does this fabrication of the imagination in Rousseau contradict liberty and natural equality as political norms? Liberty requires government by consent, but that consent can be consent *by* the imagination or consent *to* the imagination. Both elements seem necessary, as they correspond to the presence in society of different types of men, or perhaps different psychological states through which all men pass. This is why Rousseau never clearly decides between two classical political conceptions: that of an authority founded first of all on the wisdom of the rulers, and that of an authority founded first of all on the consent of the ruled; as wisdom is understood as the capacity to win men's consent by forging their imagination. In the *Contrat social* we read "obedience to the law one has prescribed oneself is liberty" (*CS, OC* 3: 365); but elsewhere we read "How then are hearts to be moved and made to love the fatherland and the laws? Dare I say it? By children's games; by institutions which are trivial in the eyes of superficial men, but which form cherished habits and invincible attachments."[25] Where, in the end, does liberty reside? In habits and attachments, or in obedience to the law one has prescribed oneself? Rousseau does not reply clearly, and never explicitly asks whether political consent achieved on the level of the imagination calls liberty into question. Rather, he proceeds as if liberty were only accessible by the imagination, and intermingles the two perspectives.

Liberal thinkers like Locke, who make consent the condition of political legitimacy, admit that consent cannot always be a deliberated act. There are weaker forms, *tacit* consents, which nevertheless do not make the governments enjoying them illegitimate.[26] But these thinkers, attached to the Enlightenment ideal, do make the citizens' reasoned choice the *aim* of politics; and this horizon of deliberated consent is a decisive criterion for judging the meaning of Rousseau's politics concerning liberty. For him, more rationality does not mean more liberty; more political transparency or less duplicity does not represent moral progress. His objective is not a society which would, like a child being educated, arrive at a

---

25 Rousseau, *Considérations sur le gouvernement de Pologne* (*OC* 3: 955).
26 Locke, *Two Treatises of Government*, sections 119–122.

sort of maturity which ultimately makes the formation of the imagination redundant. Wishing to generalize individual autonomy in the city would be acting like the *semi-learned*, like the *Philosophes* who claim to educate all men into liberty by reason.

Rousseau lets it be understood that no constitution can result from open deliberation; that it is when the *impenetrable feeling* of belonging to a collective is lost that societies dissolve. Recognizing societies' need for a founding exteriority if this feeling is to be born, the figure of the Legislator seems to go against the voluntarism of the *Contrat social* and (obviously) the revolutionary discourses which claimed it as their authority. This is why the most severe critics of Rousseau at the turn of the century are particularly attentive to this figure, seeing it as the mark of an admittedly fleeting lucidity which reveals the flaw in contractualism.[27] Let us not forget, however, that if the Legislator must be able to place his words in the mouths of the gods, the source of his authority is really human or philosophical: his greatness comes from the fact that he can legislate *in the name* of God, not that he is the instrument *of* the divine will. Nevertheless this aspect of the book demonstrates a critique of the idea of transparent self-foundation of societies, and the obliteration in the eighteenth century of a traditional political virtue: secrecy or deliberately-fostered ignorance. At the heart of the Enlightenment and the dawn of the Revolution, Rousseau, the champion of popular sovereignty, nonetheless raises the question of ignorance as a condition of authority.

One can see the uncomfortable position Rousseau's thinking was led to occupy, in debates between Enlightenment and Counter-Enlightenment, and later between revolutionaries and traditionalists. As the voice of conscience comes from Man himself, but also draws its strength from a source which is beyond him, it is always possible to emphasize one of these origins to the detriment of the other. If we stress the humanity of feeling, conscience will be understood as an injunction to Man to be the agent of his moral life, to distance himself from tradition, even to subject it to the ordeal of public discussion; if we emphasize a conscience informed by the divine, one which illuminates Man, then the initiative is taken away from him and he is carried by a necessity which has been gathered, given form and passed on by tradition. Rousseau seems to place the authority of Nature in the modern dynamic of *tearing away* from that tradition, by way of calling the theological heritage into question; but he nonetheless fights against the false certitudes of individual reason and the skepticism of dis-

---

[27] This is equally the case for Bonald as for Maistre, for example. For the latter, see *De la souveraineté du peuple* (1992: 118).

solvent questioning, in the name of a *divine instinct* and the entrenchment of men in sound prejudices which it is right to foster. According to traditionalist critics, the first movement of his thinking contributes to chaos and his individualism irreparably weakens the political and religious order; according to the promoters of revolutionary emancipation, the second movement makes him the Trojan horse of the Counter-Enlightenment.

Translated by Edward Hughes, Université Paris-Sorbonne

Works Cited

Augustine, Bishop of Hippo. *The Confessions of Saint Augustine*. Montreal: A Cardinal Edition, 1952.
Bréhier, Émile. "Les lectures malebranchistes de Jean-Jacques Rousseau." *Études de philosophie moderne*. Paris: PUF, 1965.
Chateaubriand, François-René de. *Essai sur les révolutions. Génie du christianisme*. Ed. Maurice Regard. Paris: Gallimard-Bibliothèque de la Pléiade, 1978.
Garrard, Graeme. *Rousseau's Counter-Enlightenment: A Republican Critique of the Philosophes*, Albany: SUNY Press, 2003.
Helvétius, Claude-Adrien. *De l'esprit*. Paris: Fayard, 1988.
Hulliung, Mark. *The Autocritique of the Enlightenment: Rousseau and the Philosophes*. Cambridge: Harvard UP, 1998.
Knee, Philip. *Penser l'appartenance: enjeux des Lumières en France*. Montréal: Presses de l'Université du Québec, 1995.
Locke, John. *Two Treatises of Government*. Cambridge: Cambridge UP, 1967.
Malebranche, Nicholas de. *Méditations chrétiennes*. Paris: Éditions Montaigne, 1928.
Maistre, Joseph de. *De la souveraineté du peuple: un anti-contrat social*. Paris: PUF, 1992.
Maritain, Jacques. *Trois réformateurs. Luther, Descartes, Rousseau*. Paris: Plon, 1925.
Montaigne, Michel de. *Essais*. Eds. Pierre Villey & Verdun L. Saunier. Paris: PUF, 1992.
Montesquieu, Charles de Secondat. *De l'esprit des lois. Œuvres complètes*. Vol. 2. Paris: Gallimard, "Bibliothèque de la Pléiade," 1951.
Pascal, Blaise. *Pensées. Œuvres complètes*. Ed. Louis Lafuma. Paris: Seuil, 1963.
Rousseau, Jean-Jacques. *Œuvres complètes*. Gen. Eds. Bernard Gagnebin and Marcel Raymond. 5 vols. Paris: Gallimard, "Bibliothèque de la Pléiade," 1959–1995.
Voltaire. "Vingt-cinquième lettre. Sur les *Pensées* de M. Pascal." *Lettres philosophiques. Mélanges*. Paris: Gallimard, "Bibliothèque de la Pléiade," 1961.

Stéphane Lojkine
Nature as Blind Space

1 An ambiguous concept

What does the word nature exactly represent in such an expression as "state of nature," which is precisely what knits up the whole demonstration in Rousseau's *Second Discourse*? Rousseau is explicitly referring to a twofold tradition: the recent, yet clearly delineated tradition represented by the jus-naturalists and law philosophers[1]; but also the older and less conspicuous one held by scholastics and theologians:

> It did not even occur to most of ours [i.e. our French philosophers] to doubt the possibility for a state of nature to have existed, whereas it is obvious, when one reads the sacred books, that, having received immediate enlightenment and precepts from God, the first man was not himself in that state, and when one adds to Moses' writings the faith owed to them by all Christian philosophers, one must deny that, even before the Flood, men should ever have found themselves in the pure state of nature, unless they had fallen back into that state in consequence of some extraordinary event.[2]

From the state of nature, understood as the state of man *in* nature, as opposed to the state of man in society, Rousseau has slipped to the state of *pure* nature, which refers to the *status purae naturae* that one comes across in the works of Thomas Aquinas' commentators, Cajetanus, Suares, and mostly Jansen who places that notion at the heart of his *Augustinus*. The entirely hypothetical character of the state of pure nature, from which man has immediately fallen into a state of corrupted nature, *status naturae lapsae*, comes from the scholastics; and the mode of reasoning consisting in making use of an hypothetical and unreal category, in order to deduce from it a certain type of organization or arrangement of the real, is a scholastic mode of reasoning.

Now, what does the word nature refer to in the theological concept of "the state of nature"? It is neither to nature as it is displayed before our eyes, nor to Nature as the organizing principle of the world, but to a state of nature *specific to man*, to the original nature of man, to what man is by nature: "Religion [...]

---

[1] See Robert Derathé; Victor Goldschmidt (especially 217 [ff.].).
[2] *The Second Discourse* (*OC* 3: 132). We will indicate further references after the acronym *SD* followed by the corresponding pagination without indication of volume. All translations from Rousseau are by the author of this article.

does not forbid us to form conjectures, derived from the mere nature of man and of the creatures that surround him, upon what mankind might have become, if man had remained abandoned to his own self" (*SD* 133).[3]

This abandonment is the abandonment of man without God; it hypothesizes a purely logical development of man, without Providence, a necessary hypothesis in order to establish, by contradistinction, the intervention of God through Grace, within the Christian reality to which we are witnesses: to the theological *status naturae* is opposed the *status gratiae*, to which Rousseau makes a very slight allusion here by appropriating the same structure and mode of reasoning, but emptied of its original content, as Hobbes had already done before him (Zarka 2000 [1995]).

Nature therefore does not refer to the world, or to a certain state of the world in which one should imagine the first men living. Nature is a logical category, such as the nature of a noun in grammar when opposed to its function, as when Rousseau, at the end of his *Second Discourse*, discusses "the nature of the fundamental pact of all governments" (*SD* 184) and "the nature of the Contract" (*SD* 185). Nature is an abstract tool that sends us back to a non-existent origin that one has to postulate, but that cannot be represented:

> At last, in their endless talk of need, greed, oppression, desire and pride, all have transferred to the state of nature ideas they had borrowed from society. They were talking of savage man when what they were painting was civil man [...]. The research one can pursue in this field should not be taken for historical truths, but only for hypothetical and conditional reasoning, better suited to clarify the nature of things as they are than to show their true origin, not unlike those daily offered by our physicians upon the formation of the world. (*SD* 132–113)

We are here confronted with the properly literary subtlety of the *Discourse*, which does not merely reject one mode of reasoning in favor of another, but which superimposes one upon the other. Starting from an "extremely embarrassing paradox," it builds its own representation from this logical impossibility.

On the one hand therefore, taken as a moral display of the human passions (such as need, greed, oppression... etc.), the *state of nature* is a visual delusion in which the other philosophers' discourses get caught and flounder; on the other hand, *the nature of things*, that the hypothesis of the state of nature serves to

---

[3] In a note, Jean Starobinski sends us back to Suarez, *de Gratia*, Prol. 4, c.1, n. 2, who himself quotes Cajetan.

clarify, becomes visible only if the hypothesis that makes it intelligible is maintained throughout as a logical impossibility.

"They were talking of savage man when what they were painting was civil man": when discourse becomes painting, when it makes us see what it says, it is our current human condition, the current stage of our world, that we see as though in a false, painted, scenery. It is not possible "to show the true origin": the nature of the state of nature can be apprehended only in the indirect convolutions of "hypothetical and conditional reasoning." It cannot be offered to sight or staged since to stage nature is merely to project our own world. We are therefore left on the one hand with a theatrical space, a stage, where we are in the civilized actuality of the world, and on the other hand, with an abstract, logical but invisible space, where we localize nature for want of visualizing an origin. Here Nature makes up for the lack of origin and can be patterned as the backstage of the world, constituting what we shall call a blind space.

2 The impossibility to see

We do not, we cannot see that space and, at the same time, we are required to have a mental image of it: "how will man at last manage to see himself as nature formed him?" (*SD* 122), Rousseau asks in his Preface. But then he immediately states that seeing such a thing is impossible: "let not my readers imagine that I dare flatter myself with having had a sight of what I deem to be so difficult to see" (*SD* 123). Instead of seeing, one must therefore imagine an indirect method, putting into play "reasoning" and "conjectures", and determine "what experiments would be required in order to reach full knowledge of natural man."[4]

This method is defined in contra-distinction to reading: "Leaving therefore all scientific books which teach us to see men only as they have made themselves, and pondering over the first and simplest operations of the human soul, I seem to perceive two principles that are anterior to reason [. . .]" (*SD* 125–126).

Scientific book reading makes us see only a staging of the present human condition. On the contrary, private meditation turns our eyes inward and demands that man should "at last manage to see himself as he was formed by na-

---

4 Starobinski has shown how seeing is prohibited in *Les Confessions* (*L'Œil vivant*, 1961: 93 [ff.]). Is it this autobiographical prohibition of desire that is objectified here in a philosophical formulation, or is it on the contrary a kind of theologico-political device, through which Rousseau organizes his conception of nature, that is projected into *Les Confessions* as a prohibition to see?

ture": eyes then seem to perceive "two principles anterior to reason." Turning our eyes inward, piercing through the coatings of reason – the disfigurements of Glaucus' statue (158), the successive developments through which reason "has managed at last to smother Nature" (162) – allows us to have a peep at this side of the visible, where principles lie. What is there cannot be read, nor can it offer itself to reading.

Unless there exists another book: "Oh man, whatever your country, whatever your opinions, listen to me; here is your history such as I seem to have read it, not in the books of your fellow-men that are liars, but in nature that never lies" (*SD* 133).

Nature is now defined as a space, and not as a mere category, a space that is not offered to eyes as a show but, nevertheless, can be read and submitted to conjecture. A space that would serve as a virtual book, and compensate our blindness.

Within that space, Rousseau first refuses to describe man, as we see at the beginning of the first part of the *Second Discourse*: "*I shall not trace* his organization through his successive developments, *I shall not stop at* looking into the animal System to see what he may have been at the start [...]; *I shall not examine* whether, as Aristotle thinks, his long nails were not first hook-like claws" (*SD* 134). Nature is a blind space: trying to see it is pointless and Rousseau makes it clear that it is not to be attempted. The origin is not to be looked at; better still, the examination of nature is necessarily preceded by the solemn denial of a visible origin, by the claim that any visible show of original nature is an impossibility.

It is a double negative that introduces the embryonic description of the original man, which is there only to tell us that we renounce to see him, because he is himself deprived of sight: "I shall *not* examine [...] whether, his walking on all fours, his eyes directed upon the ground and their range limited to a distance of a few steps, *did not* mark both the character and the limited range of his ideas" (*SD* 134). This limited horizon that prevents man in the state of nature from seeing and that we cannot see from our own world, to this space upon which we can only form "vague, almost imaginary, conjectures, is covered and replaced by Rousseau's own hypothesis" a hypothesis that he boldly puts forward as a false hypothesis, offering a postulated origin, a visible substitute for its impossible visibility: "I shall suppose him (man) conformed from all time as I see him today, walking on two feet, using his hands as we do ours, holding the whole of Nature under his gaze, and using his eyes to measure the vast expanse of the sky" (*SD* 134).

Nature at last shows itself as a spectacle. Man, using his eyes to measure up the vast expanse of the sky, thus delineating the range and extent of his own ability to see, is opposed to the original quadruped whose ground-bound and limited sight only signaled out the emptiness of his ideas. The spectacle of nature is necessary in order to conceive the state of nature; but it is impossible, both because we project it from our own corrupted humanity and because the natural man could not see it:

> His imagination does not paint anything for him [...]. The spectacle of nature becomes indifferent to him, by dint of becoming too familiar [...] he does not have the mental ability to wonder at the greatest marvels; and it is not in him that one should look for the Philosophy that man needs, in order to know how to observe once what he sees every day. (SD 144)

One should be able to observe what the natural man saw. But the natural man had no consciousness of seeing anything. One must therefore substitute him with a hypothetical man, "conformable from all time" and capable of observing a spectacle of which natural man was not aware.

Further on, Rousseau evokes Mandeville and his fable of the *Bees*. Mandeville provides him with a figure for this impossible original gaze:

> The pathetic image of an imprisoned man who perceives outside a ferocious beast tearing an infant from its mother's bosom, breaking the feeble limbs with its murderous teeth and tearing away the throbbing entrails of this child with its claws. What an awful commotion is it not for this witness of an event in which he takes no personal interest? What anguish doesn't he suffer at the sight, for being unable to go to the rescue of the fainting woman and the expiring infant?[5]
>
> Such is the pure movement of Nature, anterior to all reflection. (SD 154–155)

This parable, found in a book, provides an image for the principle of pity that, together with the love of oneself, Rousseau, at the beginning of the *Second Discourse*, felt he perceived after he had discarded all books... One can see that thought is always submitted to a double constraint and deliberately superimposes two contradictory modes of conceptualization, at once exacting visibility and stating invisibility, proclaiming and denying the necessity of conjecture; and, for this conjecture to function, both using and proscribing the model of books and reading. Mandeville's parable makes it possible to articulate this double movement.

Man in the state of nature is related to an imprisoned man who, from his prison cell, witnesses a performance in which he can have no active part. The

---

[5] Should we connect this image with that offered by the frontispiece engraving of the *Lettre sur les sourds* that Diderot had published in 1751?

relative positions of the prisoner watching the scene where the lion devours the child are analogous to what the audience witnesses in a dark or dimly-lit theatre, facing an illuminated, plainly visible, stage. Like the prisoner in his cell, the spectator is not personally concerned or endangered by what is happening before him. Like the cell bars, the invisible fourth wall between the stage and the audience allows him to see, but not to interfere in the play. Conversely, the woman and child do not realize that they are being watched; the prisoner remains as invisible to them as the spectators to the characters in a play; he is not in the place of the action; his place is only a point of vantage directed outward, towards the place of the action, towards the object of the performance, where the infant is being devoured by a lion.

The state of nature, the inside of the prison cell, escapes description; or rather such a description would be pointless. What Rousseau is concerned with here is no longer the "pure *state* of nature," but the "pure *movement* of nature." In other words the point is not to describe the inside of the prison cell, but to give an account of what attracts the prisoner to this external spectacle which is yet supposed to be totally alien to him. The blind space of nature (represented by the cell) is the place where the act of seeing takes its origin; but the birth of this faculty of seeing projects the person that sees outside of nature, into the movement of history, towards social horror. The emergence of society as a visible, theatrical space prepares the way to de-naturation and corruption.

3 The civil is the visible

The second part of the *Discourse* starts with a space-enclosing gesture: "The first person that, having enclosed a piece of land, bethought himself of declaring, *this is mine*, and found sufficiently simple minded people to believe him, was the true founder of civil society" (*SD* 164). Beyond the symbolic and philosophical bearing of this gesture which identifies the social state with a state of property ownership, this alteration of the relationship between man and space plays a decisive part in the passage from the blindness of nature to the visibility of society.[6] A man marks off a piece of land, lays his hand upon it and makes a speech, *This is mine*, in front of an audience, "people that are simple minded enough to believe him," who are from then on forbidden any access to this property, this scen-

---

[6] Scenic visibility, in Rousseau's thought, is always manifested as a consequence of a previously blind state. See Sampieri's analysis of chapter I of *l'Essai sur l'origine des langues* (1992, notably 231).

ic space. The foundation of society is the foundation of a scenic space; the civil organization is a theatrical organization.

At the same time, the process of conceptualization, which had so far been marked by the impossibility to see and by the working and tension of conjecture, now undergoes a radical change of model. A point of view is now established, in order to face a visible picture: "Let us therefore take things from a higher vantage point and try to gather *within a single point of view* this slow succession of events and discoveries, in their most natural order" (*SD* 164). At the same time as the philosopher gathers, unites, and orders the component parts of a social scene that he will thus be able to make us see, the historical process itself of constituting of societies is described as a process of gathering, circumscribing, and connecting, in radical opposition to the process of dissemination that characterized the state of nature. In the state of nature, men were "dispersed" (*SD* 135), they lived "scattered among the beasts" (*SD* 136) "and as there was hardly any other means to keep together than not to lose sight of one another, they were soon almost in a state of not even recognizing one another" (*SD* 147): dissemination is an essential character of the blind space, bearing the same relationship to the social state of property as, in classical painting, the vague space of the real surrounding bears to the scene, the inner stage of the representation (Lojkine 2015).

When an embryo of society emerges in nature, the faculty of looking manifests itself as directed from the space of nature towards this scenic enclosure circumscribing a civil organization, in the same way as the powerless gaze of the prisoner towards the lion devouring the child, or the stupefied gaze of the savages in front of the first man that, having enclosed a piece of land, bethought himself of declaring *this is mine.*

Society emerges out of this drawing of limits, but also out of a process of gathering, of assembling individuals together: it was "the effect of a new situation that gathered husbands and wives, fathers and children, within a common dwelling" (*SD* 168); they are now "men thus brought together, and forced to live together" (*SD* 169); they "gradually come closer together, gather in various groups" (*SD* 169); to the initial scattering there succeeds a linking process, "a few links between various families," "the linkages increase and the links become tighter."

History is a synthetic, and therefore scenic, ordering of what nature offered as a scattering: "things having reached this point, it is easy to imagine the rest. [...] I shall limit myself only to casting a glance at the human species placed within this new order of things" (*SD* 174). This ease with which one casts a glance is opposed to the delusions and impossibilities among which conjectures about the state of nature were getting lost. Here the philosopher can exert his scanning gaze at the very moment that the gathering of men together – and the beginning of relationships between them – make the faculty of looking possible in the *civil* community. It first manifests itself as looking at oneself, which degrades the love of oneself into self-love: "Then the first time he looked at himself, he felt his first motion of self-pride; then, hardly distinguishing among the respective ranks of beings, and finding himself in the first rank on account of his species, he found himself by far prepared to pretend to this rank on account of his own individual self" (*SD* 166). Looking is a splitting faculty that divides being and seeming and thus leads the way to the great stage of the civilized world and, in so doing, introduces the leaven of corruption: "Each man began looking at the others and wished to be looked at [...]; and the fermenting process initiated by this new leaven finally produced aggregates that were baleful to happiness and innocence" (*SD* 170). From then on, within society itself, the faculty of looking will degenerate and precipitate the social state towards a return to the blindness of nature. Rousseau speaks of a circle, of that "extreme point that closes the circle, adjoining the point from which we started" (*SD* 191).

4 Panoptical vision and blinded vision

Yet it is not exactly a return to the same situation as at the beginning of the *Second Discourse*: the blinded state of the enslaved and corrupted men – "the eyes of the People [...] fascinated" by their leaders (*SD* 188) – manifests itself as a picture to the wise man's eyes, to those "few great cosmopolitan souls, who can step over the imaginary barriers that divide the peoples of the world and who, following the example of the sovereign being that created them, embrace the whole of Mankind within their benevolence" (*SD* 178).

The erroneous, split up, blinded vision, is itself enfolded within a larger device, as one component piece of the conceptual picture that is being built around the love of freedom:

> The politicians make the same sophistic discourses upon the love of freedom as the philosophers upon the state of nature; from the things they see they judge very different things that they have not seen and they attribute to men a natural leaning towards servitude from the patience with which those they have under their eyes bear their own. (*SD* 181)

Concerning the love of freedom, that breaks out within the state of society as the demand of a return to nature, Rousseau once more finds the same blindness of the philosophers that he had condemned at the beginning of the *Second Discourse*, concerning the state of nature. They implement the same transposition of the current delusion with which they are surrounded, into a prior situation, a state that utterly differs from their world. In appearance therefore the loop is looped: the social picture is blurred and the splitting effect of its visibility brings back the civil space of representation to its initially scattered state of nature.

Yet, the very parallel between the love of freedom and the state of nature introduces a new operative device: the love of freedom is not a state, but a movement from the civil state towards nature. In other words it is a means, from the social space, which is the current visible one, of seeing this state of nature despite the blindness and the native paradox it is connected to. The love of freedom does not bring back the primal blindness; it pictures the movement towards that blindness and thus makes the state of nature indirectly visible:

> As an untamed horse bristles up its mane, stamps the earth with its hoof and struggles impetuously at the mere approach of the bit, whereas a trained horse suffers whip and spur with patience, the barbarian does not bend his head under the yoke that the civilized man bears without a murmur of complaint, and prefers the most stormy freedom to the tranquility of servitude. (*SD* 181)

The revolt of the Barbarian who refuses civilization is incomprehensible to the politicians who measure his nature and his behavior from what they are used to seeing, that is people whose civilization has been reduced to a debased state of servility. The revolted Barbarian springs up as a symptom of the state of nature that they cannot *a priori* understand, because it is irreducible to semiotic apprehension within the social space. In order to make it visible on the stage of representation, Rousseau resorts to the subterfuge of culture, which provides him with the images that our corrupt and weakened world could not offer him: the double epic metaphor of the untamed racehorse and of the trained horse introduces the difference between the two states within the sphere of the visible, and thus makes the state of nature visible from the state of society within which it introduces a claim for freedom through protest and revolt. However, this double image must not induce us to simply juxtapose the two concepts: it is from within the trained horse itself that one must discern the untamed one, from within the civilized man that one must detect the original Barbarian, and from within the sea-eroded statue that one must descry the primal Glaucus. To the philosopher's eye the social state is a screen that enfolds the state of nature. Not only does it make it invisible, but it corrodes, corrupts and disfigures it.[7]

---

[7] See Starobinski's analysis of the myth of Glaucus in *La Transparence et l'obstacle* (1971: 27 [ff.]).

Visibility can therefore only arise as far as we understand and keep in mind this superimposition, which makes it possible to conjecture the primal state of nature from the social symptom, through the exercise of philosophical indignation. What comes into play then is another seeing eye than the deluding and deluded eye of the moralists and politicians, a revolted eye:

> but *when I see* the others sacrificing pleasures, peacefulness, wealth, power and life itself to the preservation of this one good that is so despised of those that have lost it [i..e. freedom]; *when I see* animals that were born free and that abhor their captivity, break their skulls against the bars of their prison, *when I see* multitudes of naked Savages disdaining the European pleasures and braving hunger, fire, the sword and death in order to keep no more than their independence, I feel that Slaves are not fit to reason about freedom. (*SD* 181–182)

What Rousseau sees is unintelligible, and Rousseau himself sees it only at the cost of his own exclusion from the civil community, which he denounces as a community of slaves. These senseless, unseemly pictures, become visible to the reader only from within the movement of the Rousseauist revolt, which is a movement outward, towards nature. Rousseau still keeps his social eye at his disposal but, transporting his mind into the state of nature, he disengages himself from the delusions that go with that eye; he has not yet entirely quit the social sphere of the visible, but he has now sufficiently detached himself from it to fully bring into play the splitting power of its difference, represented by the metaphor of the two horses.

This allows for a better understanding of the frontispiece engraved in 1755 by Sornique, from a drawing by Eisen.[8] Eisen took his subject from an obscure anecdote from the *History of Travels* collated by Prévost and recorded at the end of the first and longest note of the second part of Rousseau's *Discourse*. In the late seventeenth century, the governor of Cape town, Simon van der Stel, adopted a young Hottentot savage, had him richly dressed, instructed in several languages and made him travel to the Indies. Upon his return, the young man visited a few Hottentots of his family:

> He decided to strip himself of his European attire and to clothe in a ewe's pelt. He returned to the fort in this new garb, holding a parcel containing his former clothes and, as he handed them to the Governor, he addressed him thus: *Do me the kindness, sir, of taking note that I renounce this attire for ever. For the rest of my life I also renounce the Christian religion, my resolve being to live according to the religion, the uses and manners of my ancestors. The only*

---

[8] See Utpictura18, data A9459, http://utpictura18.univ-montp3.fr/GenerateurNotice.php?num notice=A9459.

grace that I solicit from you is that I may keep the collar and the knife that I am wearing. I shall keep them for the love of you. Upon which, without waiting for Van der Stel's answer, he stole away and took flight and was never seen again in Cape Town.[9]

On the foreground of the engraving, the heap of clothes that the Hottentot has come to return functions as a symptom, pointing both to the sloughing of civilization and to the move back to nature. Above, the young man, wrapped in the skin of a ewe, points at the rejected clothes with his right arm, in accompaniment to his speech and, with his left hand, at the coast and the outer space of the sea crowded with boats, as vanishing point of his flight and return to his homeland. On the left, Van der Stel is sitting and meditating in front of his counselors, who wear a hat and are awaiting his answer. At the back of this left side, clouds are gathering above the Dutch fort.

Within the space of representation, there is no place for nature, at the very moment when the Hottentot, in the name of freedom, insists on returning to the state of nature with his parents and community. The heap of clothes, the governor and his counselors assembled as spectators of the scene offered to them by the young man, the fort and the boats, in fact all of his surroundings, inscribe him within the civil society that he claims to be fleeing. Even the outward space of the sea is swarming with Dutch boats. Only the fleeing movement and the preliminary doffing of the clothes, on the threshold of the scenic space, point to the blind space of nature. In Moreau the Younger's version of the scene,[10] the outer space is peopled with Hottentots but they are busy working for the Dutch. In Marillier's version,[11] the emphasis is laid upon the young man's flight, running past the heap of clothes. But looking back as he is towards his audience in the pose of an opera dancer, he seems to be destined never to escape. In order to conceive and represent this anthropological space of nature, it will be necessary to break from the classical scenographic frame of its representation.

Works Cited

Histoire générale des voyages, ou nouvelle collection de toutes les relations de voyage par mer et par terre [...]. Eds. Prévost et al. Vol. 5. Paris: Didot, 1748.

---

[9] *Histoire générale des voyages* (5: 175; 221, note xvi).
[10] See Utpictura18, data A8044, http://utpictura18.univ-montp3.fr/GenerateurNotice.php?numnotice=A8044.
[11] See Utpictura18, data A8045, 5.

Derathé, Robert. Jean-Jacques Rousseau et la science politique de son temps. Paris: Vrin, 1979.
Goldschmidt, Victor. Anthropologie et politique: Les principes du système de Rousseau. Paris: Vrin, 1974.
Lojkine, Stéphane. "Le vague de la représentation," Sprechen über Bilder Sprechen in Bildern: Studien zum Wechselverhältnis von Bild und Sprache. Ed. Lena Bader, Georges Didi-Huberman. Berlin: Deutscher Kunstverlag, 2015.
Rousseau, Jean-Jacques. Œuvres complètes. Gen. Eds. Bernard Gagnebin and Marcel Raymond. 5 vols. Paris: Gallimard, "Bibliothèque de la Pléiade," 1959–1995.
Sampieri, Jean-Christophe. "Le Problème de l'image dans le Chapitre 1 de l'Essai sur l'Origine des langues de Rousseau, 'Des Divers moyens de communiquer nos pensées.'" Résistances de l'image. Ed. Stéfane Lojkine, TIGRE. Florence Dupont et al. T.I.G.R.E. Paris: PENS, 1992.
Starobinski, Jean. L'Œil vivant: Essai (Corneille, Racine, Rousseau, Stendhal). Paris: Gallimard, 1961.
    Starobinski, Jean. Jean-Jacques Rousseau: La Transparence et l'obstacle. Paris: Gallimard, 1971.
Zarka, Yves Charles. Hobbes et la pensée politique moderne. 1995. Paris: PUF, 2000.

Anne Deneys-Tunney
Rousseau and Technology: The Invention of a New Ecological Paradigm

Rousseau has often been portrayed as a philosopher of nature, lost or outside of Enlightenment philosophy. In truth, work, tools, and technology are major themes of his system, and they are almost entirely ignored by today's scholars.[1] The thesis according to which Rousseau's work is entirely at odds with the Enlightenment masks everything that Rousseau owes to the Enlightenment as well as his very own contributions to the *Encyclopédie* (notably the articles and especially, in the fifth volume of the *Encyclopédie* in November 1755, the article "Economie"). It masks more particularly the fact that one finds a true philosophy of technology – apparently contradictory, but in truth prophetic for us today – in the entirety of his work, from the *First Discourse on the Arts and Sciences* up through the seventh Walk of *Reveries of a Solitary Walker*.

Rousseau is, of all the philosophers, the one to have most clearly shown that "the question of technology is absolutely not technical" as Martin Heidegger puts it in his work *The Question Concerning Technology*.[2] In other words, Rousseau was the first to understand that technology was becoming a real power for man – a political and social power – and that it was from within ethical and political thought (and beginning with the foundational concept of nature) that one had to think technology. To think both its potentially devastating effects on man and nature, "this fatal progress," or on the contrary its positive effects on human freedom in society.[3]

One can measure the originality and the modernity of Rousseau's theses if one compares them to the discourse on technology in the *Encyclopédie*. One of

---

[1] The history of philosophy as a whole has repressed the question of technology, as Bernard Stiegler (2006) has shown in *Technics and Time:* "At its origin and until today, philosophy has repressed technics as objects of thought. Technic is not thought" (1: 23). Unlike the whole of the philosophical tradition, Rousseau's work proposes a philosophy of technology, as I showed in my 2010 book. A French version of this essay was published in *Planet Rousseau*, eds. Leopold and Poppenberg (2015). I thank the editors for their gracious authorization to publish a new version of it in translation.
[2] See Martin Heidegger, *The Question Concerning Technology*.
[3] It is this paradox, which is one in appearance only, that I explore here, starting from my previous analyses.

the novelties of the *Encyclopédie*, it is important to remember, consists in making public, for the first time in human history, the totality of the knowledge and production secrets of the time. With its 11 volumes of illustration plates, its 1242 articles on different trades, on machines, on forms of human work hitherto jealously guarded by trade associations, on "mechanical arts" of which Diderot wrote 104 articles, this public, democratic, and transnational disclosure of technology is in itself a revolution. It is nevertheless surprising to note, being faced with such a project, the relative weakness of any philosophical thought about technology in the *Encyclopédie*. According to Jürgen Habermas: "Modernity originates from this key moment in intellectual history where reason was forced, by the efficiency of science and nature, to dissociate its cognitive form from its practical form." (1988: 219) It is clear that Diderot and d'Alembert's *Encyclopédie* played a major role in the appearance and in the definition of this moment. The *Encyclopédie* decisively – and likely irreversibly – yoked reason to praxis, knowledge to technique. Whereas Diderot is enthralled, in the article "*Bas*" (Stockings) by the prowess of the new stocking machine and the new freedom that it provides for the worker, Rousseau puts himself in the workers' shoes. In the seventh Walk of his *Reveries*, he paints an abominable portrait of mining and metallurgic production that reveals a completely different sensibility, one that espouses the point of view of the subordinate. Rousseau is not enthralled by the technological capabilities of ore extraction.

During his visit to Diderot in prison at Vincennes, Rousseau reads the question posed by the Dijon Academy of 1750, as to whether "the re-establishment of the Sciences and the Arts has contributed to purifying mores." Rousseau suddenly saw his entire system illuminated. As though in a flash of lightening, human history suddenly appeared to him in all of its contradiction: on the one hand, the progress of science and technology; on the other, the degradation of relationships between men.[4] These two phenomena are, Rousseau writes in his *Discourse on the Arts and Sciences*, two aspects of the same process that summons them and conditions them reciprocally. Rousseau exposes here, in his first philosophical work, the question of the moral power of knowledge, both technical and artistic. Rousseau sketches out in this short text – which is very paradoxical and even contradictory in certain respects – a model of historical genealogy starting with the following question: what has been the role of artists and of technological inventions in the history of civilization up until today? Rousseau condemns – at times vehemently – the alliance between knowledge and power. He argues, in the spirit of the theses that Michel Foucault subsequently

---

4 This is the "Illumination of Vincennes." See *Confessions* (OC 1: 350–352 [CW 5: 294–295]).

developed, that there is no autonomy between knowledge and power, in particular as concerns technology.⁵ Rousseau shows that there is a paradox: the development of certain technological capacities brings about an increase in dependence and alienation with regard to power. What is at the heart of growing technology are relationships of inequality and subordination (at the level of individuals and of States), and not a process of liberation.

The question of freedom figures prominently in Rousseau's philosophy about technology; how does (technical) knowledge hinder human freedom? In two essential ways, according to Rousseau: first, it deprives him of original freedom by chaining him to artificial needs⁶; second, it weakens religion and virtue and favors despotism. Rousseau offers, in the first part of the *First Discourse*, a genealogy of human societies and shows the constant association between technical knowledge and progress with commerce and luxury. He opposes societies that have technology (Egypt, Greece, Rome, Constantinople, and China) with those that avoided it (Persians, Germans, Rome in its first state) (*DSA* 10–13). Technological societies are morally corrupt, while those without technology are virtuous. Rousseau opposes Athens to Sparta, military values to fine arts. He accuses scientists and artists of being allies to despotism. They dull the desire for freedom and turn men into "civilized slaves" (*DSA* 7). Going against other Enlightenment thinkers who maintain there is harmony between knowledge and morality, that technological development translates into an increase of human happiness, Rousseau provocatively sings the praise of ignorance and virtue.⁷ Technology is criticized for its harmful effect on mores in the following opposition: virtuous agricultural societies vs. societies of luxury and artistic culture, and technological elitism. For example, the move to technology turns Egypt – up until then a pacifist civilization – into an imperialist nation. This point is of supreme importance: technology contains its own sinister internal logic. It is indeed technology that makes peaceful societies abandon peace, leading them to the imperialist politics of conquest. Technology produces war simply be-

---

5 Michel Foucault: "One must instead admit that power and knowledge exist in a reciprocal relationship of correlation and constitution. The great hope of the eighteenth century is for the growth of technology's effect on things to be parallel to the growth of individuals' freedom with respect to each other" *Philosophie* (2004: 385).
6 Regarding this central notion of "artificial needs" that turn men into "happy slaves," see *Discours sur les sciences et les arts:* "[politicians] extend garlands of flowers on the metal chains carried by men, squelching in them the feeling of original freedom [...] and make them love their enslavement [...]" (*OC* 3: 7). Translations of *DSA* are by the translator of this article.
7 See Rousseau's condemnation: "We saw virtue flee as their light came up over the horizon [...]" (*DSA* 10).

cause it provides the material means with which to wage it and win, Rousseau states. The logic is circular. Technology produces vices – and the vices lead to an expansion of technology.[8] On the one hand, Rousseau points to technology as a major aspect in human history that projects humanity into moral corruption. On the other, this moral corruption has already occurred, and it has produced technology.

One of the principal reasons for this complicity between moral corruption and the Arts and Sciences according to Rousseau is that scientists and artists must become accomplices to power in order to sell. It is also at this moment that the concept of inequality appears: technology produces inequality simultaneously to a general moral corruption. As we can see, Rousseau deals with technology not as it is in itself, but in the context of a moral global critique of the knowledge and the arts that it includes.

One could deduce from the *First Discourse* that Rousseau systematically opposes nature to culture and nature to technology in his philosophy. In truth, this is not the case. Rousseau seeks avenues of conciliation between the two. In his *Second Discourse*, he develops his philosophy of technology in relationship to his concept of nature, staging the savage man's transition to technology, and describing the origins of each technology. There certainly is, in the *Second Discourse*, an idealization of the "state of nature," that is characterized by autonomy, self-sufficiency, and solitude.

Rousseau invents the concept of perfectibility:

> [on] this difference between man and animal, there is another very specific quality that distinguishes them and about which there can be no dispute: the faculty of self-perfection, a faculty which, with the aid of circumstances, successively develops all others, and resides among us as much in the species as in the individual. By contrast an animal is at the end of a few months what it will be all its life; and its species is at the end of a thousand years what it was the first year of that thousand. (*SD* 142 [26])

To my knowledge, Rousseau is the only philosopher of his time to have invented a philosophical concept out of technology. It is the concept of "perfectibility" that he defines in the *Second Discourse*. Perfectibility is, with self-love ("amour de soi") and pity, one of the three qualities of natural man. Perfectibility is the capacity to perfect oneself, to transform the world around oneself and within oneself. It inscribes the history of technology, the discovery of sciences and tech-

---

[8] Rousseau understood something fundamental to our modernity, which is that technology among other things, transforms the citizen into a consumer: "Old politicians spoke always about morals and virtue; ours only speak about commerce and money" (*DSA* 19).

nologies, at the heart of the human soul. It is also essential to ask oneself what Rousseau understands by the concept of nature. Nature in Rousseau is not only the immediacy of the state of nature. It is also surpassing oneself in technology. The ostensible opposition between nature and technology in Rousseau's work is only *apparently misleading*. The reality is that the totality of his philosophical system aims to rethink nature and technology in their complementarity, rather than in opposition to each other. Technology is the realization or the objectification of the natural quality within man (along with pity and "amour de soi") that is perfectibility. This quality nevertheless has a different status from the other two. Perfectibility – and therein lies the ambiguity of the concept – is both a natural quality and what makes man come out of nature. It transforms man's relationship to nature: with it, man invents tools, discovers fire, ores, cultivates the soil, becomes a social being, etc. He can henceforth create tools, houses, cities, and weapons of war.

The long descriptions that Rousseau gives of natural technologies (hunting, fishing for the Hottentots) in the notes of the *Second Discourse*, which give the text its beauty and make of it, according to Claude Lévi-Strauss, the first foundational text for the "Human Sciences" – or what is today called anthropology –, illustrate this development of human technology. In the following passage, Rousseau compares man with monkey:

> As for the objection one could make that this deprives man of the use of this hands, from which we derive so many advantages, besides the example of monkeys, which shows that the hand can very well be used in both ways, it would prove only that man can give his limbs a destination more useful than that of Nature, and not that Nature destined man to walk otherwise than it teaches him to do. (*SD* 196–197 [69]).

This excerpt shows that an obscure finality, inside of nature, produces man's exit from nature. Another comment from the notes follows the same idea:

> A Child abandoned in a forest before he is able to walk, and nourished by some beast, will have followed the example of his Nurse in training himself to walk like her; habit could have given him dexterity he did not have from Nature; and as armless People succeed, by dint of training, in doing everything with their feet that we do with our hands, he will finally have succeeded in using hands as feet. (*SD* 197–198 [70])

In another note, Rousseau makes the distinction between carnivorous and vegetarian animals according to their teeth and digestive systems. He explains the need for man to leave the state of nature: "For as prey is almost the unique subject of fighting among Carnivorous Animals, and as Frugivorous ones live among themselves in continual peace, if the human species were of this latter genus it clearly would have had much greater ease subsisting in the state of Nature, and much less need and occasion to leave it." (*SD* 198 [71])

In the subsequent texts, *Emile* and *The Social Contract*, Rousseau looked for ways to synthesize technology and nature. In *Emile*, he describes how Emile acquires technical knowledge. The only book authorized in Emile's education is Defoe's *Robinson Crusoe*, the goal being to safeguard his autonomy and his freedom. Emile must be a subject in his relationship to technology, and never become an object for the machine. It is clear that technology is not fated to be bad or alienating. In *The Social Contract* and *Constitution Project for Corsica*, Rousseau proposes the model for a political economy based on local and self-sustaining craftsmanship and on self-sufficient moderation. One must at all costs avoid luxury, that is, dependence. The aim is a self-sufficiency and a social and economic autarky that politically recovers the freedom and autonomy of the man of the forest. In yet another note, Rousseau warns prophetically against the risks of soil depletion and deforestation caused by agriculture: "destruction of the soil, that is to say, the loss of the substance suited to vegetation, must accelerate in proportion as the earth is more cultivated and as more industrious inhabitants consume in greater abundance its products of all kinds" (*SD* 198 [70]). Rousseau is indeed the founder of ecological thinking. Similarly, in *La Nouvelle Héloïse*, the bird bath in Julie's garden (part iv, letter 11) gives a lengthy description of the long incline that enables water from Wolmar's house to make its way to the bird bath.[9] The desire here is to save water. Instead of destroying nature, technology is at nature's service.

Rousseau thus defines an ethics, a politics, and an economy of the individual and of his freedom in the world of social artefacts that he creates. Herein lies Rousseau's modernity. He understood that man needs technology to survive and develop, that it is inscribed in his nature, his history; that it can become a form of freedom – as long as the notions of individual subject (rather than object of the machine), of autonomy, freedom, and responsibility are respected. This ethical and political program remains an ideal for us today. Rousseau engendered a true philosophical paradigm-shift in opening up a new ecological paradigm, the stakes and import of which we have barely begun to understand today.[10]

In their *Dialectic of Enlightenment* Max Horkeimer and Theodor W. Adorno very virulently attacked the Enlightenment as a bourgeois ideology of science and technology. According to them, Enlightenment philosophy became, at

---

9 See Deneys-Tunney (2010), *Un autre Jean-Jacques Rousseau* (ch. vi, 115 – 120).
10 See Hans Jonas (1990). It is surprising that Jonas does not reference Rousseau's name even once, despite the fact that he is the true founder of an ecological line of thinking at the very beginning of the industrial revolution.

the dawn and then at the apogee of capitalism, a new mythology of Progress, Reason, Science and Technology that became totalitarian from the nineteenth century on. Having become calculating and positivist, this type of reason in fact pursues, more or less consciously and thanks to its technological and economic outcomes, a systematic exploitation of nature and of man, the latter having become an industrial workforce. In so doing, this reasoning turns on its protagonists, i.e. man. By converting the totality of nature and of the world to its "use-value" – this is already the Hegelian reading of the Enlightenment in *Phenomenology of Spirit*[11] – thanks to the Enlightenment, science and technology have made nature no longer the place of transcendence and myth, but a reserve of wealth to be exploited, with maximum profit, until its final destruction. Everything is henceforth reduced to its "use-value," including the most intimate feelings of individuals, such as love. Marriage within these modern technological societies where each individual is nothing but a machine without subjectivity – the same as all the others – is at the service of those super machines that are modern societies: "under the domination of industry [...] free men themselves became that 'herd,' which Hegel declared to be the product of Reason [Enlightenment]" (Horkheimer-Adorno 1974: 31). The process of totalitarian rationalization of the world and of nature by technology leads, according to them, to a moral division between subject and object, which in turn leads to the objectification of man himself. Technology constrains him to cease being – at the very moment that he becomes, thanks to technology, the master of nature. In so doing, according to the philosophers of the Frankfurt school, technology separates man from himself, from his body – having become a machine at the service of production – and from his individual subjectivity. Technology separates intelligence, or the mind, from experience, through the division of labor. Whence a general impoverishment of reason, itself turned by this process into a mortal instrument at the service of a globalized technology and economy that nobody today seems to know how to control, nor even, in some respects, understand. "The technical process, in which the subject has objectified itself after being removed from the consciousness, is free of the ambiguity of mythic thought as of all meaning altogether, because reason has become the mere instrument of the all-inclusive economic apparatus" (Horkheimer-Adorno 1993: 30 [1974: 46]).[12]

---

[11] Hegel, *Phénoménologie*, specifically the pages dedicated to the Enlightenment (1941, 2: 93–200).
[12] On this issue, see Bronner's recent response to Adorno and Horkheimer.

Rousseau is a thinker of modernity. He understood the determining role of technological development in human history. He knew that these developments are irreversible, that technology's effects go further than itself, and that it constitutes a genuine power that both risks to endanger human autonomy and freedom, and destroy nature. There is no autonomy from technology according to Rousseau – it is inscribed in man and in nature, even if it risks destroying him. Against this danger, we must, Rousseau contends, establish an ethics, a policy, and an economy that aims to preserve the autonomy of the individual and his freedom in the social world of artefacts that he produces. Therein lies Rousseau's modernity. He understood that man needs technology to survive and develop, to become a moral individual, and that it can become a form of his freedom – on the condition that the concepts of individual, subject (and not object of the machine), autonomy, and freedom be respected. This ethical and political program remains, for us still today, an ideal to be attained. Rousseau carried out a paradigm change whose conditions of realization we must now conceive.

Translated by Karen Santos Da Silva

Works Cited

Bronner, Stephen Eric. Reclaiming the Enlightenment: Toward a Politics of Radical Engagement. New York: Columbia UP, 2004.

Deneys-Tunney, Anne. "Rousseau face à la technique: l'invention du paradigme écologique." Planet Rousseau: Zur Heteronomen Genealogie Der Moderne. Eds. Stephan Leopold and Gerhard Poppenberg. Paderborn: Wilhelm Fink, 2015. 151–158.

Deneys-Tunney, Anne. Un autre Jean-Jacques Rousseau: Le paradoxe de la technique. Paris: PUF, 2010.

Foucault, Michel. Philosophie: Anthologie. Eds. Arnold I. Davidson and Frédéric Gros. Paris: Gallimard, 2004.

Habermas, Jürgen. Le Discours philosophique de la modernité: Douze conférences. Trans. Christian Bouchindhomme and Rainer Rochlitz. Paris: Gallimard, 1988.

Hegel, Georg W. F. La Phénoménologie de l'esprit. Trans. and ed. Jean Hyppolite. Paris: Aubier-Montaigne, 1939–1941.

Heidegger, Martin. The Question Concerning Technology, and Other Essays. Trans. William Lovitt. New York: Harper & Row, 1977.

Horkheimer, Max, and Theodor W. Adorno. La Dialectique de la Raison: Fragments Philosophiques. Trans. Éliane Kaufholz. Paris: Gallimard, 1974.

Horkheimer, Max, and Theodor W. Adorno. Dialectic of Enlightenment. Trans. John Cumming. New York, Continuum, 1993.

Jonas, Hans. Le Principe responsabilité: Une éthique pour la civilisation technologique. Trans. Jean Greisch. 1990. Paris: Flammarion, 2009.

Rousseau, Jean-Jacques. Œuvres complètes. Gen. Eds. Bernard Gagnebin and Marcel Raymond. 5 vols. Paris: Gallimard, "Bibliothèque de la Pléiade," 1959–1995.
Rousseau, Jean-Jacques. The Collected Writings of Rousseau. Gen. Eds. Roger D. Masters and Christopher Kelly. 13 vols. Hanover: UP of New England, 1990–2010.
Stiegler, Bernard. Technics and Time 1. The Fault of Epimetheus. Trans. Richard Beardsworth and George Collins. Stanford, CA: Stanford UP, 1998.

Masano Yamashita
Rousseau and "The Mechanical Life"

Writing in the wake of seventeenth-century Cartesian mechanistic philosophy and building on the new ideas of iatromechanism and vitalism, Enlightenment philosophers and scientific thinkers such as La Mettrie, Maupertuis and Diderot continued to view human subjectivity through the metaphor of the man-machine, whose behavior could in great part be understood as an automated series of physiologically determined reactions to the physical world. Less than fifteen years after Vaucanson first displayed his automaton machine at the Saint-Germain fair, Julien Offroy de La Mettrie published *L'Homme machine* (1747) and *L'Homme-plante* (1748), in which he polemically unseated man's dominion over the animal kingdom by emphasizing man's profound likeness to plants and animals. The machine stood as a useful heuristic tool for apprehending living organisms and was not yet considered to be antinomical to the natural world. In the second half of the eighteenth century the anthropological narrative of a man-machine develops alongside a growing interest in the rapidly developing fields of technology, designated by the Encyclopedists as the "mechanical arts." Diderot's article "*Bas*" (Stocking) and the plates designed by Louis-Jacques Goussier illustrating manufacturing workshops attest to the enthusiasm surrounding technological modernity as well as the newfound prestige of the artisan. The article "Bas" distinguishes and draws equal attention to both the "*main d'œuvre*," the human hand at work, and the "machine," marking the beginnings of an exploration of the possible relationships of continuity and supplementarity between the hand and the artificial machine.[1] The machine as both metaphor and literal object also features heavily in the work of the most exacting internal critic of the Enlightenment, Jean-Jacques Rousseau. Composed during a pivotal historical moment in which France was attentively looking on at the beginnings of the Industrial Revolution in England, three texts of Rousseau – the *Discours sur l'inégalité*, the pedagogical text *Émile*, and the unfinished work of the *Rêveries* – demonstrate the author's rich awareness of the moral and social issues stemming from the increased specialization of human professional activity and the beginnings of an industrial society. Far from presenting a critique of mechanization, Rousseau turns towards possible ways of conceptualizing the mechanic as a positive model for a peaceful, natural way of living.

---

1 Diderot, *Encyclopédie* (II: 98).

As a metaphor for man, the machine appears in an ambiguous light in Rousseau's writings. Although initially eager to dispel the importance of mechanical behavior in human conduct in an attempt to distinguish himself from determinist materialist thinkers, Rousseau's last works present a turn in his thought through the unexpected praise of the "mechanical life." In *Éléments de physiologie* (1778), Rousseau's former collaborator Diderot presented his understanding of the man-machine as fundamentally un-free through his lack of volition, arguing that man is a "pure machine, simple and passive, made up of various motivations that move him, far from having been free, he has not produced a single deliberate act of his own will: he thought, he acted, but he is as unfree as an inert body, a wooden automaton would have executed the same things as he did."[2] While Diderot integrates mechanics into his conceptualization of man, Rousseau first sought to establish a clear distinction between animal behavior on the one hand, construed to be instinctive and automated, and human conduct, emphoweringly defined by its freedom of will. Weary of the idea of soulless automatons, Rousseau reprises the early-modern fear formulated by the Cartesian physicist Jacques Rohault: "If you currently hold for certain that animals are mere automatons, aren't you afraid of one day believing that men also are mere machines?" (1671: 91).

In *The Discourse on the Origins of Inequality*, Rousseau maps out his first stance toward contemporary understandings of the man-machine by the following premise: humans possess the unique ability to consciously self-fashion their lives. Men hold the unique "power of willing, or rather of choosing, and in the sentiment of this power are found only purely spiritual acts about which the Laws of Mechanics explain nothing" (*SD* 3: 26).[3] But in spite of these universalizing claims of human freedom in his anthropological works, Rousseau's self-presentation in his later works registers the recurrent desire to live "mechanically" on automatic pilot, in a liminal state of subjectivity. In *Rousseau, Judge of Jean-Jacques*, "J. J" is exposed as leading "this almost automatic life" (*D* 1: 146), "working almost mechanically" (146), his "habitual state was and always will be inertia of mind and mechanical activity" (147). His daily activities comprise mostly of copying music, going on walks and herborizing. His manner of living escapes the traditional categories of narrativity: a plotless life that requires few procedures of deliberation, undergoing little to no variations and marked by

---

[2] Diderot, *Éléments de physiologie*, *Œuvres complètes* (XVII: 485–486).
[3] All references to Rousseau's texts, unless otherwise noticed, are from *CW*. Indications of the volume number will be followed by pagination for the first citation, and then only by page numbers.

passivity. In this negative conception of human life, Rousseau goes so far as to assimilate the self with the vegetal order, writing in a letter to François-Henri d'Ivernois "one of these mornings I will become a plant myself."[4] What are the ideological and moral implications of Rousseau's identification to plant life? What remains of the self when it is emptied of its rationality and agency? The following pages will focus on how Rousseau's original understanding of the mechanical in human life allows him to fashion a stoicist practice of daily existence that paradoxically rests on the figure of the human automaton.

It is a commonplace to note that Rousseau's relationship to nature inaugurates a mode of subjectivity that will soon be characterized as Romantic. However, Rousseau scholarship has often omitted to precisely situate Rousseau's self-identification to inanimate life forms and his apology of the mechanical within the specific development of an Enlightenment ethics.[5] Critical towards the instrumentalized use of the natural world in pharmaceuticals, animal dissection, and the industrial exploitation of mines for economic profit, Rousseau's frequent herborizations and fervent espousal of botanical study reveal a radical desire to become absorbed into nature. Herborizing at l'Ile Saint-Pierre induces a transformation of Rousseau's self into a passive, plant-like entity that cancels out the typical spatial-temporal and psychological markers of personhood. Recording plants and flowers into a herbarium, the botanist preserves an ethical stance towards nature though an anti-utilitarian refusal to transform its properties. Eschewing a position of mastery, Rousseau positions himself as a precursor of deep ecology.[6] In the *Confessions*, the botanist's activity is not only directed toward the observation of nature, but also involves a radical experience of the limits of subjectivity through a movement of absorption that negates the distance between observer and the object of observation, resulting in a curious mimesis: on the island of Saint-Pierre, Rousseau becomes a plant. Second, human historical time and teleological action find themselves suspended through the practice of herborization: "To wander nonchalantly in the woods and in the country, here and there to take up mechanically, sometimes a flower, sometimes a branch; to graze on my fodder almost at random, to observe the same things thousands of times, and always with the same interest because I always forgot them, was enough for me to pass eternity without being bored for a moment" (*C* 5: 537).

---

4 Letter to François-Henri d'Ivernois, dated 1 August 1765 (1976, *CC* 26: 130).
5 On the widely accepted idea of Rousseau as the father of Romanticism, see Babbitt (1947) and Taylor (1989). Jean-François Perrin has been one of a few recent critics who have been attentive to Rousseau's articulation of mechanicity and nature in his ethical reflections. See Politique du renonçant: le dernier Rousseau du Dialogue aux Rêveries (2011: 185–201).
6 See Lane and Clark (2006).

The aimless wandering of the botanist disregards and nullifies teleological logics of progress and productivity through the invention of an alternative, disinterested practice of time and space. While Schiller laments toward the end of the eighteenth century, "Today Necessity is master, and bends a degraded humanity beneath its tyrannous yoke. Utility is the great idol of our age, to which all powers must do service and all talents swear allegiance,"[7] Rousseau transforms the mechanical into a positive index of virtue, serving as proof of a life lived according to the precepts of nature. "J. J."'s repetitive and monotonous mode of existence is "natural, because it is not the work of either effort or reason, but a simple impulsion of temperament determined by necessity. The sole merit of the person who yields to it is that he gave in without resistance to nature's bent [...]" (D 1: 146). Living in harmony with nature, according to this explanation, requires an act of submission on the part of the subject and therefore correlates to the moment of his passivization. "J. J."'s penchant for botanizing is rendered as a passive action that is socially therapeutic and deeply ethical: "it is great wisdom and even great virtue to give myself up to pastimes which gratify me. It is the means of not letting any germ of revenge or hatred spring up in my heart; and given my destiny, to still find delight in any amusement, it is surely necessary to have a natural temperament quite purified of all irascible passions" (R 8: 58).

In the *Confessions*, the simplicity of life experienced at Montmorency further points to the virtues of a mechanical existence, "that even and simple life, outside of which there is no happiness whatsoever for me" (C 442). The attributes of this mode of existence are in fact identical to those found in the experiences of state-of-nature's man, whose life is described in the Discourse on the Origins of Inequality as "simple, uniform et solitary." Surrounded by pets and a simple-minded woman (Thérèse Levasseur), Rousseau recounts his sojourn at Montmorency as an idyllic, prelapsarian interlude that allows him to reconnect with nature. He reminisces: "what good café au lait did I take there tête-à-tête with my Therese! My cat and my dog gave us company. This retinue alone would have been enough for me for my whole life, without ever experiencing a moment of boredom. There I was in the terrestrial Paradise; I lived there just as innocently, and I tasted the same happiness" (437).

Thérèse is what Deleuze and Guattari (1991) would call a "conceptual protagonist" (8). Standing for a degree zero of civilization as an uneducated manual laborer by trade (a *lingère*), Thérèse figures in Rousseau's work as an unalterable

---

[7] Schiller (2004, Letter 2: 26). Adapting a Foucaultian lens, Pierre Saint-Amand (2003) persuasively reads Rousseau's praise of idleness and "désœuvrement" as a subversive form of resistance to utilitarian, modern society.

product of nature: "Her mind is what nature has made it; cultivation and effort do not take hold there. I do not blush at all to admit that she has never known how to read very well, although she writes passably." (*C* 5: 278–279) Limited in her abilities, a savage amongst men, she cannot read time nor count money, standing at the periphery of a venal, precapitalist society obsessed with tracking monetary transactions and the accumulation of wealth: "She does not know either how to count change or the price of anything." (*C* 279) Her ignorance of financial matters stands in contrast to the rapaciousness of her mother, Madame Levasseur, whose parasitical existence weighs heavily on Rousseau and interferes in his relationship with his fellow *Philosophes*. Thérèse's intellectual shortcomings – "so limited and if you wish so stupid" (279) –, her lack of cultural capital, are revealed in sum to be moral virtues. Her ignorance of clock time and bookkeeping allow her, and by proximity, Rousseau himself, to live according to the dehistoricized rhythm of nature. Rousseau registers the symbolic importance of his life with Thérèse as the moment from which "I decided to live from day to day from then on" (*C* 347); in spite of "the stupid shame of not daring to show myself with Therese in public [...] we made little country walks tête-à-tête and little afternoon snacks that were delightful to me. [...] This sweet intimacy took the place of everything for me; the future no longer touched me or touched me only as the present prolonged: I desired nothing but to ensure its endurance" (279). Living in a depthless temporality with no sense of futurity, Thérèse and Rousseau have a daily life reminiscent of the peaceful existence of primitive man, whose "soul, agitated by nothing, is given over to the sole sentiment of its present existence without any idea of the future, however near it may be, and his projects, as limited as his views, barely extend to the end of the day" (*SD* 28).

In 1754 Rousseau kept a travel-log during a boat trip undertaken with Thérèse and the Genevan Jacques-François de Luc's family, which will later serve as the source of inspiration for the descriptions of Vaud and Chablais in his epistolary novel *Julie or the New Heloïse*. The travel-log contains a series of cursory notations that solely record the natural functions of eating and sleeping, and elide the pronominal subject so as to underscore the mechanistic activities of repose and nourishment:

> Sunday dined on the grass near Hermance.
> Slept at the Chateau of Coudrée.
> Monday dined on the grass near Ripailles.
> Slept at Meilleraie.
> Tuesday slept at Bex.
> Dined at Pisse-Vache.
> Slept at Saint-Maurice.

> Dined at Aigle.
> Frugal repast of hospitality.
> Isn't there something in Homer worthy of my trip?
> Tuesday dined at Villeneuve.
> Slept at Vevai.
> Wednesday dined at Cuilli.
> Slept at Lausanne.
> Thursday dined and slept at Morges.
> Friday dined at Nion and slept at Eaux-Vives. ("Travel notebook" 12: 62)

The low register of the *carnet de route* is, however, elevated through a reference to Homer that occurs midway through the travel log: "Isn't there something in Homer worthy of my trip?" Rousseau ponders rhetorically in the midst of listing the various places where he lodged and dined. The seemingly elementary actions of dining and sleeping implicate the deeply humane and symbolic relationality at work in the practice of hospitality. The mechanical notations yield to the richness of human exchange and the social development of natural pity, described in *The Discourse on the Origins of Inequality* as the point of origin of "all the social virtues" (*SD* 37) which include "generosity, Clemency, Humanity [...] Benevolence and even friendship" (37). Here the mechanical serves as a screen for the most developed manifestation of human potential: the appreciation for the unconditional acceptance of strangers into one's home.

Within the framework of natural life, music copying also stands as an exemplary activity: it consists of honorable "manual work" (*D* 1: 136) that procures Rousseau his financial independence and moral autonomy, establishing him as a humble yet dignified and self-sufficient "artisan" (147) The psychological wellbeing and anonymity related to music copying are set in contradistinction with the travails of the writer-artist identified by the public as the celebrity "Jean-Jacques." Rousseau laments in the seventh walk: "I felt the fatigue of mental work and the importunity of an ill-fated renown [...]" (*R* 8: 58) The character of "J. J." is attributed a lengthy prosopopeia in the second *Dialogue* wherein he opposes the idle pleasures offered by music copying to the torment of writing: "Thinking is very painful work for me, which tires, torments, and displeases me. Working with my hands and letting my head rest refreshes and amuses me" (*D* 139). Through music copying Jean-Jacques is transformed into a machine of sorts, copying over eight thousand pages of music in six years.[8] This human machine is, however, atypical. It is imperfect, producing multiple errors and requiring constant rectification. The man-machine "J. J." does not stand in for eco-

---

[8] J.-J. Rousseau, *Dialogues* (*OC* 1: 831).

nomic efficiency or optimized output: "He works slowly and ponderously, makes many mistakes, erases or starts over ceaselessly; all of which forces him to charge a high price for his work even though he feels its imperfection more than anyone [...]" (D 145).

The irregular workings of Rousseau's body are taken to carry pedagogical value for the general public. The health issues that plague his body, variously referred to as his "poor machine,"[9] "my machine in decay" (C 207) are so unusual and numerous that he requests an autopsy to be performed in his testament. His self-writings contain a formidable laundry list of physical and mental ailments that include urological difficulties, vapors, heart palpitations, vertigo, and tinnitus as well as a warning guide for the perils of old age. Though he critiques the practice of animal dissection as repugnant in the *Rêveries*, the posthumous analysis of his faulty machine is recommended as a public service due to the unusual nature of his illness:

> The strange malady which has been consuming me for so many years [...] is so different from other illnesses of the same kind that I believe it'll be of import to public utility to examine it in its seat. That is why I wish for my body to be opened up by skilled individuals, if at all possible and I am joining here a note on the nature of my illness [...].[10]

The human machine is conceived by Rousseau as a fragmented object, open to visual scrutiny and waiting to be integrated in a grid of knowledge. The call for an autopsy draws attention to the limitations of self-knowledge and particularly to those of the self-applied study of anatomy, which is linked in Rousseau's personal case history to ill-understood pathologies and states of hypochondria. In contradistinction to the materialists' understanding of human nature which tends to undermine the very notion of subjectivity, the Rousseauist trope of man-as-machine serves to highlight the importance of singularity in personhood. Each human machine is irreducibly distinct and asks to be understood on its terms.

> To finish off, having made a little physiology enter into my readings, I began to study anatomy, and passing in review the multitude and the action of the pieces that made up my machine, I expected to feel all of it become unhinged twenty times a day; far from being astonished as finding myself dying I was astonished that I could still live, and I did not read the description of any malady without believing I had it. (C 207)

---

[9] Rousseau, "Lettre à M. de Malesherbes," 26 Jan. 1762 (OC 1: 1138).
[10] Rousseau, "Testament de Jean-Jacques Rousseau, Citoyen de Genève" (OC 1: 1224–1225). My translation.

Rousseau's health problems, his erratic body-machine, are tellingly presented as hindering his enjoyment of society, but on the other hand do not come in the way of his sensuous experience of nature. His urinary-tract ailments prevent him from keeping the company of kings and genteel ladies. Yet, as cumbersome as it is, Rousseau's body serves as the propitious site of a communion with a divine nature. The disabled body is indeed able to enjoy a full relationship to the natural world. Rousseau's "incommodities" figure then mostly as a social handicap, troublesome in worldly society: "This infirmity was the principal cause that kept me isolated from the social circles, and which prevented me from shutting myself up in a room with women" (C 318).

Rousseau's conception of the mechanical in human life shows a marked departure from the conventional imagery of the early modern man-machine. Often viewed as a reflection of the perfection of Nature, the Cartesian man-machine is admirable for his harmonious and predictable order: "God constructed our body as a machine and desired for it to function as a universal instrument, always operating according to its own laws," Descartes wrote in *Entretien avec Burman* (1953: 1380). The spectacle of nature, according to naturalists such as Buffon, offers a reassuring proof of the divine order. Rousseau, however, chooses to emphasize the irregularity of natural machines and in particular, the frailty of his own organism. Rousseau's lack of efficiency as a music copyist is for instance seen as secondary to the pleasure procured by repetition and the mere activity of copying music. The refusal to comply with a utilitarian telos involves an alternative understanding of temporality: clock time and its correlative considerations of productivity and utility are discarded through the reiterated practice of non-progressive action. Further, copying music involves a mechanical task that serves to safeguard human freedom. It allows Rousseau to avoid entering into a relationship of economic dependence by refusing the patronage offered to him by sovereigns and permits him to uphold relative poverty as a virtue in a historical moment that increasingly fosters the promotion of luxury as contributing to human happiness (Voltaire's poem *Le Mondain* typifies this latter trend). In short, music copying stands as a core component of Rousseau's practical philosophy. The self-sufficiency procured by manual labor is lauded in *Emile*, where Rousseau recommends that the imaginary pupil Emile, who is of noble birth, learn the trade of carpentry. He lauds the choice of "a true trade, a purely mechanical art in which the hands work more than the head [...]" (*E* 13: 345). For Rousseau, cultivating the human hand can serve to consolidate independence of mind. Further, the carpenter hones his mental competence and aesthetic judgment, thereby bringing into play and harmonizing various functions of human abilities. The trade of carpentry "requires skill and industry from the worker; and while the form of the work is determined by utility, elegance and taste are not excluded." (*E* 351). However, not all types of manual labor are deemed to be equal. In spite of Rousseau's praise of the countryside and critique of rural depopulation, the farmer-peasant is ultimately presented in *Emile* as a negative model of servitude. Raised in a constrictive patriarchal community, the peasant remains in a state of tutelage, accustomed as he is to obeying the dictates of the *pater familias*. His way of living, based on unthinking imitation, thus runs counter to the freedom of the noble savage. The peasant, "doing always what he is ordered or what he saw his father do or what he has himself done since his youth, works only by routine; and in his life, almost an automaton's, constantly busy with the same labors, habit and obedience take the place of reason for him" (*E* 255).

The preface of *La Nouvelle Héloïse* brings a resolution to the oppressive power dynamics that arise from the unilateral relationship between fathers and sons amidst the peasantry by proposing the novel itself as a substitute parent, who would take on the role of educator in the peasants' transformation into "Patriarchs" (*Julie* 6: 17). Bemoaning the lack of pleasure taken by peasants in "cultivating their fathers' patrimony in the distant countryside, to which they consider themselves more or less exiled by the modesty of their fortune" (16), the interlocutor named "R" proposes offering *Julie* as a psychagogic remedy for the peasantry: "When they are through reading [...] everything around them will seem to take on a more cheerful outlook; their duties will become nobler in their eyes; they will rediscover their taste for the pleasures of nature [...]" (16–17).

In a similar vein, professional activities linked to the manufacturing industry that do not require any sort of mental involvement are discarded as lobotomizing agents of alienation. They reify man by transforming him into a commodified automaton: "Finally, I would not like those stupid professions in which the workers, without industry and almost automatons, never exercise their hand at anything but the same work – weavers, stocking makers, stonecutters. What is the use of employing men of sense in these trades? It is a case of one machine guiding another" (*E* 351).

Earlier at the onset of middle age, Rousseau pointedly made the commitment to remove his watch in his decision to radically reform his way of living: "The moment when he got rid of his watch, renouncing all thought of becoming rich in order to live from day to day, was one of the sweetest days of his life. Heaven be praised, he cried in a fit of joy, I won't need to know what time it is any longer." (*D* 1: 142). It is by discarding his watch that Rousseau is able to equilibrate his quotidian. In *Rousseau, Judge of Jean-Jacques*, "Rousseau" recounts the extremely regular and monotonous daily routine of "J. J." whose life appears set on repeat mode, in an eternal present:

> Nothing is more uniform than his way of life. He gets up, goes to bed, eats, works, goes out and returns at the same hours, without willing it and without knowing it. All days are cast in the same mold. The same day is always repeated. His routine takes the place of all other rules: he follows it very precisely without fail and without thought. This weak inertia does not influence only his indifferent actions, but his entire conduct, even the affections of his heart [...]. Moreover, habit does not lead to boredom for him. He would live forever on the same food, repeat the same tune endlessly, re-read the same book always, see only the same person always. Finally, I never saw him develop distaste for anything that had once given him pleasure. (D 144–145)

Does this benign, quasi-animalistic existence constitute a self-exemption from civic participation? In his adapted translation of Shaftesbury's *Essay on virtue*, Diderot had condemned the solitary lifestyle as socially destructive through his portrayal of an imaginary loner who could stand in for Rousseau in his midlife years, indicting "this living automaton [...] an individual, who by his loneliness and his inaction, would lead directly toward the ruin of his own species."[11] In an historical period which postulated man's natural sociability as one of his most salient and fundamental characteristics, Rousseau's mechanical *solitaire* polemically appears as a wild anomaly. Yet the simplicity of Rousseau's mechanical lifestyle carries moral value as it is intended as an antidote to the complex machinery, and smoke and mirrors governing contemporary civil life. Filled with distractions and noise, modern life has, according to Rousseau, transformed desires into needs and substituted self-sufficiency with blind alienation. He himself favors "the man of nature, without exhausting his weak forces building tabernacles on earth, enormous machines for happiness or pleasure, enjoys himself and his existence without much worry about what men think of it and without much concern about the future" (D 1: 159). He introduces a distinction between natural, ensouled human automatons, and denatured man-machines who have been desubjectivized and de-individuated, controlled by a powerful few who have taken on the role of master-puppeteers *maîtres à penser*. In the novel *Julie*, Saint-Preux's letter to Julie describing the inhabitants of the French capital acerbically brings attention to the automated, performative motions of soulless Parisian fops who are seen to be elusive and fickle, morally and intellectually lazy: they are "machines that do not think, and are made to think with springs" (D 6: 192). Though the "editor" of the epistolary novel, as the stand-in for the voice of reason, distances himself from Saint-Preux's indictment of the French by critiquing the overwrought, juvenile nature of his commentary, the trope of the urban Frenchman as denatured automaton repeatedly appears in Rousseau's

---

11 Diderot, *Essai sur le mérite et la vertu*, *Œuvres complètes* (1: 291).

narrative presentations of the *Philosophes'* machinations against him. Their understanding of the masses as a machine to be manipulated points to their Machiavellian conception of the emergent public opinion (whose irrational nature is antinomical to the rational public sphere which is allegedly coming into existence in the second half of the eighteenth century) and modern information theory. The anonymous and self-reproducing nature of these groups are daunting for their formidable, elusive power:

> [...] the public [...] is led by guides who are continually renewed in the groups that have taken a dislike to me. Individuals die, but not collective groups. The same passions are perpetuated in them, and their ardent hatred – as immortal as the Demon which inspires it – is active as always. When all of my individual enemies are dead, Doctors and Oratorians will still live; and even if I had only those two groups as persecutors, I could be sure that they would not leave my memory in greater peace after my death than they leave me during my lifetime. (R 8: 6)

The blind passivity of denatured automatons is the main conceit behind *Emile*'s understanding of group psychology. The multitude "now judges only according to the views of those whom it believes more enlightened than itself. It approves not what is good but what they have approved" (*E* 13: 513). As attested in Rousseau's last literary self-embodiment as a "solitary walker," while the natural automaton appears as a solitary individual, the automatons that can be found on the streets and public gardens of Paris only manifest themselves as a collectivity. Soulless and deprived of reason, they are the amorphous puppets of the *philosophes*: "I understood that in relation to me my contemporaries were nothing more than automatons who acted only on impulse and whose action I could calculate only from the laws of motion. [...] I no longer saw in them anything but randomly moved masses, destitute of all morality with respect to me" (*R* 8: 72). By understanding the mechanical nature of the public's reaction towards him, Rousseau is able to become detached from the emotional turmoil involved in his ostracization. The stoic attitude that results from the insights of this social analysis marks an evolution from Rousseau's worried stance towards his contemporaries in the *Confessions*, where he repeatedly marked the desire to challenge the viewpoint of his contemporaries and attempted to establish a legal framework of judgment that would vindicate his version of events and his understanding of himself. Robert Osmont, in his annotation to the Pléiade edition of *Rousseau juge de Jean-Jacques,* relates this newly appeased perspective on the relationship between Rousseau and contemporaries to an insight presented in a letter written in March 1770 wherein Rousseau affirms a neutral, quasi-scientific attitude towards his adversaries: "I see the evil man who persecutes and diffames me, as I would see a rock detach itself from a mountain and come squash me. I would push him away if I had the energy, but without anger, and then I would leave him there without paying him another thought."[12] This newfound stoicism allows the ostracized writer to confidently embrace the locus of passivity; the eighth walk of the *Rêveries* presents a definitive ethics of being-in-the-world: "I understood that since all I had yet to do on earth was to regard myself on it as a purely passive being, I ought not to use up, in futilely resisting my fate, the strength I had left to endure it" (*R* 73). As a response what he perceives to be to a denatured society governed by a small handful of atheistic determinists, Rousseau pointedly turns to the mechanical as the gateway to a spiritual experience that brings him closer to divinity. Indeed, the liminal state of personhood, posited between the vegetative and the human corresponds to a passive state of mind that pertains to the spiritual practice of quietism.[13] But how does the figuration of the mechanical in Rousseau's self-portraiture connect with the rest of his works? The reader of Rousseau will notice that the idleness and repetitiveness presented in his later works as the most salient characteristics of his life practices actually run counter to the precepts posited in *Emile*. In *Emile*, Rousseau condemned habits as a sign of infirmity, either of the elderly or of those who are constitutionally weak: "the power of habit is very strong on the old and the idle" the narrator cautions. In a critical gesture of self-awareness, the *Dialogues* place "J. J." into the aforementioned category of the weak and the old:

> Never did a man more fully bear, right from his youth, the yoke that belongs to weak souls and the aged, namely that of habit. It is through habit that he likes to do again today what he did yesterday, without any other motive than that he did it yesterday. Since the path has been cleared, he has less trouble following it than making the effort to go in a new direction. It is incredible to what extent this laziness of the will subjugates him. It can even be seen in his walks. He will always repeat the same one until some motive absolutely forces him to change. (*D* 144)

The author's own lifestyle is linked with senility and lack of memory. Since habits are understood as exacerbating men's natural inclination towards laziness, the young Emile for his part is raised to only expect the unknown: "This way of life [the regime of habits] is good only for weak souls and weakens them more from day to day. [...] ... the only habit useful to men is to subject themselves without difficulty to reason. Every other habit is a vice" (*E* 304). Emile's lifestyle is engineered by his tutor to be constantly active and changing: "He does not

---

[12] Rousseau to Pierre Laurent Buirette de Belloy, Monday, 12 March 1770 (*CC* 37: 326), cited by Robert Osmont (*OC* 1: 1681, note 2 for page 823).
[13] Perrin notes the quietistic strain in Rousseau's practice of self-abandonment to nature (2011: 195).

know what routine, custom or habit is. What he did yesterday does not influence what he does today" (*E* 304). So how does Rousseau account for the divergences between his own way of living and his imaginary ideal pupil's? Rousseau's understanding of the demands of each age of life provides an answer. Emile's negative education is based on the insight that the stadial nature of child development demands malleability and patience. Children's moral growth does not necessarily follow the pace of their physical evolution: their sense of self-understanding and grasp of relationality remain limited for a considerable length of time. It is not until Emile sets out on a journey and leaves his family and home behind as an adult that he will be forced to thinking self-reflexively about the place he occupies in the world. As a full-fledged adult entering the last phase of life, Rousseau understands that copying music and herborizing allow him to live in harmony with the natural world. He hence espouses mechanicity as a willed mode of being-in-the-world and a key component of the technologies of the self that he fashions for himself dating from his mid-life "reformation." Young Emile's relationship to the world, however, is non-reflexive. His experiential lack of contact with affective matters disallows him from embodying Rousseau's natural automatist ethics.

Rousseau extends the explicatory system of human automatisms to include the vagaries of the life of feelings, so that the human heart itself is understood as a machine. This is the main subject of the sixth walk of the *Reveries of the Solitary Walker*, which begins with the maxim: "There is hardly any of our automatic impulses whose cause we could not find in our heart, if only we knew how to look for it" (*R* 49). Prior to Freud's programmatic "discovery" of the unconscious, Rousseau addresses the subject of the mechanical in the context of unexplained patterns of behavior which emerge in daily life. The exordium of the sixth walk asserts that the analysis of the mechanical holds the key to self-knowledge. The object of investigation of the sixth walk are the detours that Rousseau finds himself "automatically" (49) taking on his daily walks around Paris "near the Enfer tollgate exit" (49). Is there a reason behind this seemingly mindless physical action of taking an alternative itinerary in one's daily stroll? Upon reflection, Rousseau discovers that these detours are motivated by a desire to avoid running into a young handicapped beggar who obliges him to exchange niceties with him and expects some loose change in return for the small talk. Initially interacting with the young boy with great pleasure, his feelings turn sour when their interactions lose their spontaneous nature and become an obligation defined by a relationship of bondage, part and parcel of a "chain of duties" (50). As noted by Marie-Hélène Huet, Rousseau describes himself in this walk as having lost his humane capacity for pity in his dealings with the street urchin.[14] After having developed the concept of "natural pity" (*SD* 36) in *The Discourse on the Origins of Inequality*, Rousseau turns to the topic of *bienfaisance* (charity) and the potential alteration of pity in the *Reveries*. In the *Second Discourse*, Rousseau had posited the two passions of pity and self-love as the main affects that structure man's natural defense mechanisms. Pity tempers our self-interest and is responsible for the feeling of fellowship: it "is a natural feeling which, moderating in each individual the activity of love of oneself, contributes to the mutual preservation of the entire species. It carries us without reflection to the aid of those whom we see suffer [...] (*SD* 37). The *Discourse* repeatedly insists on the irreflective, spontaneous quality of the sentiment of compassion. Although the secularized practice of charity is presented by Rousseau as one of the pleasures of human experience, pity is in the end susceptible to becoming deformed in the face of societal obligations. He sadly notes in the sixth walk: "I came to understand that all natural tendencies, including beneficience itself, carried out or followed imprudently and indiscriminately in society, change their nature and frequently become as harmful as they were useful in their first direction" (*R* 8: 50).

As Diderot explains in the *Encyclopédie* entry for "Machinal," the adjective "machinal" can be applied to describe human behavior that appears to be without volition and lacking in thought. However when one examines daily actions closely, one can observe the experiential, cognitive dimension of automated reactions. Diderot elucidates the phenomenon of the "mechanical" by underlining the learned nature of automated behavior. Dissecting the physical motion of breaking a fall, he remarks that although the "MACHINAL" does pertain to "what the machine executes by itself, with no participation of our will"; "I think that this artifice is the suite of an infinity of experiences undertaken since our earliest youth, that we learn almost without noticing, of falling as softly as possible from our earliest years, & no longer knowing how this habit was formed, we believe, at a more advanced age, that it is an innate quality of the machine; this idea is a chimera" (IX: 794). In Rousseau's case, the growing unpleasantness of the forced exchanges with the disabled boy forces him to examine what Pascal would call the "reasons of the heart." If the "heart has reasons that reason ignores," Rousseau interrogates the nature of automatisms as an underappreciated yet key segment of an Enlightenment anthropology and self-analysis wherein the mechanical is demonstrated to obey a covert logic of nature that spiritualizes matter.[15]

---

[14] Huet notes: "The pleasure to give, he realizes, has become an unbearable form of duty. Rousseau's natural capacity to feel pity, or to yield to a feeling of pity, is dead." (2003: 123)

[15] Pascal, *Pensées* (1999: 473). Translation is mine.

Works Cited

Babbitt, Irving. *Rousseau and Romanticism*. Boston: Houghton Mifflin Company, 1947.
Deleuze, Gilles, and Félix Guattari. *Qu'est-ce que la philosophie?* Paris: Minuit, 1991.
Descartes, René. *Œuvres et Lettres*. Ed. André Bridoux. Paris: Gallimard, 1953.
Diderot, Denis. *Œuvres complètes*. Ed. Jean Varloot et al. Paris: Hermann, 1987.
Diderot, Denis, and Jean L. R. d'Alembert. *Encyclopédie; ou Dictionnaire raisonné des Sciences, des Arts et des Métiers*, etc. 17 vols. Paris: Briasson, 1751–1765.
Huet, Marie-Hélène. "Altered States." *Approaches to Teaching Rousseau's* Confessions *and* Reveries of the Solitary Walker. Eds. John C. O'Neal and Ourida Mostefai. New York: MLA, 2003. 121–126.
Lane, Joseph H. Jr., and Clark, Rebecca R. "The Paradoxes of Rousseau and Deep Ecology." *Political Theory* 34.1 (2006): 62–94.
Pascal, Blaise. *Pensées*. Ed. Philippe Sellier. Paris: Classiques Garnier, 1999.
Perrin, Jean-Francois. *Politique du renonçan*: le dernier Rousseau du Dialogue aux Rêveries. Paris: Kimé, 2012.
Rohault, Jacques. *Entretiens sur la philosophie*. Paris: Michel Le Petit, 1671.
Rousseau, Jean-Jacques. *Œuvres complètes*. Gen. Eds. Bernard Gagnebin and Marcel Raymond. 5 vols. Paris: Gallimard, "Bibliothèque de la Pléiade," 1959–1995.
Rousseau, Jean-Jacques. *The Collected Writings of Rousseau*. Gen. Eds. Roger D. Masters and Christopher Kelly. 13 vols. Hanover: UP of New England, 1990–2010.
Saint-Amand, Pierre. "*Rêveries* of Idleness." *Approaches to Teaching Rousseau's* Confessions *and* Reveries of the Solitary Walker. Eds. John C. O'Neal and Ourida Mostefai. New York: MLA, 2003. 127–131.
Schiller, Friedrich. *Letters upon the Aesthetic Education of Man*. Whitefish, MT: Kessinger, 2004.
Taylor, Charles. *Sources of the Self: The Making of the Modern Identity*. Cambridge, Mass.: Harvard UP, 1989.

II **Politics and Ethics: Beyond the Nature/Culture Polarity**

Paul Audi
Rousseau's Ethical Freedom

In Book II of *Emile*, Rousseau writes: "the first of all goods is not authority, but freedom." And on that subject of freedom, he immediately makes himself clear: "The truly free man wants only what he can, and does what he likes. That is my fundamental maxim" (*E* 309).[1]

If this maxim is fundamental for Rousseau's ethics, we need to understand it properly. But merely uttering it already evokes a question: is being free, "truly free," just a matter of doing what we like? In fact, Rousseau was hardly satisfied with such a trivial formula; he made a point of prefacing it with a condition relating to the *limitation* of the human will. So by limiting the will – in other words, by controlling its expression, mastering the way it unfolds, or more exactly *measuring* how it unfolds against unitary physical and mental power, against the "I can" (as Husserl would put it) – do we achieve "true" freedom?

* * *

It is useful, even necessary, to illuminate Rousseau's fundamental maxim with the help of another statement, to be found a little further on in *Emile:* "I always have the power to will, but not the strength to act" (*E* 586).

Why choose this other sentence? And first, as a preliminary question, how are we to understand this double dichotomy – power/strength on the one hand, and will/act on the other?

To grasp Rousseau's conception of action, we must first be careful not to confuse what Greek metaphysics, with its single concept of *dynamis*, constantly and inextricably mixed up. *Here*, strength is *not* power: strength is exerted (on occasion), power is possessed (all the time). In other words, power is a constituent of the personal subject; the "I" is an essential "I can" – and the "I can" depends only on itself. As for the strength which partakes of this power that nothing can limit from within, and which Rousseau called "without limit" (*E* 588), we should say that it is in essence "relative." For strength to be relative means that although the "I'" is powerful in its essence and identifies with its *power to act*, nonetheless it is not necessarily *strong*. In its very power, it can just as well be *weak*. What's more, the relative categories of cause and effect cannot be applied

---

[1] All quotations from Rousseau's texts refer to *Œuvres complètes* (*OC*); all citations will indicate page numbers after acronyms, without volume numbers. All translations of Rousseau's texts are by the translator of this article.

to power without distortion; yet they suit the essence of strength perfectly. "Strength" is only really exerted when, on the one hand, its exertion is grounded in its intrinsic "power" to take hold of itself and thus to possess itself for ever; and on the other hand, it is related to something other than itself. This something-else (which is nonetheless of the same nature) is the *testing element* of strength, given that by "resisting" it, by *opposing* another strength to it, it makes its own strength apparent – that strength which otherwise would have remained quite simply *potential* (i.e. a matter of power).

Thus if any strength is to appear as what it is, it must depend in part on a Power which makes it possible in itself. But equally, this exerted strength is only linked and related to another strength, so that there is never a strength which is single and solitary in its exertion; every strength which is exerted here and now is itself and other-than-itself, every strength is at least "double," and its actuality – or activation, as we should no doubt say – sets up *de facto* a *rapport de forces* in which it can only experience itself *as* itself when confronted with *what can* or *what has the force to* resist it.

Possible, or virtual, resistance is the very essence of active strength, of the effective *vis*. This is why there is hardly any virtue – if it is true, as Rousseau says in his letter to Franquières of 1769 that "the word virtue means strength" (*LF* 1143) – that is not by definition heroic (or, as Rousseau puts it in his *Lettres morales*, "There is no virtue without combat, there is none without victory" (*LM* 1143).) Those are the primary conditions of virtue – which, according to a fine phrase from the *Discours sur les sciences et les arts*, is "the strength and vigor of the soul" (*DSA* 8). But as I have already said, that strength still only becomes effective provided its intrinsic, constitutive Power – the 'I can' which deploys it – mobilizes it immediately and totally. That requires it to take possession of itself, to enter and remain in itself. Strength, then, is part of a Power that enjoys possessing itself eternally, which is to say in the present. It also means that all power worthy of the name is by its essence *joyful* and what it *enjoys* is first and always itself. In these conditions, those are the reasons why the strong never stop rejoicing in their strength: in exerting their strength, they enjoy that joyful power that gives their strength the possibility of being what it is, a strength that *strives* to achieve something desired and possible.

Strength has to strive because it is desire. Strength is nothing less than the power *of desire*. And that makes it a potentially weak power. Stressing this is in no way redundant, since – as Rousseau kept saying in every possible way – "it is man's weakness which makes him sociable" (*E* 503), it is his weakness which strengthens the attraction in him of "irascible, hate-filled" passions that give rise to "purely negative pleasure" (*D* 670) and that range from *amour-propre*, that hopeless desire to set oneself apart from others by preferring oneself to them, to the most violent attempts to outdo them. That "all wickedness comes from weakness" (*E* man. Favre, 77) means this weakness is also a strength, a terrible, formidable strength, since it partakes as such of the acting subject's Power-to-act.

But the question morality raises is this: how are we to circumscribe, even "reduce" this weakness which is the source of all wickedness? As for the question of ethics, it asks how fortitude ("*force d'âme*") can lead to happiness.

This is where we discover the principles of action on which Rousseau sought to found his ethics. If the question of ethics is traditionally, "what are we to do?" Rousseau would reply, "reach a point of self-sufficiency where one no longer has any need to do anything at all." But is that possible?

The "I want" can very well fail to free itself from the 'I can' which gives it being. In other words, Desire can very well fail to emanate from the Power which is its source. When does this non-liberation take place? When is there absence of emanation? Only when action is not essential, which in life would be exceptional (since living is always doing something). For Rousseau this is only the case with the sage. The sage is the one who can afford, as a living creature, not doing anything. Rousseau's sage is the being who no longer experiences the need to act – and that means: who feels no lack and has no desire. Rousseau says the sage "enjoys without acting" (*D* 845); unaffected in any way by any lack, he is also the being for whom "desire and enjoyment are [...] one and the same" (*D* 857). The sage neither acts nor desires: he enjoys. He enjoys his power without limits, and at the same time he is "impassive like God himself" (*R* 999). Which is as much as to say that he is sufficient unto himself, enjoying his self-love. To enjoy an unlimited enjoyment, which is at the same time a power without limits, is to rejoice endlessly over it. Thus, the sage is the being who delights endlessly in himself. True, his achievement as a human being makes him the figure (the image, the representation) of the achievement of life itself. Not only is his own self the self-hood of life itself, but this self itself is life in its higher achievement. It follows that the sage is both the being whom life itself delights, and the being in whom life enjoys itself.

On the other hand, if someone acts it is because of a desire (to achieve something). Desire is the *source* which mobilizes action – it is not its *object* (the distinction between objet and source is an essential one).

The object of an action is something possible and desired, something possible that one seeks to achieve and that is *lacking in reality*. But is there desire because there is a lack? No! For Rousseau (and this is sufficiently remarkable to be strongly underlined) it is not the (lacking) object that decides on desire, but the opposite; it is desire that decides on the (lacking) object. That object is even *cre-*

ated by the way the "I can" (the subjective power) is experienced in the moment when it resolves to act.

Not only is desire defined only *secondarily* for Rousseau as seeking to satisfy a lack, but neither the content of desires nor the sort of ability they articulate in action interest him. What interests him is the *relationship* between the two and the *type* of subject-of-action this relationship leads to: *strong* or *weak*. For Rousseau's perspective is strictly ethical, and the happiness or sadness of the subject-of-action depends on that weakness or strength *in action*.

In his ethics Rousseau pursues a single goal: that humans who are caught amid thousands of contradictory desires should finally do as they will. To that end it is essential that 1) desire should *proceed* from power itself, and 2) it should not *exceed* the power it emanates from; the "I want" should find its *measure* in its source, in the "I can" which gives it being. To borrow an expression from Claudel, we could say that the sage is the living being who *never loses touch with the source*.[2]

* * *

Let us return now to that sentence from *Emile* which is guiding our reflections: "I always have the power to will, but not the strength to act."

The "I" in this sentence is a *subjective being*, whose subjectivity is made up of both *abilities* and *desires*. Three mental faculties are generally distinguished: thinking, imagination and feeling, but the power of subjectivity is far from being limited to those three. The desires this being is *capable* of developing on the outside, and the abilities he/she is also *capable* of exercising upon the world, have to take possession of themselves to be able to *support an action*. But by virtue of *what* does an ability or a desire take possession of itself? The answer is, by virtue of its own *power*. Since this power is not proper to this or that ability, nor to this or that desire, but transfixes each of them, we could say that it is "of a piece" with the soul as a whole. What is the principle of the soul which at the same time makes the soul into a power? According to Rousseau it is *self-love*.

In French self-love (*amour de soi*) is an expression that contains a grammatical genitive. But that's a purely grammatical snare. In reality (I mean in the subjective phenomenon of self-love) there is no relation between love and the Self: the Self (the unity and uniqueness of the subjective power) only exists by the attachment of the soul (life) to itself, and only for as long as that attachment continues. In other words the power of the "subject" ensues from the attachment of

---

2 Claudel (1967: 164). Note that what, for Claudel, is a question of aesthetics is for Rousseau a question of ethics.

life to itself. That does not mean that strength or weakness have the same source. These are exclusively produced and realized through action. The paradox of Rousseau's doctrine of the soul (life) is that in *amour de soi* the relation is grammatical, not real, whereas in that other form of self-love, *amour-propre*, the relation is real but not grammatical (there is no genitive in the expression *amour-propre*): the relation is the way the individual targets and pursues *self-interest* – at this level of analysis it matters little whether that personal (selfish) interest is well or badly understood, sincere or artificial.

Unlike *amour-propre*, self-love achieves that movement in the soul by virtue of which some ability, seeking to exert itself, takes possession of itself. This self-possession is demonstrated by way of a certain self-affection, we could even say a "self-enjoyment" which in itself is identical with "suffering oneself." We must be careful not to confuse "suffering oneself" with any particular suffering; the "suffering" which is proper to the self-affection of self-love only ever indicates the *absolute original passivity* which is the form self-love always takes. We could just about call this original passivity Suffering, as long as we take care to distinguish it from any sort of sorrow or pain. But whatever name we give it, we must understand that when we talk about the Self, Power and Affectivity are the same thing. Yet when it is actualized, Power is always declined according to two different modalities, strength and weakness. Likewise when *it* is actualized, Affectivity is declined in two different modalities, enjoyment and suffering. So strength and weakness can cause both suffering and enjoyment, accordingly. But according to what exactly? According to the *desire* which is awakened in the light of an *action*.

What in fact do we do, on the subjective level, when we act? Acting supposes the emergence of a *desire* which by definition aims to realize something which is considered as possible. From the point of view of subjectivity, acting is situated at the convergence of Desire and Power. Desire solicits Power and leads it into action. One faculty plays a particular role in this convergence: imagination. For it is imagination that projects that which is desired and possible, and leads Power to try to realize it. Reason has nothing to do with it at this stage; it will strive to bring to light the imagination's *duplicity*, that "Achilles's spear" as Rousseau called it, which can lead the soul to perdition just as well as it can save it.

Where is the source of desire? Let me make clear immediately that by "source" I mean, not its *raison d'être*, but the subjective condition of its possibility.

Either we consider that desire is added to Power from the outside, like another power. To say that a desire is added to Power from outside is to say that its *source* is something other than Power. But what source? There is only one, magnified by a whole tradition which has sought to determine the causes of desire:

something which is *lacking*. Here this *lack* appears as the sole, veritable source of desire. Desire is consequently defined as the search for satisfaction. It seeks to fulfill an original lack. In the beginning there is a *negativity*, which desire works to overcome.

Or, second possibility, we think that desire proceeds from Power itself. In this case its source cannot be anything other than Power, i.e. *self-love*. Then desire responds to an unparalleled affective *plenitude*, an "excess of the self," for self-love (which is not a relationship) contains no negativity within itself, no internal differences or gaps. Inasmuch as in this case again the source of the "I can" is no different from that of the "I want," we have to conclude that the two are not separate. In fact desire *emanates* from Power and *frees itself* from Power as soon as Power is *carried into action*, i.e. put to work to achieve something possible, projected before the consciousness by that troubling faculty, the imagination.

"Your freedom, your power, only extend as far as your natural strength and no further; all the rest is only slavery, illusion, prestige" (E 308). This sentence is also from *Emile*, and shows that freedom and power do indeed go together in Rousseau's mind. But inasmuch as power and desire also go together for Rousseau, we should recognize that the *desired possible* for him represents the dimension where human freedom always unfolds. But this freedom itself is always – I mean essentially – *troubled*. It is troubled because the possible is *projected* by a freedom which desires, and for that very reason it relies on the activity of the *imagination*. Imagination is such that it never feels so "troubled" (Rousseau's epithet – *inquiète* – used in the *Confessions* [C 41]) as when it "lays out for us the measure of things which are possible," as he explains in *Emile* (E 304).

Thus freedom arises, and is manifest, as that *desire* which, sometimes answering to the name of "will," always gives itself something that is possible and measures itself against it – with the sometimes baleful complicity of the imagination. But as Emmanuel Levinas says, we still have to "liberate[s] freedom from the arbitrary"[3] for it to be fully itself. This is the task undertaken by what I call the ethical renewal of action, which enables the subject of the action to take into itself, and give itself, the desired possible. This act, the equivalent of a resolution, confers a supplementary meaning to what Rousseau conceives in terms of a *balance* of the powers of subjectivity. By *constituting* this balance, we in fact do nothing other than to *restitute* it, if it is true that by harmonizing "want" and "can" we make the "want" itself effectively and resolutely "possible"; the subject *fait sa volonté* (does as he will), as it is expressed, in French particularly, which

---

3 Levinas, *Totality and Infinity* (85).

shows that to be free is to be resolute, and to be resolute is to be capable of doing as one wills. Indeed Rousseau spells this out in *Emile:* "The only one who does as he wills is he who, in order to do so, has no need to add the arms of another to his own: from which it follows that the first of all goods is not authority, but freedom" (*E* 309).

* * *

There is hardly any first-person action where the very fact of acting does not arise from life, i. e. from the feeling of existence. So this action has its own tonality. To say that every action is 'tonally' determined does not mean that the particular affective tonality of the action results *from* that action; it precedes the action as its most intimate and least obvious mobilizing force. Under the influence of this pure affectivity by which we are *born to life* (Rousseau's expression, found in the *Rêveries*), the "I can" which we all are, fundamentally, at every point of our being, feels capable of action and does act. Rousseau summarizes this in these terms: "self-love is the most powerful and, in my opinion, only motive which makes men act."[4]

That said, is not acting first of all *desiring* to act? Where does such a desire for action come from? What is its *raison d'être?* Rousseau affirms that desire is born of a *feeling of insufficiency* experienced by the "subject" of the action – an insufficiency whose singular, major effect is to make power weak, and weakness wicked.

There are two things to point out here.

1) The relationship which connects Power with Desire is an essential, even a structural relationship, one which characterizes the individual's subjective life from within.
2) Whoever desires, desires "more" than whatever they currently possess, otherwise they would not desire. But what they possess, before all else, is their own *power to act*. Unlike "need" which proceeds from a *lack* they seek to satisfy, Desire is born of an excess which it strives when appropriate to "contain" as far as possible. How is that plenitude to be "contained"? By desiring, precisely. With Desire ("I want"), Power ("I can") seeks to free itself from the very Power it is. But as this excess (of Power) is nothing less than irreducible (Rousseau says *inexhaustible*), Desire always works to exceed it, to exceed its natural "too-muchness" (*excédence*, in French). And it only needs to fail to feel invaded by *angst* right away.

---

[4] Letter to the Abbé de Carondelet, 4 March 1764 (*CC* 19: 199).

What, then, is this Desire whose existence does not depend on an already-given object? What is it to desire, when the "subject" of the action, according to Rousseau's astonishing description, is "blind on every point," someone "born blind who cannot imagine what sight is" (*LM* 1092)?

To desire is always to "want" more than the too-much one already is, and suffers from being. But Desire, which itself is born of Power, can only free itself from Power with the *help* of Power. Desire can only desire what its own power permits it to desire. And yet in desiring, Desire also (and above all) aims to exceed its own power. Only, by wanting to exceed it in this way (i.e. in wanting to free itself from *itself*), Desire always finally runs up against what is outside its scope. That is its essential, intrinsic limitation. Its limitation is the result of its own Power; and when that Power is aligned with Desire it is a form of impotence for Desire itself: a suffering, a weakness, opening the way to the baneful procession of sad, hate-filled passions, as well as to all sorts of wickedness. This is the foundation of the necessity of Rousseau's wisdom, and here we recognize the great originality of his ethics and morality. For that wisdom invites us to learn and understand what constitutes the "more" on which our Power to act can be broken. That is why this wisdom can be expressed in a single sentence, of absolutely capital importance: "Let us measure the radius of our sphere and stay in the center, like the insect in the middle of its web; we shall always be sufficient unto ourselves and never have to complain of our weakness, for we shall never feel it" (*E* 305).

But how are we to do that? How are we to achieve self-sufficiency?

At the heart of the relationship which connects Desire structurally with its own Power, Rousseau discovers a law of internal regulation or proportionality, whose determinations are in fact variations – or, better, forms – of subjectivity (that subjectivity which is founded solely on self-love as an immanent structure of affectivity) according to *pleasure* or *pain*. This is how the feeling of insufficiency is born from a painful disproportion (and that of sufficiency from a happy equalization) between desire and what puts it into action, i.e. between strength and its power, between *want* and *can*. In Book II of *Emile*, Rousseau presents the law that modulates the equilibrium of those two constituents of subjectivity, desires and abilities. Referring to the phenomenon of pain, he notes: "It is [...] in the disproportion between our desires and our faculties that our misery consists." And concerning the modality of joy: "A sensitive being whose abilities were equal to its desires would be an absolutely happy being" (*E* 304).

On the basis of this "differential" between "what I can" and "what I want" Rousseau traces the main lines of an ethics of affectivity which in itself has no objective or general character, no pre-established axiological content. The project which governs its constitution knows nothing of commandments or imperative regulations. Addressed to the individual "in particular" according to his subjective power and will, which are singular on every occasion, this ethics only recommends one single thing – though a crucial one. It recommends learning to *know oneself* so as to be able to establish an equal proportion between Desire (limited) and Power (without limit) which determine – together – the feeling of existence that always belongs to the individual. This ethics founds its reality on the totality of subjective "potentialities" that constitute the unity of the individual who acts. For that individual, faculties are nothing without the desires that express them, and desires are nothing without the faculties that exercise them; the two together constitute his "individual" nature. So this ethics is the bearer of internal regulations that apply to the affectivity of the "ego"; it is the complete opposite of any kind of transcendental normativity.

But for this regulation to take place in practice, it is important not to privilege one or another faculty to the detriment of the others. It is just as important not to bridle this or that desire to the advantage of another. The recommendations of ethics have to be based on life's own prescriptions, as they are expressed *singularly* in each person by the ontological relationship between power and desire. And the goal of those prescriptions is not to urge a reduction of desire in order to gain greater power, or the opposite; nor do they tend towards encouraging the total extinction of one or the other, since the only result would always be frustration and sadness. If this ethics is not to have effects which are the opposite of what it aims at – "true happiness" – on the contrary whoever agrees with its principle must only be concerned with the free and harmonious development of his desires in accordance with his own faculties. One of Rousseau's most important texts declares:

> In what, then, does human wisdom or the path to true happiness consist? It is precisely *not* in diminishing our desires; for if they were less than our power, part of our faculties would remain idle and we would not enjoy the totality of our being. Nor does it consist in extending our faculties, for if our desires meanwhile extended more, we should only become more miserable: but it consists in diminishing the excess of the desires over the faculties, and in putting power and will in perfect equality. Only then, with all forces in action, can the soul nonetheless remain tranquil, and man be well-ordered. (*E* 304)

No doubt, defined by a law of internal regulation (or moderation) – a law which can be modulated in terms of the *particular constitution* of whoever is inspired by it – Rousseau's wisdom would have had every chance of appearing quite "speculative" (like Spinoza's *Ethics*) if it had not given rise to a concrete characterization of life. The possibility of this concrete characterization of life explains how, between the abstract generality of the rule and the extreme particularity of its "application," Rousseau made room for a "typology" of individuals who are concerned (or not) by the rule. In addition to the different forms of the ontological structure power/desire, Rousseau took account of a modulation of that same structure, according to whether it defines "strong" or "weak" beings. He asked, "When one says that man is weak, what does one mean?" And he replied "The word weakness indicates a relationship of the being to which it is applied. One whose strength exceeds its needs, be it an insect or a worm, is a strong being; one whose needs exceed its strength, be it an elephant or a lion; be it a conqueror or a hero; be it a god; is a weak being" (*E* 305). Determining the strength of the strong whilst only considering its power, only its capacity, its aptitude in general, is to deny oneself access to the specificity of its being, what it is in reality. For it is what it *really* is as a living being. And since, for Rousseau, "to live is not to breathe, it is to act, to make use of our organs, our senses, our faculties, of all the parts of ourselves which give the feeling of existence" (*E* 253), it is never merely in living *praxis* (when, feeling one is oneself in every point of one's being, "all the [subjective] forces [come] into action" (*E* 304) that the *nature* of one's soul, a nature which depends in part on the content of one's desires, can or should finally be revealed. Thus the strongest soul from the point of view of power (a god, for example) can be the weakest from the point of view of its action and the desires which govern that action. For what is essentially at stake in action and ultimately in the very fact of living (since to live is to act) is *ratio*, the "differential" or mutual modification of power and will, faculties and desires, potency and needs, which gives the "free agent" its incomparable self-hood (ipseity).

The need for such ethical "balancing" comes from the fact that the inner feeling by virtue of which our Power to act is built is never identical with itself; it is never in itself constituted in an identical, "definitive" or "permanent" way. Nor should we be surprised that when Rousseau seeks to define weakness in his text, he always feels obliged to mention its opposite (and vice versa). In the absolute subjectivity of action, strength "is" weakness and weakness "is" strength. Yet the two are not confused; they relate to a unitary foundation which makes it possible to identify both the strong soul and the weak soul. Rousseau calls this common basis *"force"* and *"puissance"* in turn – terms which indicate the Power without limits of the feeling of self ("without limits," as nothing external to the self can limit it).

So we should say: power is the "strength," always virtual, by virtue of which strength is exercised or actualized here and now. Power gives shape to (i.e. makes possible, in their very specificity) both strength and weakness – which incidentally is why weakness is also a "strength" or, better, a power. Or again: if strength and weakness – these "ways of characterizing the soul," explained in the last resort by relationships of proportion which regulate the "can" and the "want" – can lend themselves to categories relating to an objective temporality (such as the beginning and end of the action, its cause and effect), or if they can be explained in terms of production of the will, this cannot be the case for *power* which in its very immanence is always virtual – or "permanent," as Rousseau says of "the sweet enjoyment of life" (*LF* 1141) in the living present of life, where it is gathered up in itself as a constitutive "nature" and its "potentiality."

So what are we to conclude? First, that the weak are only miserable inasmuch as their desires exceed their power. And then, that the strong are only happy inasmuch as they desire that of which they are capable. However, since the power of the "I can" resides just as much in a weak being as in a strong one, we should add that a god can be weak just as an insect can be strong – we just have to adequately grasp the structural relationship which *applies* to this or that *being*. The strong, then, are those who exert the power they possess according to their own possibilities. Their action is in accord with the enjoyment of their pure self-love, and this accord is a factor of rejoicing. The weak, on the other hand, still have strength (the power of their "I can") but cease to enjoy it as they are overtaken – or exceeded – by the passion of a desire or the ardor of a need they are unable to meet. They cannot exert any strength, other than that which makes it possible to turn against themselves in despair (against the self-love that is the first principle of the soul, of life) until, by dint of laboring against themselves, being dissatisfied with themselves, the weak lose all respect for what they do and what they are. Rousseau sums up this point in *Emile*, saying: "It is our passions which make us weak, because to satisfy them would require more strength than nature gave us" (*E* 426).

But in the end what does it mean to cease to enjoy one's power to act? It does not mean ceasing to experience it in oneself – as we have seen, the *permanence* of that experience is essential to subjectivity. So why do the weak cease to "enjoy" it? Because the feeling of existence which they always already suffer as living beings has turned out to be unbearable. No longer enjoying themselves or life in itself, finding themselves insufferable, suffering from their insufferability, the weak suffer from the fact that there is too much of themselves and that they are too much *to* themselves; in a word, they suffer from being "too-much." Rousseau says this is why they "fear and flee" themselves and "make merry by rushing outside" themselves (*E* 597). They fear the suffering which they embody in every point of their being, and which reveals and gives them to themselves. They fear life, which overtakes them on all sides. They are terrified by the *position* into which they are thrown by the insurmountable passivity of the feeling of existence. And, fearing themselves, they flee. "Where they are" is not where they want to be. And so they rush outside of themselves; they cloud the crystalline transparency of their hearts. In short, they desire, start to move – act. There is no action in the true sense of the word which is not intrinsically tainted, if not moved, by the despair of existing and thus by that self-love which, far from being the opposite of despair, makes it intrinsically possible.

In opposition to *idleness*, where we learn to "enjoy [our] innocence" (*R* 1046) as a "sufficient, perfect, full happiness, which leaves no void in the soul which it feels any need to fill" (*R* 1001) – in opposition to the "precious idleness" to which Rousseau admitted wanting to "devote" his entire life, action is essentially connected to need or regret, to the future or the past. It is always, in one way or another, associated with suffering, dissatisfaction and the immediate need to "provide" for it. Indeed for this reason every action turns out, deep down, to be onerous in its achievement, as it is entirely determined by a "despite," and shot through with a current of idleness which permanently undoes it, makes it "difficult" and makes us obstinate in our efforts. But if every act is transfixed by an essential, irreducible fatigue, it is because it is always presided by a weakness. Following Rousseau as he elaborates this question, we could even gladly conclude that activity is to be put solely to the account of the weak – the weak person who is always presented as "agitated" and "troubled." But nevertheless here it is a weak person who intends to get enjoyment by means of his action. So much so that his/her acts lead ineluctably to reflection, with a view to evaluating the means to be put to work, and to appropriate them to the ends at which the faculty of knowledge aims. This is why *Emile* declares: "The innate desire for wellbeing, and the impossibility of fully satisfying that desire, make [men] endlessly seek new means of contributing to it. This is the first principle of curiosity; a principle which is natural to the human heart, but whose development only takes place in proportion to our passions and our enlightenment" (*E* 429). And so, according to the doctrine set out in the *Second Discourse*, "whatever the moralists say, human understanding owes a great deal to the passions which, by common accord, owe a great deal to understanding too: it is by their activity that our reason is perfected." And so, as this text of prime importance adds, "we only seek to know because we desire to enjoy, and it is not possible to conceive why anyone without desires or fears would take the trouble to reason" (*SD* 143).

The "theoretical" elaboration which leads to action thus throws the anxious subject into the externality of representation, where it becomes possible to find reasons which justify the action in one's own eyes and in the eyes of others – not without sometimes awakening, in return, the bitter taste of failure and increasing one's weakness in proportion to the development of one's bad conscience. For indeed it is because of this impotence that the "I can" harbors deep within its omnipotence, because of this passivity that enables us to differentiate that omnipotence structurally from any strength, as from any act of the will, that the exhausting feeling of failure ends up indelibly soiling every one of our actions, and that guilt found the way to insinuate itself constantly in Rousseau's troubled consciousness. On the other hand we can see more clearly what led him to think that only the perfectly happy individual – the self-sufficient ego – can enjoy its innocence like the natural man or the *promeneur solitaire*. For in an ontological (not moral) sense, someone is only innocent who turns out to be denuded of all will, who remains fundamentally inactive. So it is no accident if, for Rousseau, walking or daydreaming are the best expressions of this extinction of will, or of the desire for something – this "inactivity" which is equal to the impassivity of a living god and identical to the enjoyment of the fact of living. As the "Rousseau" of the *Dialogues* remarks, when "daydreaming, one is not at all active. Images arise and combine in the brain as in sleep, without the help of the will: we let all that go where it will, and we enjoy without acting. But when we want to stop and fix objects, order and arrange them, it is something else; we are involved. As soon as reasoning and reflection come into play, meditation is no longer repose; it is a most painful action, and that is the pain which is the terror of Jean-Jacques, the very idea of which overcomes him and makes him idle" (*D* 845).

So when Rousseau delights in admitting to Malesherbes that "active life has nothing to tempt me, and that I would agree a hundred times to do nothing rather than do something despite myself" (*OC* 1: 1132) what he says has much more than autobiographical value. In fact he is reflecting his deepest conviction, that "doing nothing is the first and strongest passion of man after self-preservation. If we look carefully we see that even amongst ourselves, everyone works to achieve rest: it is still idleness which makes us industrious" (*EOL* 401). Just as we ought to use our reason the better to define its limits, we work despite ourselves in order to work no more. The *raison d'être* of work is to achieve rest: "We only work in order to have pleasure. This alternative of pain and pleasure is our veritable vocation. Rest, which serves as relaxation from past work and encouragement to more work, is no less necessary to man than work itself" (*Julie* 470). I should say that it is all the more so if it is true that we only ever work in order to get pleasure – that pleasure, that rest forming in a certain way the *telos* of humanity, a provisionally industrious humanity, since technical progress seems from day to day (or from century to century) to help bring humanity closer to that "end"...

To the two questions, "why does work have only one concern, that of coming to an end?" and "why does idleness occupy the same position as self-love?" we can thus unhesitatingly answer that it is so because we always act *despite* – despite the impotence of the feeling which determines our power to act and makes its action possible; despite the impossibility for that power to overcome *itself*;

and so, despite the passivity which is essentially inherent in it. Despite ourselves, in a word. When we act, in a way we leap over our shadow, because that shadow seems to us to have more weight than our own body and it becomes so intolerable that we have only one desire, to leave it behind. But in fact it is only apparently a leaping-over, since when we act we only ever land on our own two feet, "where we are," just as when we think "our little lights can only reach as far as our hands, two feet ahead of us" (*LM* 1092) i.e. no further.

To put it another way: we act although, and because, we are essentially passive with regard to our being, as our "nature" has placed us passively on the level of life's immanence. It is within this conceptual framework that the emblematic story of humanity recounted in the *Second Discourse* takes on its full scope, one which is like a story of the weak – or to put it more precisely, a story of the weakness of the "strong ones." And it is also in contrast with the same conditions of historical "becoming" that the remarkable pertinence of Rousseau's wisdom becomes apparent. For it has no other ambition than to invite the soul to take itself into itself, into its own constitutive power, so as to unfold its desires and its intentional "faculties" in conformity with its own subjective possibilities. This is when the power of the soul becomes a virtue, the strength and vigor of the soul – *fortitude*. Once this "power to will" that the soul "always" has within itself, and with which it identifies, is asserted as that which it can be *satisfied* with in order to be itself (i.e. as that which it can enjoy without obstacles), isn't it in fact its role to be able to take hold of itself, to take possession of its being, and by that possession – or repossession in itself – to become a strength capable of exerting what the soul "wants"? When the soul *can* do what it *wants*, it is a fact that it only acts in accord with itself, in conformity with its own nature – excellently, in other words.

What, then, is fortitude? It is what Rousseau, from the first *Discourse* on, defined as virtue *par excellence*, the equivalent of the being-in-exercise of subjective omnipotence; it is demonstrated on the outside, against another strength (the strength of weakness), the affective and dynamic structure of subjectivity, its fundamental "I can."

Now, if it facilitates the exercise of the power to act by arousing its excellence, are we to say as a result that the ethics of rejoicing constitutes the supreme accomplishment of our essence? That is of course what I would affirm, whilst nonetheless specifying that this accomplishment of subjectivity in fact rests on the implicit recognition of what is intrinsically capable of weakening the individual and making him despair, and which thus should be "overcome." This is why Rousseau never stopped declaring that "self-knowledge" is essential to ethics, that it is what makes virtue possible in practice. What indeed does it mean to know oneself, if not seeking to discover the inner enemy we harbor deep inside ourselves, and to understand how we are always setting up obstacles to our own enjoyment of life, to our eternal self-love? To know one's "self," it is true, requires us to take account of what damages and weakens the soul, of what leads it to despair, flight and self-alienation. To "know" oneself is to recognize what is born along with oneself, with one's own self-love and happiness in existing: self-suffering, which proceeds from self-love, for all that (as this love drives us up against ourselves without respite) we cannot *not* love ourselves, and we die of being unable to free ourselves from this inner stranglehold which edifies and exhausts us at the same time, it is so inexhaustible and indestructible.

But with what intention are we to know ourselves? If it is right to "go into oneself," it is in order not to be beaten down, not to let ourselves be felled either by the inherent "vicissitudes" of life when its tribulations exceed our strength, or by the inner trial we endure invincibly, even though we are not at its very origin. If it is right to "go into oneself," it is because deep down, despair is not the opposite of self-love but only its *other side*; for despair is born in the soul as soon as one realizes that one never ceases to be bound, delivered and eternally driven back to oneself, to that "Self" which keeps running up against itself, wanting constantly to overtake itself ("exceed itself") – for better and for worse.

Translated by Edward Hughes, Université Paris-Sorbonne

Works Cited

Claudel, Paul. *Art Poétique*. *Œuvre poétique*. Ed. Jacques Petit. Paris: Gallimard, "Bibliothèque de la Pléiade," 1967.
Levinas, Emmanuel. *Totality and Infinity: An Essay on Exteriority*. Pittsburgh: Duquesne UP, 1969.
Rousseau, Jean-Jacques. *Correspondance complète de Jean-Jacques Rousseau*. Ed. Ralph A. Leigh. 52 vols. Geneva: Institut et Musée Voltaire; Madison: U of Wisconsin P; Oxford: Voltaire Foundation, 1965–1998.
Rousseau, Jean-Jacques. *Œuvres complètes*. Gen. Eds. Bernard Gagnebin and Marcel Raymond. 5 vols. Paris: Gallimard, "Bibliothèque de la Pléiade," 1959–1995.
Rousseau, Jean-Jacques. *Les Confessions*. Ed. Bernard Gagnebin et Marcel Raymond. *Œuvres complètes*, vol. 1. 1959. [C]
Rousseau, Jean-Jacques. *Discours sur les sciences et les arts*. Ed. François Bouchardy. *Œuvres complètes*, vol. 3. 1964. [DSA]
Rousseau, Jean-Jacques. *Émile ou de l'Éducation*. Ed. Charles Wirtz et Pierre Burgelin. *Œuvres complètes*, vol. 4. 1969. [E]
Rousseau, Jean-Jacques. *Essai sur l'origine des langues*. *Œuvres complètes*, vol. 5. 1995. [EOL]

Rousseau, Jean-Jacques. *Lettre à M. de Franquières*. Ed. Henri Gouhier. *Œuvres complètes*, vol. 4. 1969. [*LF*]

Rousseau, Jean-Jacques. *Lettres morales*. Ed. Henri Gouhier. *Œuvres complètes*, vol. 4. 1969. [*LM*]

Rousseau, Jean-Jacques. *Julie, ou La Nouvelle Héloïse*. Ed. Henri Coulet and Bernard Guyon. *Œuvres complètes*, vol. 2. 1961. [*Julie*]

Rousseau, Jean-Jacques. *Les Rêveries du promeneur solitaire*. Ed. Marcel Raymond. *Œuvres complètes*, vol. 1. 1959. [*R*]

Rousseau, Jean-Jacques. *Rousseau Juge de Jean Jaques*. Ed. Robert Osmont. *Œuvres complètes*, vol. 1. 1959. [*D*]

Pasquale Pasquino
Remarks on Rousseau's Dictatorship: Between Machiavelli and Carl Schmitt

Rousseau devotes one of the chapters of the fourth book of *The Social Contract* to the Roman magistracy of *dictatorship*. With an important exception, which I shall consider briefly at the end of this article, this text seems to have been overlooked by most Rousseau specialists.

As a preliminary remark, I need to observe that we are faced here with the well-known conundrum, stressed for instance by Charles E. Vaughan and Robert Derathé, of the role of Roman references in the architecture of the *Social Contract*.[1] Needless to say, I will discuss neither this complex question nor Rousseau's preference for Sparta and Rome over democratic Athens in the *First Discourse*. I shall simply quote an excerpt from the *Lettres écrites de la montagne*, in which Rousseau summarizes the content of his *Contrat Social*, presenting this synopsis as a "short and faithful analysis of my Book": "Finally in the last Book [the fourth one] I examine, by means of comparison with the best Government that has existed, namely that of Rome, the public order [the form of government, *police* in French, from the Greek *politeia*] most favorable to the good constitution of the State [...]" (*OC* 3: 809 [*CW* 9: 233]).

Be that as it may,[2] chapter 6 of Book 4 of the *Social Contract* speaks in very positive terms about the dictatorship. On this question there is no important literature.[3] Rousseau, who was considered by Hans Kelsen – likewise by many others – the most important theorist of modern democracy,[4] seems inaccessible

---

[1] For Derathé, see Rousseau (*OC* 3: 1495). For Vaughan (1915), *The Political Writings of Jean-Jacques Rousseau* (2: 109, note 1).

[2] On Rousseau and Rome, see Postigliola (1992: 227–245).

[3] I must note that Saint-Bonnet (2001) accurately discusses Rousseau's doctrine of dictatorship in *L'État d'exception* (274–284). He nonetheless starts his commentary with the claim that "Ce constat abrupt [the reference is to the *inflexibilité des lois* at the beginning of the chapter on dictatorship that *peut en certains cas les rendre pernicieuses*] porte un coup colossal à l'édifice de Rousseau pour qui 'la première des lois est de respecter les lois'" (274). Still Saint-Bonnet sees, correctly in my opinion, the absolutist character of Rousseau's sovereignty that makes his republic (*vulgo* democracy) compatible with the dictatorship. A point which makes very plausible the Rousseauian legacy in Carl Schmitt's political thought. In his article "Diktatur," Ernst Nolte (1972) mentions in passing Rousseau's chapter on dictatorship with the interesting observation that this traditional Roman institution "für den Sohn der Republik Genf [...] einen durchaus aktuellen Vorbildcharakter [hat]" (906).

[4] "Rousseau, perhaps the most important theorist of democracy," in H. Kelsen (1929: 85).

when he prizes dictatorship, which is a word nowadays disqualified due to its association with the experience of twentieth-century authoritarianism, despotic regimes such as communism or fascism. Thus the chapter is somehow forgotten, covered by a willed veil of ignorance.

My essay is divided into three parts. In the first section, I briefly summarize Machiavelli's doctrine of dictatorship. In the second part, I comment on Rousseau's text by comparing it with the one of the Florentine secretary. The third section is devoted to Carl Schmitt's analysis of the chapter that is, to my knowledge, the only important analysis of it before the recent commentary by Saint-Bonnet.

1 Machiavelli

My starting point is Machiavelli, not only because of my knowledge of his work, but because it seems evident that his conception of the Roman dictatorship was present in the mind of the author of the *Social Contract*.[5] I am not going to enter into details,[6] I want only to make some general remarks to explain the *reason d'être* of the doctrine of dictatorship in the major political work of Ser Niccolò: *The Discorsi on Livy*.

Dictatorship is a natural idea for a theorist of classical republicanism. By this I mean a political thinker supporting the idea that the best political regime is the *mixed politeia* in the Aristotelian-Polybian tradition and notably the Roman republican constitution, where *patricii* and *plebei*, *grandi* and *popolo*, in the Machiavellian language, were sharing the direct exercise of political authority. In emergency situations,[7] the polyarchic/pluralistic decision-making structure of the republican/mixed regime with its different veto powers, can serve as an obstacle to tackling what Machiavelli called *accidenti straordinari* – extraordinary events. Hence, there is a need to wake the dormant but constitutional magistracy of dictatorship – according to the Roman model – in order to guarantee the *salus rei publicae* in front of unforeseeable threats which cannot be tamed by the regular architecture of public magistracies. This necessity for

---

5 See McKenzie (1982), where incidentally the question of the dictatorship is never mentioned.
6 See my article "Machiavel: dictature et salus reipublicae" (2010).
7 The nature and *raison d'être* of the "emergency" is a complex question that I cannot discuss here. It is possible to claim that it implies the action of internal or/and external enemies of the republic.

a dictator has to do with the circumstances that the principle of collegiality[8] and various mechanisms of veto within a mixed government produce, what Machiavelli called *moto tardo*. This slow and balanced decision-making process of the mixed government represents a relevant danger vis-à-vis an event that constitutes a threat to the survival of the republican order. Thus Machiavelli had good reasons to prize the Roman magistracy,[9] since it allows temporary suspension of the regular constitutional regime in order to protect and preserve it. It must be emphasized that this is an allowance to suspend, not to modify. The classical Roman dictatorship was a *conservative-preservative-stabilizing* institution, not a transformative one according to the later Marxist conception. The dictator was the guardian of the republican *status quo*.

This point was formalized canonically – introducing an historical misinterpretation[10] – by Theodor Mommsen (1888), who in *Römisches Staatsrecht*,[11] distinguishes the original dictatorship from the *dictatura rei publicae constituendae causa* of Sylla, who would have used this magistracy not to defend and stabilize the republican mixed government, but rather to modify it, altering the conservative function of the dictatorship as a defense of the constitutional *status quo ante* in a sort of transformative constituent power.

Returning to Machiavelli, I want to stress again the strong connection between the dictatorial magistracy and the pluralistic structure of the republican system, as well as the need for the establishment of an institutional insurance mechanism to preserve this pluralistic order, in the eventuality of a danger requiring a short regression to a monistic form of government – the true antonym of the republic – which would include the *suspension* of fundamental guarantees of citizens rights' like the *tribunicia intercessio* and the *appellatio ad populum*.

The last instantiation of this type of ancient magistracy was the *dittatura* exercised in Venice by Daniele Manin in 1848–1849 in the desperate and vain attempt to rescue the *Serenissima Repubblica* from the siege of the Austro-Hungarian army.[12]

---

[8] "La dictature étant un remède aux inconvénients de la collégialité" (dictatorship being a remedy to the inconveniencies of collegiality) observed for instance Theodor Mommsen in *Le Droit public romain* (livre deuxième – Les magistrature. La dictature).
[9] Notably in Chapter 34, Book I of *Discorsi on Livy*.
[10] See Nippel (2012); Carl Schmitt (2011).
[11] Theodor Mommsen, *Römisches Staatsrecht* (2: I, 141–172; 703–705).
[12] The Venetian assembly voted "Resistance at all costs!" and granted Manin unlimited powers. See Ginsborg (1979).

2 Rousseau

Now, notwithstanding what Rousseau tells us in the *Lettres écrites de la montagne* on the Roman republic, the constitutional/institutional structure he presents in the *Social Contract* is not republican, but Hobbesian. Rousseau is, *from the institutional, constitutional point of view*, the only point of view I am considering here. He is not the intellectual heir of the *Machiavellian Moment*,[13] but rather a political thinker who accepted the Hobbesian conceptual revolution, which destroyed the classical anatomy of the city introducing the modern ideology of equal rights. This claim that some share and some do not is not immediately understandable. The words "republic/republicanism" have a variety of possible meanings that are inevitably a source of confusion.

Machiavelli is in my opinion the last great thinker of the classical Aristotelian tradition, a tradition that gave a prominent role in its political theory to the *mere tes poleos*, the constitutive parts of the city, and conceived of the *ottima republica*, i.e. the best form of government, as a pluralistic institutional structure, attributing to each *part of the city* (*grandi* and *popolo*, in his language) a share in the government.[14] The Hobbesian revolution conceptually abolished social ranks and estates, and established the principle of equal individuals and a *society without qualities*, or without natural *ranks* or *estates* if you prefer, and finally without legal privileges. Rousseau is certainly the heir of this revolution and thus could not think of the dictatorship as a suspension of the mixed government in the Machiavellian sense, especially since, moreover, the word *government* in Rousseau was used simply to qualify a subordinated function, a *pouvoir commis*, in the architecture of his vertical separation of powers. In his odd presentation of the Roman government in Book iv there are, by the way, neither Consuls nor Senate[15]! Thinking of the Roman magistracy, he had to have something different in mind than what the classical supporters of mixed government were looking for. Indeed, if we read Rousseau's text on dictatorship we find a slightly different perspective and a new type of preoccupation.

I'm not going to present here a detailed close reading of chapter vi of book iv. I wish only to highlight some crucial points regarding the commonalities and

---

[13] J. G. A. Pocock (1975); on Rousseau and republicanism see L. Foisneau (2007).
[14] This form of polyarchy is distinctly different from the doctrines which are known under the etiquette of separation of powers, since they speak, at least since James Madison, of separation inside the governmental structure, not of the society as such. Federalism has nothing to do with the Aristotelian parts of the city.
[15] Elsewhere Rousseau refers to the Senate (*The Social Contract*, iii, 10) but in Book iv it does not play any significant role.

differences between the Florentine and the citizen of Geneva concerning dictatorship (*OC* 3: 455–458).[16]

Rousseau starts from a point of view similar to Machiavelli's: the danger of a crisis that can produce *la perte de l'Etat* – the ruin of the State. He also speaks of the problem of "the order and slow pace of legal forms," which most likely refers to the regular functioning of the political system. But he uses expressions such as "inflexibility of Laws,"[17] and "cases [...] that the Legislator has not foreseen" that are in a sense original to Machiavelli, even though Rousseau repeats the topic of *suspension* of the ordinary functioning of institutions. After reading these sentences, it is not clear if Rousseau was thinking of just an institutional mechanism to speed up the decision-making process in moments of danger and crisis – a sort of monarchical provisional power – or, as I tend to believe, something more than that, something which would make his conception of dictatorship an original contribution to the doctrine and render it compatible with the post-Hobbesian constitutional doctrine. Much depends on how we understand the word "laws." If, as it seems possible, the laws are the equivalent of the Machiavellian "ordini," meaning the constitutional structure of the political regime that Rousseau called (in a sense different from the tradition) *république*, then a new question appears: what produces the "slow pace of legal forms" in the Rousseauian decision-making process?

Elements of an answer may come from the passage in which Rousseau explains the two modalities of the *commission*,[18] the delegated power represented by the dictatorship.

The *first one* consists in concentrating the executive power (*l'activité du gouvernement*) in a single agent to establish a provisional monarchical/monocratic form of the *executive*. The structure of the sovereignty is intact. This case has no clear equivalent in classical doctrine since the distinction between sovereignty and government (executive power) is specific to Rousseau and we cannot find a real equivalent of it in Machiavelli. We see here that the author of the *Social Contract* is trying to adjust classical doctrine to his own.

The *second form* or modality is more radical and consists in the suspension of the sovereign power – legislative power. The dictator is an organ who can do everything, but not enact laws. He may suspend the existing laws but cannot cre-

---

16 For the English translation, see Rousseau, *Of the Social Contract and Other Political Writings* (2012: 118–120).
17 Here there is probably an echo of the issue of the King's prerogative discussed notably by Locke. On this point please see my article "Locke on King's prerogative."
18 The expression *commission* to characterize the power of the dictator comes from J. Bodin's *République*, Book I, ch. 8.

ate new ones (see the parallel in art. 16 of the French Gaullist constitution).[19] Here again we see the effort of inserting the classical doctrine of emergency powers into the new theory of the government based on the vertical/functional separation of powers where the legislation coincides with the sovereign power and the government is a subordinated power.

This short analysis shows clearly enough that here again the dictatorship in its two versions is a mechanism of stabilization of the new political order that no longer has a direct connection with mixed government.

In a sense Rousseau seems to believe that his *republic* is as fragile as the classical one. Like its homonym, the Machiavellian *republica*, the institutional construction of the author of the *Social Contract* seems to have to cope with enemies that can threaten the political order and need to be fought with special institutions.[20]

3 Carl Schmitt

In 1921 Carl Schmitt published his first important academic book (after *Gesetz und Urteil*, 1912) the one which established his academic reputation and was at the origin of his professorship at the University of Bonn, one of the best for Germans who were not Lutheran. Carl Friedrich (1930) notably published a very positive review of this book on dictatorship. Here Schmitt, whom I would call with Wilfried Nippel a sort of *conservative Rousseauian*, presents a detailed commentary of Rousseau's doctrine (*Die Diktatur* 116–129). His reading of the text is very similar to the one I offered here. Two points nevertheless deserve special attention since they allow us to see the usage that Schmitt makes of Rousseau for his own political and constitutional theory. A usage that is also a "twist," like the one that Rousseau performed on Machiavelli's doctrine.

Schmitt insists not only upon the circumstance that the Rousseauian dictatorship is a *commission*, a delegated power, but, more importantly, on the alleged opposition between law and power ("Recht und Macht," 1921: 123). Schmitt's language is ambiguous. True, the dictator – in the more radical version of this figure – acts in a condition of suspension of the laws. But he exercises a *constitutional* magistracy with specific competences, limits, and the

---

19 This is the meaning of the 4th alinéa: "L'Assemblée nationale ne peut être dissoute pendant l'exercice des pouvoirs exceptionnels."
20 A similar preoccupation in a different context characterized also the new democracies in the twentieth century; see Karl Löwenstein (1937).

unique goal of the reestablishment of the conditions for the functioning legal-constitutional order. It may be suggestive to oppose law and power, but we cannot forget that the "power" is here entirely subservient and functional to the preservation of "law," the legal-constitutional republican order. But Schmitt is interested in the opposition between two figures of Rousseauian political theory: the dictator and the legislator. The first one exercises power *extra* and *contra legem*, to use Locke's language of the King's prerogative. The latter, the legislator, suggests law without the power to enact it; he has the initiative, not the effective function of the constituent power. The fusion of the two figures (in addition to the popular ratification of the constitution) generates what Schmitt defines in 1921 as *sovereign dictatorship*, the revolutionary figure of the *constituent power*, a crucial topic of his *Verfassungslehre*. From this point of view, it is absolutely evident that Schmitt's constitutional theory depends on Rousseau and the French revolution.

4 Coda

I do not need to offer a conclusion to this fragment of an archeology of emergency powers. But it seems clear that chapter 6 of Book iv of the *Social Contract* constitutes the link in the chain and the possibility of migration of the classical idea of dictatorship from the ancient doctrine of mixed government to the modern theory of representative government, *vulgo* democracy.

A quote from Joseph Schumpeter's classical book on democracy is clear evidence of this migration:

> […] democracies of all types recognize with practical unanimity that there are situations in which it is reasonable to abandon competitive and to adopt monopolistic leadership. In ancient Rome a non-elective office conferring such a monopoly of leadership in emergencies was provided for by the constitution. The incumbent was called *magister populi* or *dictator*. Similar provisions are known to practically all constitutions, our own included: the President of the United States acquires in certain conditions a power that makes him to all intents and purposes a dictator in the Roman sense, however great the differences are both in legal construction and in practical details. If the monopoly is effectively limited either to a definite time (as it originally was in Rome) or to the duration of a definite short-run emergency, the democratic principle of competitive leadership is merely suspended. If the monopoly, either in law or in fact, is not limited as to time – and if not limited as to time it will of course tend to become unlimited as to ev-

erything else – the democratic principle is abrogated and we have the case of dictatorship in the present-day sense. (296)[21]

Works Cited

Bodin, Jean. Les Six Livres de La République de J. Bodin Angevin: A Monseigneur Du Faur Seigneur de Pibrac, Conseiller du Roy en Son Privé Conseil. Paris: Chez Jacques du Puys, 1578.

Foisneau, Luc. "Rousseau et les républicanismes modernes: Présentation." Les Études Philosophiques 83.4 (2007): 409–541.

Friedrich, Carl J. "Dictatorship in Germany?" Foreign Affairs 9.1 (1930): 118–132.

Ginsborg, Paul. Daniele Manin and the Venetian Revolution of 1848–49. Cambridge: Cambridge UP, 1979.

Kelsen, Hans "On the Essence and Value of Democracy." *Weimar: A Jurisprudence of Crisis* Eds. Arthur J. Jacobson and Bernhard Schlink. Berkeley: U of California P, 2000. http://ark.cdlib.org/ark:/13030/kt209nc4v2/.

Löwenstein, Karl. "Militant Democracy and Fundamental Rights." The American Political Science Review 31.3–4 (1937): 417–432; 638–658

McKenzie, Lionel A. "Rousseau's Debate with Machiavelli in the Social Contract." Journal of the History of Ideas 43.2 (Apr.-Jun. 1982): 209–228.

Mommsen, Theodor. Römisches Staatsrecht Zweiter Band, Leipzig: Hirzel, 1888. http://www.mediterranee-antique.info/Auteurs/Fichiers/MNO/Mommsen/Droit_Romain/ T30/DPR_308.htm

Nippel, Wilfried. "Saving the Constitution: the European Discourse on Dictatorship." Footsteps of Herodotus: Towards European Political Thought. Ed. Janet Coleman and Paschalis Kitromilides. Firenze: L.S. Olschki, 2012. 29–49.

Nolte, Ernst "Diktatur." Geschichtliche Grundbegriffe, Eds. O. Brunner, W. Conze, R. Koselleck. Stuttgart: E. Klett, 1972.

Pasquino, Pascal. "Machiavel: dictature et salus reipublicae." Raison(s) d'état(s) en Europe. Ed. by B. Krulik. Bern, etc.: Peter Lang, 2010. 11–34.

Pasquino, Pascal. "Locke on King's Prerogative." Political Theory 26.2 (1998): 198–208.

Pocock, J. G. A. The Machiavellian Moment: Florentine Political Thought and the Atlantic Republican Tradition. Princeton, N.J.: Princeton UP, 1975.

Postigliola, Alberto. La Città Della Ragione: Per Una Storia Filosofica Del Settecento Francese. Roma: Bulzoni, 1992.

---

21 In a footnote to *Capitalism, Socialism and Democracy*, Schumpeter adds: "In ancient Rome whose term we are in the habit of misusing, an autocracy developed that for several centuries displayed certain features not dissimilar to those of modern dictatorships, though the analogy should not be pushed too far. But that autocracy did not make use of the republican office of dictator except in one case, that of G. Julius Caesar. Sulla's dictatorship was simply a temporary magistracy created for a definite purpose (constitutional reform). And there are no other but quite 'regular' cases."

Rousseau, Jean-Jacques. *Of the Social Contract and Other Political Writings*. Ed. C. Bertram. Trans. Q. Hoare. London: Penguin Books, 2012.
Rousseau, Jean-Jacques. The Political Writings of Jean-Jacques Rousseau. Ed. C.E. Vaughan. 1915. Oxford: Basil Blackwell, 1962.
Saint-Bonnet, François. L'État d'exception. Paris: PUF, 2001.
Schmitt, Carl. "'kommissarische' und 'souveräne Diktatur'. Französische Revolution und römische Vorbilder." Ideenpolitik. Geschichtliche Konstellationen und gegenwärtige Konflikte. Ed. H. Bluhm et al. Berlin: Akademie Verlag, 2011. 105–139.
Schmitt, Carl. Die Diktatur: Von den Anfängen des Modernen Souveränitätsgedankens bis zum Proletarischen Klassenkampf. München und Leipzig: Duncker & Humblot, 1921.
Schumpeter, Joseph A. Capitalism, Socialism, and Democracy. 1942. New York: Harper & Row, 1975.

Simon Critchley
Politics and Religion in the Social Contract

There is a paradox of sovereignty in Rousseau. *The Social Contract* from 1762 arguably provides the definitive expression of the modern conception of politics, namely an egalitarian conception of association rooted in popular sovereignty: the only sovereign in a legitimate polity is the people itself. In other words, Rousseau provides an entirely *immanent* conception of political legitimacy. This finds clearest expression in his conception of law: namely, the only law that can be followed in a legitimate polity is the law that gives itself through acts of the general will. In other words, law must be self-authorizing and correspond to autonomy.

Yet – and here's the paradox – what authority can law have if it is self-authorizing? This question leads Rousseau to the famous problem of the legislator: namely, in order for law to have authority over a community it becomes necessary to posit the existence of a legislator who stands outside that community: a foreigner, a stranger who initiates the constitutional arrangements of a polity, as Rousseau himself might have done with his plans for Corsica and Poland. Namely, the autonomy of law needs a heteronomous source in order to guarantee what some see as law's empire.

The dependence of an immanent conception of legitimacy on some transcendent instance becomes even more acute in Rousseau's treatment of the relation between politics and religion, which is my focus here. On the one hand, in the early draft of *The Social Contract*, the Geneva Manuscript, Rousseau insists that the question of legitimate political institutions is a philosophical issue that must not be resolved theologically. Yet, on the other hand, the published version of *The Social Contract* concludes with an infamous discussion of civil religion, namely those political articles of faith – which include a belief in a beneficent deity and an afterlife – that Rousseau believes are necessary in order to provide the motivational set of moral intuitions that will affectively bind together a polity and ensure that citizens take an active interest in the process of collective legislation that constitutes a self-determining political life. Such is the source of Rousseau's appeal to Voltaire in 1758 that there should be a catechism of the citizen, analogous to the articles of Christian faith, that would underpin the functioning of any legitimate polity.

Following Louis Althusser's essay on *The Social Contract* in *L'Impensé de Jean-Jacques Rousseau* closely,[1] I see Rousseau's extraordinarily inventive thinking as marked by a series of *décalages*, displacements, moments of tension, ambiguity or seeming contradiction, which, for me, find a particularly intense focus around three key concepts: politics, law and religion. An avowedly immanent conception of political autonomy requires an appeal to transcendence and heteronomy that appears to undermine it. But perhaps the truth is more complex. The logic of Rousseau's writing is a movement of articulation and disarticulation.

* * *

There are two versions of the book that has come to be known as *The Social Contract*, although as we will see, this title is a misnomer. There is no contract in the usual sense, understood as an agreement between two independently existing parties. Prior to the 1762 published version, Rousseau finished a manuscript, in his fairest handwriting, that was in a condition to be sent to the printer. It has come to be known as the *Geneva Manuscript*. Precise dating of this text is difficult, although it might well originate from 1755, and thus follows hard on the heels of *The Discourse on the Origin of Inequality* and the *Discourse on Political Economy* that were both published in 1755, although the writing of the *Second Discourse* was completed in 1754. What is fascinating about this first version of *The Social Contract* is the *décalage* that opens up around the question of politics and religion.

Consider two philological puzzles: firstly, Rousseau writes a compelling opening chapter to the *Geneva Manuscript* on the necessity for political institutions, which is simply suppressed in the published version. But why? Secondly, although the text of the *Geneva Manuscript* is written in Rousseau's best hand, a chapter called "On Civil Religion" is scribbled in an almost indecipherable hand on the text's verso. It is probable that this text was written in 1761, as Rousseau was drafting the final version of *The Social Contract*. So, doubts and uncertainties about whether the subject of politics can be raised without reference to religion frame the entire agonized writing and conceptual organization of *The Social Contract*, particularly what happens in Book iv.

In addition, Rousseau's doubts extend to the very title of his book on politics. He initially thought of it as a work on the need for and nature of political

---

[1] I thank Anne Deneys-Tunney for alerting me to this text and discussing it with me some years ago. Unless otherwise indicated all quotations from Rousseau are from vol. 4 of *CW*; *SC* will refer to Gourevitch's edition and translation of Rousseau's *Social Contract* (1997).

institutions. Rousseau begins the *Geneva Manuscript* with the words, "Let us begin by inquiring why the necessity for political institutions arises" (76). The fair version of the *Geneva Manuscript* has the Platonic subtitle, 'Essay about the Form of the Republic,' where 'form' would seem to recall the Platonic concept of *eidos*. Although Rousseau changes the published subtitle of *The Social Contract* to "Principles of Political Right," the allusion to Plato is arguably retained as the latter is one variation on one version of the *Republic's* bibliotekal subtitle, *peri dikaion politikos*, concerning the right or just ordering of human affairs in the state or Republic. But the full extent of Rousseau's wavering about the title of his book on politics is brought out by Victor Gourevitch (1997), when he writes that the manuscript title page of the *Geneva Manuscript*

> [s]hows "Of the Social Contract" crossed out and replaced by "Of Civil Society", which is again crossed out and replaced by the original "Of the Social Contract"; the second line reads "or"; and the third line gives as subtitle "Essay on the Constitution of the State"; 'Constitution of the State" is then crossed out and replaced by "The State", which is then also crossed out, to leave the subtitle to read "Essay on the Form of the Republic". In the definitive version, the subtitle became "Principles of Political Right." (*SC* 296–297)

Rousseau was clearly in two minds about the title and subtitle of his book, perhaps in more than two minds. But in order to bring out the full extent of Rousseau's uncertainty about the relation between politics and religion, I would like to lay out carefully the argument of the initial chapter of the *Geneva Manuscript*, "On the General Society of Mankind," in sixteen steps based on a close reading of the text. Rousseau's question is: why does the need for political institutions arise? Why indeed *does* the need for political institutions arise?

1. The initial answer is because, "nature's gentle voice is no longer an infallible guide for us" (77). That is, human beings have become denatured and alienated. This, of course, is the argument of the *Second Discourse*. Furthermore, life in the innocence of nature would leave human beings without any society as there is no communication.
2. We have become social and therefore, according to Rousseau's logic in *The Discourse on the Origin of Inequality*, miserable and wicked. We have entered Hobbes' state of war, which Rousseau equates with the state of nature.
3. Nature cannot be a guide to how society should be run, this is a "true illusion" (78) or "veritable chimera" (*SC* 155). Rousseau is resolutely against any conception of natural law, as he was in *The Discourse on the Origin of Inequality*.
4. We therefore find ourselves in a social state of independence or a violent individualism governed by private interest alone. Contra Mandeville in "The Fable of the Bees" or Pope in "An Essay on Man," there is no alliance be-

tween private interest and the public good. On the contrary, for Rousseau, private interest and the public good pull in opposite directions.
5. So, the question then becomes: how do we persuade the personage that Rousseau calls, "the independent man"? (79) That is, how might the person of private interest, the Hobbesian rational egoist (a straw man if ever there was one), the character that Rousseau identifies with Diderot's "violent reasoned" (82), act out of the common good rather than private interest?[2]
6. One powerful option is divine will. This is rejected as Rousseau asserts that it will lead to fanaticism. The multitude will never grasp the sublime morals that God imposes upon us, but will create "Gods as senseless as itself" (79).
7. Therefore, Rousseau suggests, "Let us set aside the sacred precepts of the various Religions whose abuse causes as many crimes as their use may prevent" (80). He goes on to argue that we should not appeal to theology in determining the good, but should return to the philosopher what the theologian has imperfectly understood. He continues, and this is crucial: "Let us restore to the Philosopher the examination of a question which the Theologian has never dealt with except to the prejudice of humankind" (80).
8. Yet the philosopher will send us back to the concept of the human race or humankind *(le genre humain)*, which is a concept that rightly invites Rousseau's suspicions. The philosopher will claim that the human being should address himself to the greatest good or – and this is how the central term of Rousseau's political theory is casually dropped into the *Geneva Manuscript* in a seeming allusion to Diderot – the general will.
9. How does the "violent reasoned" or "independent man" respond to the philosopher? He will assert that it is not a question of teaching him "what justice is, but of showing me what *interest* I have in being just" (80, my emphasis). What is the connection between justice and the interest in justice? *Cui bono?* as Hobbes writes, recalling Cicero (474). In other words, it is not a question of the philosophical justification of the good, but rather the subjective *motivation* to act on the good. Recall that Hobbes's answer to this question in *Leviathan* is that my interest in justice is in order to leave behind "that miserable condition of Warre" (117).
10. There are other obvious problems with an overly philosophical approach to politics. The general will is "a pure act of understanding" (80) that requires that each citizen become a philosopher of sorts. For egalitarian reasons, Rousseau wants to avoid Plato's elegant solution to this problem with the

---

[2] On the attribution of the character of the "violent reasoned" to Diderot's article for the *Encyclopédie* on "Natural Right" from 1755, see *CW* 4: 235–236.

idea of the philosopher king. He asks, "Will the average man be capable of deriving his rules of conduct from this manner of reasoning?" (80) Also, might we not mistake our inclinations for the general will? "Will he listen to the inner voice?" (80) But if such an "inner voice" or conscience is only formed through the habit of judgment in relation to the laws that govern a given society, then such a conscience cannot serve to establish such laws. How, therefore, do we avoid error in moral reasoning?

11. There is no obvious way of avoiding error. There is no Socratic *daimon* or Augustinian divine voice to which we can appeal, as conscience is only formed when human beings become sociable, that is, when they have already become narcissistic and miserable. We cannot, for the same reason, appeal to the principles of right that may govern the society we live in, for we might well be the dupes of that society, as we do not know anything else. Mushrooms grown in the dark cannot be trusted to judge the quality of sunlight. Such is the "champignon" problem in political philosophy.

12. What to do, then? Rousseau writes, in an extraordinarily eloquent passage that concludes the Chapter, and I quote at length:

> But although there is no natural and general society among men, although men become unhappy and wicked in becoming sociable, although the laws of justice and equality mean nothing to those who live both in the freedom of the state of nature and subject to the needs of the social state; far from thinking that there is neither virtue nor happiness for us and that heaven has abandoned us without resources to the corruption of the species, let us endeavor to draw from the ill itself the remedy that should cure it. By means of *new associations* let us correct, if possible, the lack of a general association. Let our violent interlocutor himself be the judge of our success. Let us show him in *perfected art* the redress of the evils which beginning art caused to nature: let us show him all the misery of the state which he believed happy, all that is false in the reasoning which he believed solid. Let him behold in a better constitution of things the worth of good deeds, the punishment of bad ones, the endearing harmony of justice and happiness. Let us enlighten his reason with new knowledge, fire his heart with new sentiments, and let him learn to increase his being and his felicity by sharing them with his fellows. If my zeal does not blind me to the enterprise, let us not doubt that if he has the fortitude of soul and upright sense, this enemy of humankind will in the end abjure his hatred along with his errors, that the reason which led him astray will bring him back to humanity, that he will learn to prefer to his apparent interest his interest rightly understood; that he will become good, virtuous, sensitive, and in sum, finally, instead of the ferocious brigand he wanted to be, the most solid bulwark of a well-ordered society. (81–82 [*SC* 159], emphasis mine)

It is a fascinating passage. What is being imagined here is an art of politics. Such an art attempts to show "in perfected art" the reparation of the ills that "beginning art caused to nature." Anachronistically perhaps, the logic of Rousseau's argument recalls Jacques Derrida's analysis of the *pharmakon,* which ambivalently means both poison and cure. Rousseau insists that we must endeavor to "derive from the evil the remedy which will cure it." The art of politics is not *creatio ex nihilo*, or a work of genius, but the imagining of what Rousseau calls "new associations" that will remedy the lack of a general association. That is, given that we live in the aftermath of the catastrophe that "beginning art caused to nature," namely the development of society away from a state of nature towards a state of war and violent inequality, the cure is not a return to nature, but a turn to art: an art of politics that is capable of shaping new associations. Art against art, then. Of course, this is nothing new. In the Introduction to *Leviathan*, Hobbes compares the commonwealth to "an Artificiall man" (10, 491). If God said during creation, "Let us make man," then the art of politics is the fiction of an artificial man complete with an "Artificiall soul" that will animate the "Body Politique" (9).

13. What is fascinating about the opening chapter to the *Geneva Manuscript* is that we can see how the argument of *The Social Contract* was initially intended to persuade the skeptic, the violent reasoner, the social narcissus living in state of war described at the end of *The Discourse on the Origin of Inequality*. It is a question of providing something that will motivate the violent reasoner to act in the light of the general will and "bring him back to humanity" (82) and act on the general will, in relation to public rather than merely private interest.

14. The argument about religion comes full circle here. In order to force the violent reasoner to act on the general will we cannot rely on religion, on the coercive power of will of God, as this would lead to fanaticism. What seems to be required is a philosophical answer to a practical dilemma. Yet, at the end of *The Social Contract*, in the chapter on civil religion scribbled on the verso of the *Geneva Manuscript*, Rousseau acknowledges the motivational inadequacy of a purely philosophical account of politics and offers the picture of a political religion. In so doing, Rousseau implicitly accepts the limits of any Platonism in politics and comes much closer to Hobbes than is usually thought.

15. Perhaps this is why Rousseau eliminated the original introduction to his book on politics and the chapter on religion was added to *The Social Contract*. Is the necessity for religion the Platonist's cry of despair? Is that faint noise we hear at night from the downstairs apartment the sound of Socrates' sobbing? Or is it rather the quiet ironic Straussian chuckling at the very idea that philosophers might be kings? It is difficult to discern through the floorboards of millennia of interpretation and misunderstanding.

16. These are unanswerable, indeed paralyzing, questions. This much is clear, though: there is a need for fictions other than philosophical in order to unite

the general will with the interest to act on that will and bring the "enemy of mankind [...] back to humanity." The "perfected art" of politics that will permit the formation of "new associations" requires new forms of what I will call *fictional force* that might address the problem of motivation in politics. For those tempted to see Rousseau "a lisping Kant" (*SC* xxxviii), it should be noted that this is the problem that Kant never solves in his ethics: namely, how to combine the legitimacy of practical reason – the universality of the moral law – with the motivation to act on that law. Insofar as Kant's critical system is written under the sign of the primacy of practical reason, the problem of motivational force is arguably what undoes that system, the rationalism of Kant's ethics and any Neo-Kantian moral rationalism, such as Habermas's discourse ethics. As Rousseau writes in a political fragment reminiscent of Hume: "The mistake of most moralists has always been to consider man as an essentially reasonable being. Man is a sensitive being, who consults solely his passions in order to act, and for whom reason serves only to palliate the follies his passions lead him to commit" (70).

Where does this leave us? In the wider argument from which this talk is extracted, I try to show the "actuality" of Rousseau by tracing the intrication of three concepts in his work: politics, law and religion. I follow a series of conceptual *décalages* around which Rousseau's system is staged, where the condition of possibility for any legitimate form of political association requires the externality of the legislator for its authorization and the transcendence of civil religion for its sacralization. Sadly, this condition of possibility is also the system's condition of impossibility and we have Rousseau's political argument unravel in a rather improbable conception of civil religion.

But it might lead elsewhere.

As I said at the beginning, Rousseau establishes the modern conception of politics: popular sovereignty, or free association rooted in equality. Furthermore, by following the *décalage* machine of Rousseau's text, I think we are afforded a decisive recognition of the *fictional force* that is essential to politics. In Hobbes's words, what gives life and motion to the body politic is an "Artificiall *Soul.*" Politics is, in the literal sense, a *poetic* task concerned with the construction of fictions. The question is whether we might speak of the possibility of a supreme fiction in politics, a fiction that we know to be a fiction, yet in which we can still believe. But that, as they say, is another story.

Works Cited

Althusser, Louis. "Sur *Le Contrat Social* (les décalages)." *L'Impensé de Jean-Jacques Rousseau. Les Cahiers pour l'Analyse* 8 (1967): 6–42.
http://cahiers.kingston.ac.uk/vol08/
Althusser, Louis. "Sur *Le Contrat Social*." Houilles, France: Manucius, 2009.
Hobbes, Thomas. *Leviathan*. Ed. Richard Tuck. Cambridge, N.Y.: Cambridge UP, 1991.
Rousseau, Jean-Jacques. *The Social Contract and Other Later Political Writings*. Ed. And trans. Victor Gourevitch. Cambridge, UK: Cambridge UP, 1997. [*SC*]
Rousseau, Jean-Jacques. *The Collected Writings of Rousseau*. Gen. Eds. Roger D. Masters and Christopher Kelly. 13 vols. Hanover: UP of New England, 1990–2010.
Rousseau, Jean-Jacques. *Social Contract*. Ed. Roger D. Masters and Christopher Kelly. Trans. Judith R. Bush et al. *Collected Writings*, vol. 4. 1994.

Mira Morgenstern
Alienation and Freedom: Rousseau and Transcending Nature/Culture Dualism

1 Introduction

The tricentennial of Rousseau's birth presents the opportunity to evaluate more than just the legacy of an eighteenth-century thinker and his relevance to the concerns of the twenty-first century. More broadly, readers of Rousseau are called to weigh the significance of liberal political thought to the postmodern challenges of the twenty-first century. In a world where dictatorships take on the coloring of democratic systems; where political processes can obscure instead of enable liberty; can politics be said to be the pathway to freedom?

These are particularly sensitive issues in evaluating Rousseau's thought, especially because Rousseau insists on his own honesty and openness as a way of justifying the credibility of his revolutionary arguments. But how can twenty-first-century students of Rousseau assess a political thinker who seems to contradict himself? How can modern interpretations ascribe value to an author whose works are happily cited by adherents of opposing political systems with contradictory values and outcomes?

The broad nature of these questions underlines the fact that Rousseau's thought has always conjured fundamental doubts regarding conventional justifications of power allocations, whether socially- or politically-based. Most recently, twentieth-century scholarship on Rousseau has often entangled itself on just these topics. Indeed, one can argue that this emphasis is not surprising, given that these subjects appear to go directly to the issue of what Rousseau actually means in any particular work. By the same token, these queries inevitably interrogate whether meaning in Rousseau's writing is – or ever can be, for any author – stable.

The broad swathes of this divide are already well-known: is Rousseau an Enlightenment *philosophe* in the style of Montesquieu, or a cultural conservative like Burke? Does he emphasize individual or community? Does Rousseau promote individual self-expression or conformity to a state-mandated ideal of citizenship? Does Rousseau insist that the individual must choose between being a man or a citizen?¹ Or does his thought unite the extremes of both left-wing and right-wing politics by emphasizing state control of all the citizens?²

Perhaps ironically, Talmon's fusion of the oppressive tactics and democratic (in his view, "doublespeak") values that he finds in Rousseau is reflected far more benignly in those scholars who take a more complex approach to the putative "contradictions" or "fusions" in Rousseau's thought. These modern thinkers insist that Rousseau transcends the simplistic dualisms attributed to him by those conventional critics whose interpretations of Rousseau leave disabling contradictions in their wake.³ Rather, taking seriously Rousseau's own awareness of the complexity of language and the difficulty of expressing oneself with perfect clarity at all times,⁴ these more nuanced approaches understand that Rousseau's work must be taken as a whole to be properly assessed; and not artificially read as a series of quotations that are pulled out of context.

Following the more complex path traced by these more expansive readers of Rousseau, but going beyond the "blander" readings of Rousseau that the thematic approach can sometimes engender, this paper utilizes a dialectical reading of Rousseau's works that deals directly with the uncomfortable dissonances that Rousseau describes in both everyday life and political/philosophical circumstances. This method allows the excitement and revolutionary implications of Rousseau's thought to shine through even three centuries after his birth. This is particularly apparent in an idea that appears throughout Rousseau's essays and literary endeavors: the concept of alienation.

2 Alienation in the State of Nature

Rousseau's description of the development of the human being in the State of Nature seems to introduce pre-civilized human existence as simply individual, without any social aspect. But in Rousseau's telling, things soon become more complicated. Despite Rousseau's emphasis on the monadic *individual* in the State of Nature, Rousseau claims that human beings start to recognize and to cooperate with each other only once they have distinguished themselves cognitive-

---

1 "[H]is [Rousseau's] insistence that one must choose between the two models, between man and the citizen" (Shklar 1969: 5).
2 Jacob Talmon (1961: 38–50).
3 Lévi-Strauss (1962); see Starobinski (1971).
4 Rousseau writes of the impossibility of utilizing words with consistency all the time: in book ii of *Émile* (*OC* 4: 345, note [1991: 108, note]). All translations of Rousseau are my own, unless otherwise indicated.

ly as a species different from other animals (*SD, OC* 3: 166–167). Thus, human beings, by Rousseau's account, first develop *group* identification with their species before acquiring separate, individual identities of their own.[5]

The development of this identification occurs as the result of a series of systematic, even analytical, moves. According to Rousseau, Savage Man (in one of his later incarnations) reflects upon himself in an orderly manner, so as to increase his practical security vis-à-vis the potentially dangerous animals that surround him in the pre-governmental State of Nature (*SD* 136). Following that process, he extends his circle of comparison to include those two-legged creatures that he finds remarkably similar to himself. Finally, man exercises his heretofore latent powers of imagination in order to give expression to a generalized and vocalized call for help at a point when he feels himself to be in (mortal) danger (*SD* 148).[6] It is only after this point that Rousseau presents the development of what we would understand as the various incarnations of individual differences, which Rousseau describes as the evolution of desires and possessions that establish human beings' distinctiveness from one another.

In Rousseau's view, the alienation – or distanciation – inherent in the activation of the imagination plays a major role in heralding these changes. Rousseau presents alienation as constitutive of man's imaginative process, because imagination, by definition, involves thinking *about* a person or situation at some remove from the immediacy of lived experience. As a result, man now perceives himself – and consequently, the creatures around him – as objects of analysis.[7] Once man extrapolates from his own reactions – demonstrating pity for someone who needs help – and attributes these same responses to creatures similar to himself (based on their physical resemblance to him), man identifies the objects of his cry and calls them his "*semblables*" (fellow creatures/counterparts) (*SD* 165–166). Moreover, the pity activated by the imagination extends itself to form the basis of permanent social cohesion:[8] the imaginative juxtaposi-

---

[5] In "The Mirror Stage as Formative of the Function of the I as Revealed in Psychoanalytic Experience" (1949), Lacan traces a parallel development in the ego-formation of the (very) young child, who similarly comes to identify him/herself in the mirror after first recognizing a familiar companion during that same event (2001: 75–82).

[6] Prior to this, the existence of Savage Man is characterized by Rousseau specifically by the non-realized quality of the imagination dormant in him (*SD* 144).

[7] The analysis of metaphor here owes a great deal to Miller (1992), especially chapters 1–2.

[8] The point is that pity, in its first and more primitive manifestation, operates as a basic instinct; it is only later that its social implications are fully realized. See in this connection Morgenstern, *Jean-Jacques Rousseau and the Politics of Ambiguity*, especially 55–80. This point, stated generally in *The Discourse on the Origin of Inequality*, is more specifically developed in *Émile*, where Rousseau writes, "[I]t is only imagination which makes us feel the fills of others" (*E* 517 [1991:

tion of the human recognition of the self vis-à-vis the acknowledgement of the other allows for the development of lasting, and not just temporary, social cooperation (*SD* 166–167).

The combination of self-reflection with the imagination enables man to solidify the connection between himself and his fellow creatures. This imaginative act of comparison, establishing the interactive individual and communal notions of "self" and "other," also heralds a deepening of man's intellectual attainment. By dint of comparison, man is now able to enter into the mind of his *semblable* and to make assumptions not only about the *semblable*'s (anticipated) psychological reactions (pity), but also about the *semblable*'s (presumed) intellectual abilities. The cry for help is thus not merely a hopeful request, but also a sign of assurance that solutions to difficult problems exist, can be found, and can be actualized by mankind.

While insisting on the existence of group identification *prior* to the development of individual consciousness, Rousseau does not valorize group coherence over individual identity; that is to say, he does not succumb to the hierarchy that so often accompanies categorization. Thus, Rousseau maintains that the individual and social spheres cannot be understood as exclusively separate phenomena. Rousseau portrays the evolution of human uniqueness through Natural Man's deliberate engagement with the dialectic engendered by the encounter between the self and the other.

Rousseau's understanding of the self and the other imputes to both concepts a shared reflexive and reflective ground. This, for Rousseau, is anchored in the possession of free will. According to Rousseau, the presence of free will presupposes a being who can reflect upon his choices.[9] Rousseau states this quite openly in his definition of liberty near the beginning of *The Discourse on the Origins of Inequality:* free will, says Rousseau, allows man to "recognize *himself* [as] free" (*SD* 142, my emphasis). For Rousseau, liberty is not the expression just of a self-referential intellectualism. In addition, by affording man the possibility to reflect

---

231]). Significantly, this statement is made when Émile is being taught the principles of socialization.

9 Rousseau takes account of the different roles that man's moral liberty plays in his decision-making throughout the various stages of his anthropological development. Rousseau points out that moral liberty is not present in its full strength at every juncture of this process: in the beginning steps of men's evolution, liberty is present mainly as potentiality and is not fully operative; towards the end of man's development in the State of Nature, and in an ironic twist, liberty may be utilized even to eliminate freedom for the vast majority of humanity (this is the perpetration of the false social contract, as presented in *The Discourse on the Origins of Inequality,* 177).

upon himself, liberty, as embodied in free will, concretely structures the way man views the world and operates within it. Implicit in Rousseau's argument is that the ability of man to consider himself – to conceptualize himself as a being about whom it is possible for him to reflect – marks man as a creature of moral dimensions even before he formally enters into the political sphere. For Rousseau, alienation in its most positive aspects makes the human being a creature capable of moral thought, political choice, and intellectual problem-solving.

3 Alienation: Loving Me, Loving You

As the State of Nature advances, man's encounter with the other engenders entanglements of its own. These are largely the result of the effects of the imagination that is activated by man's encounter with the outside world. Complications ensue because the imagination that creates the circumstances of man's alienation can also imperil man's humanity.[10] At first glance, however, this point appears problematic, because it seems to contradict our prior understanding of alienation, which credits the *advance* of Natural Man's individual and social potential in the State of Nature precisely to a measured amount of alienation (as evident in Natural Man's ability to distance himself enough to be aware of his own and of his fellow man's identity, and subsequently to cooperate with them). In *The Discourse on the Origins of Inequality*, the complex tensions between these two combative and yet linked notions of alienation form the context for man's subsequent development in the State of Nature and beyond. Throughout this process, Rousseau traces the social and political implications of the link between the imagination and alienation, particularly as these are expressed in the founding movement of society: the onset of love.[11]

---

10 This is implicit in Rousseau's definition of alienation, which he understands as "giving or selling [...] renouncing one's liberty [...] [is] incompatible with human nature" (*CS* book i, ch. 4; *OC* 3: 355–356).
11 In this, Rousseau differs markedly from Hobbes, who bases man's hopes to attain what he wants on man's own industriousness (*Leviathan* I, ch. 13, 188). For Hobbes, the possibility of fulfilling one's desires obviates the question of happiness, for if one is free to attain what one wants, one can choose what to pursue and how much to pursue it according to one's own sense of personal happiness. Happiness is, in a very concrete sense, what one makes of it. For Rousseau, however, this hope is based on a fallacy because man's desires are inherently incapable of satisfaction. It is not, as for Hobbes, a question of man's diligence, which would make the attainment of man's desires a factor of his own skill and perseverance. Rather, for Rousseau, the very nature of this pursuit reflects the essence of the Tantalus experience: "the object that

As Rousseau sees it, natural affection, growing out of man's recognition of his *semblable*, becomes concretized in the State of Nature with the institutionalization of living arrangements. This development is centered on the construction of huts. According to Rousseau, the permanent nature of these domiciles fosters the growth of exclusive romantic love between the heretofore (merely) functional pairing of the conjugal dyad. Subsequently, the gradual incorporation of ritualized meetings/performative events nurtures the feelings of romantic love among the younger generation. This in turn gives rise to manipulative relationships, whose primary goal becomes not the expression of personal sentiment, but the exercise of individual power (*SD* 169).

While the exercise of power may seem antithetical to the romantic love that serves as its breeding ground, Rousseau's account demonstrates that both stem from man's ability, developed early on in the State of Nature, to turn a reflective eye upon himself through a series of deliberate comparisons between the self and the other. In addition to the problem-solving abilities and developmental strides that man has already accomplished by this sort of reflective "alienation," another logical extension of man's ability to look at himself from the outside is man's newly-developed ability to consider other people's reactions to him at their increasingly important social encounters outside the huts.[12] This yields important advances in man's psychological and social self-calibration. Man can now develop his own sense of control and awareness of his own abilities; among which Rousseau emphasizes man's new capability of foresight (*prévoyance*). In addition, thinking about others in this context presents to man an opportunity of possible profit and power.

---

appears under the hand flees more quickly than one can pursue it." To be sure, it is possible to read the *Leviathan* as being far less sanguine about the probabilities of achieving happiness: for one thing, while Hobbes does point out that man can designate that which he needs to acquire in order to achieve happiness, this in and of itself is no guarantee that man will therefore achieve his aim, much less a more generalized goal of stable happiness. After all, consonant with Hobbes's definition of life as motion, is the idea that man's desires, too, infinitely grow. Nevertheless, there is a fundamental difference between Hobbes's and Rousseau's respective assessments of happiness and the likelihood of the individual human being to achieve it. For Hobbes, happiness is something that the individual can define for himself, can calibrate to his own assessment of his present energies to attain that goal and can therefore hope to achieve. Thus, it is possible to conjecture that for Hobbes, happiness does not have to be an ever-elusive goal. For Rousseau, on the other hand, happiness by definition eludes human beings precisely because of the fact that they are not divine (*E* 503 [1991: 221]).

12 Rousseau characterizes this man in the State of Nature as being the "Spectator of himself" (*SD*, n15 to 154; *OC* 3: 219).

Despite the varied possibilities that now open up for Rousseau's Natural Man, Rousseau depicts this situation as full of moral traps. On one level, reflection can offer an individual scope for creating his own future, free of the perhaps unfair trappings that fate and circumstances have already established for him. It becomes possible even to engineer the active process of choice so as to appear to be the passive object; or even, potentially, to move between both of those roles, as the advantages of each particular situation dictate. But at the same time, the sort of success now available to Natural Man inevitably involves a process of self-manipulation: the individual is forced to present him/herself as a function of what s/he imagines other people would value, just in order to elicit the desired reactions from his/her fellows.[13] Strategically-inspired manipulation yields to philosophical obfuscation, as the lines between the energetic selector and the quiescent focus of desire become increasingly blurred.

The complication of the difference between the chooser and the chosen, and between analysis and manipulation – in other words, the exploitation by and among the various selves and others that constitute society – carries with it important implications for moral judgment, as well as for the structure and function of political power. In Rousseau's depiction of this process in *The Discourse on the Origins of Inequality*, the clouding of moral distinctions – does appearance reflect reality? or mask it? – gives rise to successive levels of dehumanization. If one cannot really be the best, one has to fool the other person into believing that one is.[14] This has important social – and romantic – implications.

Consequently, the love which is originally portrayed in *The Discourse on the Origins of Inequality* as anchored in a positive regard for oneself – Rousseau calls this *amour de soi* and sees this as the basis of a healthy (romantic) relationship with another person – deteriorates into a warped imitation of itself, which Rousseau names *amour-propre*. In the process, says Rousseau, this distorted version of love causes the closest of human relationships to degenerate into the process of marketing a product – oneself – rather than presenting an opportunity to ex-

---

13 Thus, for example, a person with qualities that are considered less attractive may utilize his ability to speculate about other people's likely (negative) reactions to those qualities by presenting himself in a way that would minimize the (perceived) negative impact of those qualities. This would afford him a better chance of shaping a more advantageous future for himself: "[O]ne had to show oneself, for one's own advantage, [to be] other than what one [actually] was [...]" (*SD* 174).

14 In his famous distinction between authentic "being" and misleading "appearance," Rousseau makes it clear that the failure to distinguish between the two is not a matter of happenstance. Rather, this blunder results from "cheating trickery" (*SD* 174).

pand one's being by entering into someone else's soul.¹⁵ As depicted in *The Discourse on the Origins of Inequality*, the aim of *amour-propre* is to gain one's own advantage, rather than to achieve greater happiness for all concerned. The result is that man becomes a fictive being, recreating himself as an illusory image in order to attract someone else. His existence becomes entirely relative, a function of his estimate of the other person's perception. Instead of carrying his own being entirely with himself (*SD* 136), in the manner of the authentic Savage Man, man is now reduced to being the slave of someone else's perception of him.¹⁶

But even with the obvious differences between *amour de soi* and *amour-propre*, Rousseau sees moral ambiguity in both. Rousseau points out that *amour-propre*, normally highlighted as the "evil" type of love, also carries with it certain positive traits, such as patriotism.¹⁷ Similarly, *amour de soi*, portrayed by Rousseau as linked to the natural instinct of self-preservation (and thus retaining a measure of inherent goodness) (*SD* n15, 219), can potentially degenerate into selfishness and even homicide.¹⁸ Rousseau also finds that both *amour de soi* and *amour-propre* contain within themselves different varieties of the dialectic between the self and the other. Thus, Rousseau argues that even the healthy expression of *amour de soi* embodied in the love of another human being can easily function in an egotistical fashion, serving merely as an excuse for self-gratification, which is another term for *amour-propre*.¹⁹ For Rousseau, even the seemingly polar expressions of love are actually implicated in each other.

The ambiguities of love do not remain merely personal in nature. They also contain important social implications, some of which are explored in Rousseau's romantic novel, *La Nouvelle Héloïse*. In this novel, the protagonists persist in viewing the categories of self and other not only as manipulable, but also as im-

---

15 It will be recalled that *amour de soi*, on which love of another is based, is characterized by "the force of an expansive soul" (*E* 523n [1991: 235n]).
16 As Rousseau notes, people now need to interest other people in their own lot in order to survive (*SD* 174–175).
17 See Morgenstern (1996: 124).
18 Rousseau's point, elliptically made, is that *amour de soi*'s emphasis on the self has the potential to lead to homicide; and that it is pity that moderates this enhanced sense of self existing within *amour de soi* (*SD* 156).
19 Thus, as we will see further on, Rousseau presents one reading of romantic love as excessively self-involved: "Lovers see only themselves; are concerned only [...] with themselves" (*Julie*, part 3, letter xx; *OC* 2: 372).

penetrable, essences.[20] As the narrative moves forward, however, it is precisely the porousness between the self and the other that provides much of the tension between Julie and Saint-Preux. The first sections of this story trace the anxiety with which Julie registers her growing awareness of her love for Saint-Preux. While both of these protagonists love each other, they react differently to the challenges that love poses to the fragile boundaries of the self: Saint-Preux glories in losing himself in his beloved, but Julie is frightened of being deprived of her own individuality.[21]

As the novel progresses, Julie further presses the perplexities of the self-other dynamic of love. She interrogates the extent to which romantic involvement, while appearing to focus on the other person rather than on the self, is actually selfish in that it deflects attention from the larger responsibilities owed to society as a whole (*Julie* 372). The narrative tension of *La Nouvelle Héloïse* deepens as Rousseau does not simply accept Julie's solution to this moral conundrum, which is to valorize communal stability exclusively above personal happiness.[22]

Beyond the plot-based intricacies of the narrative, Rousseau's larger theoretical argument is that facile declarations based on dualistic views of the world do not work, either on the practical level or on the more theoretical plane. Rousseau insists that instrumentally simplistic solutions, based on an exclusivist or category-bound approach to resolving complex matters, are likely to exacerbate problems rather than solve them in a positive manner. This occurs because dualistic understandings of the world tend by nature to overlook the complex variety of the human needs of *all* the participants who are involved. Consequently, these unsophisticated solutions fail to take account of the underlying tensions that give rise to the personal and social dissonances that had engendered these different requirements in the first place. As a result, these conflicts, when ignored, simply explode.

In *La Nouvelle Héloïse*, this turmoil is evident at Julie's death, when the estate at Clarens begins to disintegrate. If the death of just one family member im-

---

20 This is essentially the situation presented in *Discours sur l'Inégalité*, where each individual is portrayed as positioning him/herself in order to increase his/her real "worth" in the eyes of the other. In this context, the categories of self and other are portrayed as subject to manipulation but never as being transformed in their respective essence. That is to say, people in the (beginning of the moral disintegration of the) State of Nature, as depicted by Rousseau in the image of the dances in front of the huts, perform for each other but never truly interact or interrelate.
21 See the discussion in Morgenstern (1996: 96–101).
22 In the novel, Julie claims that love is not an inextricable part of a happy marriage, and insists that she is content in her loveless marriage to Wolmar (*Julie* 372).

perils the existence of the entire family/estate organization, it becomes clear that the collapsing structure has little moral coherence to begin with.[23] Implicitly, Rousseau contends that the complexities of the self-other dialectic must be faced, and not avoided, if one is to live a fully authentic life, maximizing humanity in both the personal and political arenas.

4 The Politics of Borders

The struggle over the proper boundaries between the self and the other, as expressed in the paradoxes of alienation, similarly underlies Rousseau's understanding of the dynamic of the political sphere. Rousseau accords a central place to alienation in the establishment of the political sphere. In fact, Rousseau defines the founding movement of the ideal polity as "the *total alienation* of each associate with all his rights to the whole community" (*CS* i, ch. 6, 360; my emphasis).

At first glance, placing alienation at the center of the polity's founding seems both counterintuitive and irremediably flawed; after all, in the State of Nature, alienation appears to set into motion the very contradictions that prove inimical to the social fabric in the first place. As Rousseau depicts it, the social inequality that develops as a result of the posturing and pretensions encouraged by the development of romantic love becomes entrenched with the passage of time and the subsequent concentration of wealth in the hands of the (relative) few.[24] The rich utilize the novelty of these circumstances to persuade the poor that social stability is best achieved under a government pledged to uphold the sanctity of property. As it happens, however, the inequality now ensconced in law yields upheavals of its own so that, in the end, despotism – the supreme inequality – itself ironically evokes the absolute equality of all, as everybody is equally oppressed by the totalitarian dictator.

Despite what can conventionally be viewed as a major "contradiction" in Rousseau's thought – alienation is deemed both "good" and "evil" in developmental/political terms – Rousseau manages to avoid this conundrum. By presenting alienation as having both "positive" (in the sense of analytic, problem-solving) and "negative" (in the sense of morally destructive) aspects, Rousseau

---

[23] For more on this point, see Morgenstern (1996: 213–214).
[24] See the discussion in *Discours sur l'inégalité*, where alienation causes man to manipulate the process of love, so that love degenerates into jealousy (169), which in turn prepares the way for the introduction of oppression and exploitation (177). This situation leads to social anarchy, where society collapses into a Hobbesian state of war (*SD* 187, 190–191).

appears to slice this Gordian note neatly in two. But one difficulty remains. After Rousseau presents, in one fell swoop, the destructive nature of negative alienation as it develops out of human machinations and prevarications, one would expect Rousseau similarly to provide one inevitable depiction of the ideal polis established with the positive manifestation of alienation.

But Rousseau does not do that. Rousseau remains aware that much mischief can result from this single-minded approach, and not just from misidentifying a category as salutary when in fact it is not (Rousseau's emphasis on Julie's misapprehensions regarding the importance of love both as it relates to her own life, and to the larger community of which she is a part, underlines this point). In addition, Rousseau demonstrates that the act of classification itself, in its beguiling simplicity, often misrepresents itself as the morally "pure," and hence ideal, solution to the more messy complexity of real-life issues involving the actual varieties of human nature. Consequently, perhaps mindful of the complicated lines and tensions between self and other that he evokes throughout his political and literary writings, Rousseau formulates not one, but two visions of the (positive sort of) alienation that can establish the authentic political state.

Rousseau's intellectual move here is important and it is worthwhile grasping the salience of his approach. Rousseau's insistence on presenting dual roots or manifestations of central human developments – whether these are linguistic,[25] emotional,[26] or political – emphasizes Rousseau's claim that the intricacies of social and psychic phenomena marking human relations defy the limits of conventional categorization. Thus, in politics, the focus of this essay, Rousseau insists on the total alienation of everything to the state, leaving no private sphere extant (CS 360). But at another juncture, Rousseau appears to advocate founding a state through the mechanism of partial alienation, leaving some private area of choice outside of politics for the citizens (CS 373). The apparent contradictions in Rousseau's formulations appear to challenge the requirements of logic.

---

25 In *Essai sur l'origine des langues*, Rousseau gives differing accounts of the two types of primal language: the warm, passionate speech of the South, and the cold, instrumental voice of the North. Similarly, Rousseau also puts forth two different versions of the first form of human speech in *Essai sur l'origine des langues*, and *Discours sur l'inégalité*, respectively. See Morgenstern (1996) for a coherent explanation of this seeming philosophical sloppiness on the part of Rousseau.

26 In *Discours sur l'inégalité*, Rousseau similarly writes of two kinds of love that are both presented as fundamental: *amour de soi* and *amour-propre*. In like manner, Rousseau gives two seemingly jarring accounts of "pity," and includes pity, as well as self-preservation in his account of "the" fundamental human instinct.

Understanding Rousseau's difficult ideas requires contextualizing Rousseau's statements in terms of his understanding of the politics and pitfalls of categorization. For Rousseau, each type of alienation associated with politics, whether total or partial, contains a particular advantage – and an accompanying disadvantage – for the construction of the politically authentic state. Total alienation on the part of each citizen sets up a political system where there is no conflict between self and other, since each individual citizen is subsumed totally in the whole. As a result, total alienation guarantees the state loyal and obedient citizens.

At the same time, however, total alienation cannot ensure a passionate commitment to the state on the part of these same citizens. This is because the eradication of individuality also entails the lack of distinctive passion, of the intense caring, that is an inherent part of each person constituted as a separate being. Can an enterprise as complicated as the state exist and flourish without the passionate commitment of its citizens? Rousseau appears to think not: in *Political Economy*, he writes that "a man who would have no passions would certainly be a terribly bad citizen."[27]

A state based on partial alienation would solve this problem, as each citizen would retain enough of his private individuality to be able to commit passionately to the state. But a state based on partial alienation faces challenges of its own. The very structure of partial alienation that allows its citizens voluntarily to dedicate themselves fervently to the state also carries with it the danger that the interests of the individual self may triumph over the well-being of the collective other,[28] leading the state to disintegrate into an empire of selfishness. In either case, alienation highlights the tension between the self and the other that can destroy the possibility of their fusion. Whether total or partial, alienation in politics still reflects, to some degree, the opposition between the unique self and the communal other, jeopardizing their accommodation of each other in an ideal society where personal and political authenticity should harmoniously coexist.[29]

---

27 *Discours sur l'économie politique* (*OC* 3: 259).
28 "As soon as somebody says about the affairs of state, 'What difference does it make to me?' one must assume that the State is lost" (*CS* first version; ii, ch. 4, 330).
29 In the end, Rousseau does advocate strengthening the state's emotional cohesion and thus long-term survival by establishing it on a strong sense of *amour de soi*, that expands upon individual emotion to include the entire State within its bounds: "The individual 'me' extended over the whole is the strongest link of the general society" (*CS*, first version, book ii, ch. 4; OC3: 330). One could also argue that, in the end, Rousseau deems it more likely that a state based on partial, rather than total, alienation will enjoy an extended and dynamic existence. This is because partial alienation takes into account the realities of human nature, and valorizes (in the Lockean

In order to ensure that the dynamism of self and other in the political sphere be mutually reinforcing instead of reciprocally destructive, Rousseau takes great care to describe the process by which the ideal polity should function. Rousseau calls the principle underlying this method the General Will, and describes it as "an act of pure understanding, reasoning in the silence of the passions" (*CS* first version, 288). But defining the General Will – the true will of the people – becomes difficult, chiefly because the people do not always realize their "pure understanding:" i.e., they do not always grasp what they truly want (*CS* 380). Often, in fact, the knowledge necessary to arrive at the General Will is manipulated and falsely presented, and thus is itself compromised.[30]

As a result of this intellectual manipulation, the Will of All (a numerical plurality/majority that can masquerade as what the people as a whole really want) often can be mistaken for the General Will (the true best interest of the people), even though the Will of All is antithetical to the General Will in both function and content. According to Rousseau, this confusion can happen because the Will of All deludes the people about the real substance of their happiness. In so doing, the Will of All destroys the possibility for authentic self-government. An even more dangerous situation arises when the Will of All comprises an actual majority of the people, and thus can lay claim to a seeming legitimacy for its self-serving point of view. This notion of the Will of All may be understood in Madison's terms as a majority faction, which is "adverse [...] to the permanent and aggregate interests of the community as a whole."[31]

Rousseau's evaluation of the complicated dynamic between the General Will and the Will of All does not end here. Making things even more difficult, and true to his nuanced appreciation of the intricacies of human existence, Rousseau does not depict even the Will of All as irrefutably bad. Despite the harmful tendencies of the Will of All when deployed in the political sphere, Rousseau views its existence is a practical imperative, possessing important positive political implications. As Rousseau notes, even in the ideal polity, people are born with individual wills of their own before joining the polis and subsuming their own per-

---

sense) the maximization of individual property and security that motivate the founding of the polity in the first place (*CS* 360). For more on this topic, Morgenstern (1996: 147–157).

30 See the discussion of *Discours sur l'Inégalité* in Morgenstern (1996: 162–164). Rousseau points out the empirical usefulness of the arts and sciences, employed by corrupt governments to distract their subjects by throwing "garlands of flowers" to mask the brute reality of their oppression (*DSA*, *OC* 3: 7).

31 James Madison, Federalist #10, in Rossiter (1961).

sons within the General Will.³² Rousseau writes that this selfish sense of individuality is indispensable for the recognition of the General Will; as Rousseau points out, the General Will is revealed in contradistinction to the Will of All, which historically is the prior phenomenon.³³ Consequently, the existence of the Will of All is a (historical) prerequisite for the discovery of the General Will.

This complex process of the political engagement of the General Will, and its contradistinction to the earlier establishment of the Will of All, finds its emotional/psychic counterpart in Rousseau's description of the concept of alienation. Ostensibly, as we have seen, alienation in Rousseau's theoretical writings has (mainly) negative connotations: on the personal level, it leads to people's estrangement from each other (this is the negative human relationships resulting from *amour-propre*); and on the political level, it negates what Rousseau considers to be the essence of humanity.³⁴

But as we have already seen on the individual psychic-psychological level, the very same alienation that sponsors human estrangement (resulting from *amour-propre*) can be reconfigured as the ability to step outside the conventional "box" of imprisoning limitations and to distance oneself enough from the minutiae of actual circumstances in order to think creatively about problems and their solutions. Similarly, the negative alienation of liberty that can render the inauthentic polity morally reprehensible can also be recalibrated as the authentic alienation of the *Social Contract*. In its ideal political realization, this kind of alienation actually allows for the humanization of politics, enabling each individual to go beyond his/her own selfish desires and support what is best for the community of individuals comprising the polity.

---

32 Certain readers of Rousseau contend that Rousseau wants people to identify primarily as indivisible parts of a greater whole ("citizens") rather than as unique individuals. Readers of this persuasion often cite the texts of *Essai sur le gouvernement de Pologne* (particularly *OC* 3: 966) and *Discours sur l'économie politique* (especially *OC* 3: 260) as proof. But in that very same work, Rousseau also acknowledges, more realistically, that (hopefully) "[individuals] [...] would *finally* achieve loving [their fatherland] with the exquisite sentiment that every lone person has only for himself" (*OC* 3: 259; my emphasis). In other words, even at his most "communitarian," Rousseau acknowledges the primacy of individual feeling that must anchor social sentiment.

33 Rousseau notes that it is precisely the varied nature of personal differences that necessitates the art of politics. As Rousseau points out, if everyone would automatically think in the same manner and reach the same conclusions, the common interest would naturally obtain without any further complications (*CS* 371n). Here again, it is worth noting the resemblance to Madison's remarks *in Federalist* #10 on the necessity of politics to establish a framework within which human individualities can flourish without destroying each other.

34 See footnote 10 above.

Thus, in the context of the ideal polity, the citizen must possess a highly-nuanced proclivity for complexity in order to arrive at the General Will. In Rousseau's polis, the citizen needs simultaneously to manage multiple levels of consciousness: s/he must acknowledge his/her own individual selfish desires, while at the same time recognizing and advocating for the best (and often divergent) interests of the community as a whole.[35]

This highly-developed tolerance for intricacy that Rousseau urges, the multiple levels of consciousness demanded of each and every citizen, means that the realization of the authentic polity presupposes people living as a community that demands constant engagement of self and other; of each self reflexively, and of each self with the individual others that it encounters, as well as with the corporate community of others to which it also belongs. Life in Rousseau's polity is complex, because the natures of each self and of each other perennially evolve.

5 Conclusion

While talk of change may make for philosophical comfort, the reality of constant flux seems to yield impractical obstructions for politics. How can the stability necessary for the existence of a political system develop in an environment of perennial dialectic? How is a philosophically coherent life possible if the stability of categorization is jettisoned?

In answer, Rousseau reminds us that the seemingly comforting certainties of stability can quickly transform themselves into the constraining knots of convention. The familiarity of the surrounding "box" can easily become the enclosure that we cannot escape. According to Rousseau, while categories provide us with the building blocks of systematic thinking, we must guard against the possibility that they eliminate the transcendence both engendered by and needed for human creativity.

As a political and social theorist, however, Rousseau has one more question to answer: how is it possible to inhabit the conventional world and not be ham-

---

[35] Rousseau notes that "[T]here is not one person that does not appropriate the word 'everyone' to himself, and who does not think solely of himself in voting for all" (CS 373). In *Rousseau's Social Contract*, Gildin (1983) offers an illuminating example to explain the simultaneous presence of both individual and collective consciousness within the citizen: the situation where the individual would like to avoid the extra expenses of the pollution-control device, yet recognizes the necessity of these devices for the well-being of society as a whole. For further discussion of this topic and Gildin's solution, see Morgenstern (1996, especially 160–166).

strung by its conventions? How does one maintain transcendence in environments defined by their limitations?

Rousseau actually deals with this issue in the very same literary work in which he demonstrates the faulty nature of philosophical categorization. In *La Nouvelle Héloïse*, Julie's (self-)destructive reliance on the accepted understandings of self and other in her quest for love is countered by her more practical-minded cousin Claire. Claire, a wealthy widow, is, like her name suggests, remarkably clear-sighted. Accordingly she does not let herself be persuaded by Wolmar's (absolute) categorization of all venues and ideas originating outside of Clarens as negative. As an independent widow, Claire uses her economic resources and free time to travel and to become acquainted with foreign political systems.[36]

The fact that Claire views the foreign as positive is important, because it allows her to break free of those categories which, in the eighteenth century, are perceived either as inevitable (the minimally-acceptive position) and/or "natural" (the strongly-acceptive position). Because Claire understands that no category is truly transparent, she is able to actualize her freedom as a function of her ability to find (limited) autonomy in the interstices that lie behind the façade of meaning.[37] Thus, Claire manages to create a distance between her public persona and her private self.[38] In effect, Claire manages to bring about in her life what Richard H. Brown recommends for the postmodern skeptic who doubts the attainability of honesty or authenticity on either the personal or political level: the practice of dialectical irony (1992: 172).

Claire's utilization of irony does more than underline Rousseau's nuanced comprehension of the perplexities and politics inherent in categorization. In addition, Claire's placement in foreign cities as she writes her letters of exploration and growth hints at Rousseau's understanding of women as harbingers of authentic revolution in modern times. Importantly, the women in Rousseau's works who are portrayed as negotiating the vicissitudes of politics – even in, and particularly in, their own lived experiences of daily life – serve, in different ways, as emblems of hope for Rousseau. To be sure, few women are depicted as triumphing completely over the corrupt social/political systems that surround

---

[36] See for example, Claire's letter on the political system in Geneva and on the situation of women there (*Julie*, part 6, letter v), and the letter she elicits from Saint-Preux on French and Italian music (part 2, letter xxiii).

[37] For more on Claire and her unique approach to maintain as much authenticity as possible in an inauthentic world, see Morgenstern (1996: 219–223).

[38] Claire herself mentions the "coquette" and the "merry widow" as two parts that she has played (*Julie* 408).

them: in the end, Julie dies, and Claire (just) persists in "keeping on" with no guarantee of (political or personal) redemption.[39] Nevertheless, even in their partial failures, these women make us aware that a fully human life demands targeted, conscious activity on many different levels, so that the individual human being is not swallowed up by the existing categories of power. In that sense, even Julie's failure to survive alerts the reader to the warning signs that she misinterprets in her role as chatelaine of Clarens: Julie fails to apprehend, as Rousseau remarks in the *Social Contract*, that peace is not inevitably the sign of a perfect life; perfect peace might also betoken the stasis of the dungeon (*CS* 355).

To be sure, Rousseau understands that the struggle against received ideas entails serious risks. The potential instability of this process is understandably frightening for those who value guarantees of achievement, no matter of what sort, over troublesome and challenging uncertainties. Still, Rousseau insists on engaging these perils in order to champion humanity in his promotion of dynamic engagement in political as well as personal matters. In this context, the courage of Rousseau's female personages highlights the extent to which Rousseau prefers the possible (partial) failures of action to the implicit perfection that is technically attainable through quiescence and passivity in the face of the conventional classifications of thought and practice that are regarded as either inevitable or right. In combating the self-justifying and mutually-exclusive dualisms of conventional thought and practice, Rousseau demonstrates the essential inhumanity of these inadequate divisions that ultimately doom their practitioners to failure.

In the final analysis, Rousseau remains wary of solutions that, however temptingly, exchange liberty for stability: he warns against this transaction in his *Essay on Poland*.[40] Anticipating Hegel's concept of dialectic – although perhaps in not as univalent a style as his successor – Rousseau insists that the complexities of human choice are in constant and evolving dialectical relationships with each other, yielding a plethora of human options and possibilities. As Rousseau sees it, the dialectical character of this political process engages its protagonists in the freedom-seeking nature of its goals. Thus, this kind of politics can mitigate the prospect of its processes being hijacked to torpedo the very freedoms that they are supposed to promote. Politics structured in this way embod-

---

39 Another central feminine figure in Rousseau's *œuvre*, the unnamed schoolmaster's wife in the *Lettre à d'Alembert sur les spectacles*, who symbolizes the middle and lower classes' (ignorant) acceptance of the inauthentic lives imposed upon them by the dominant powers of society, remains enthralled by the lies propagated by the exploitative society that keep her in her place.
40 "Repose and liberty appear incompatible to me; one must choose" (*OC* 3: 955).

ies the realization of meaning that is perennially negotiated, rather than uniformly predetermined. This kind of politics allows all of its participants, both individually and communally, to singly and together create the full potentialities of their separate and common humanities.

Works Cited

Brown, Richard H. *Society as Text: Essays on Rhetoric, Reason, and Reality*. 1987. Chicago: U of Chicago P, 1992.
Gildin, Hilail. *Rousseau's Social Contract: The Design of the Argument*. Chicago: U of Chicago P, 1983.
Hobbes, Thomas. *Leviathan*. Ed. C B. Macpherson. Harmondsworth, UK: Penguin, 1985.
Lacan, Jacques. "The Mirror Stage as Formative of the Function of the I as Revealed in Psychoanalytic Experience." *Ecrits*. Trans. Bruce Fink. New York: Norton, 2006.
Lévi-Strauss, Claude. "Jean-Jacques Rousseau, fondateur des Sciences de l'homme." *Jean-Jacques Rousseau* (1962): 239–248.
Madison, James. "Federalist #10." *The Federalist Papers*. Ed. Clinton Rossiter. New York: New American Library, 1961.
Miller, Donald F. *The Reason of Metaphor: A Study in Politics*. New Delhi: Sage Publications, 1992.
Morgenstern, Mira. *Rousseau and the Politics of Ambiguity: Self, Culture, and Society*. University Park, Pa: Pennsylvania State UP, 1996.
Rousseau, Jean-Jacques. *Emile*. Trans. Allan Bloom. New York: Penguin, 1991.
Rousseau, Jean-Jacques. *Œuvres complètes*. Gen. Eds. Bernard Gagnebin and Marcel Raymond. 5 vols. Paris: Gallimard, "Bibliothèque de la Pléiade," 1959–1995.
Shklar, Judith N. *Men and Citizens: A Study of Rousseau's Social Theory*. London: Cambridge UP, 1969.
Starobinski, Jean. *Jean-Jacques Rousseau: La transparence et l'obstacle*. Paris: Gallimard, 1971.
Talmon, Jacob L. *The Origins of Totalitarian Democracy*. NY: Mercury 1961; repr. Norton 1970.

Yves Charles Zarka
Rousseau and the Sovereignty of the People

There is a particular point in the history of sovereignty whose scope is of considerable importance when the notion of "sovereignty of the people" appears in political discourses. In a way it would not be extravagant to state that the entire modern history of sovereignty hinges on this concept, even in those thinkers whose absolutely explicit intention was to show that the notion of sovereignty of the people was unsustainable or fundamentally unviable.

What I show here is how Rousseau was responsible for a turning-point in the history of sovereignty *through* ambiguities and paradoxes, not in spite of them. This turning-point is due to the fact that he makes the sovereignty of the people the very figure of political actualization, whereas before the notion only represented a potentiality. With Rousseau we go from a virtual or potential sovereignty of the people to an actual sovereignty of the people. But this actualization (as we shall see in more detail in what follows) is a paradoxical composition of absolute and relative, sacred and profane, ideal and real, non-historical and historical. This paradoxical composition would only be untangled after Rousseau. In other words a critique of Rousseau's sovereignty had to take place so that the sovereignty of the people could become the real principle of historical democracies.

Rousseau's thinking constitutes a turning-point to the extent that it founds a new concept of sovereignty of the people, which has occupied the center of political thought up to today. Yet I also argue that this theory of sovereignty of the people is precisely the one which had to be given up. It is from this sovereignty that societies had to be liberated – and it was to be no easy matter – to open the way to the historical experience of real democracy, i.e. a de-sacralized conception of the sovereignty of historical peoples, capable of being embodied in real juridico-political institutions.

1 The non-actual sovereignty of the people

Rousseau did not invent the notion of sovereignty of the people, far from it. It can easily be shown that the notion has a long history. To consider only the modern era, we should note that the protestant Monarchomachs made use of the notion in the last part of the sixteenth century. What should be noticed, however, is that before Rousseau, the sovereignty of the people was thought of as a possible foundation for the legitimacy of political power, only then to be immediately neutralized. While the sovereignty of the people is named, it is at the same time immediately defused of its entire politically-explosive charge. For the Monarchomachs in particular it is indispensable to go via the people's representatives – that is, the magistrates. The people's sovereignty is not exercised directly, but only actualized by mediations whose function, precisely, is to prevent the people from becoming an autonomous force, which it would be impossible to master.

In other words theoreticians of sovereignty before Rousseau mostly attempted to show that the sovereignty of the people cannot be actualized by itself – or at least that if it can be actualized, it is only in the act which deposes or alienates it, provisionally or permanently. Sovereignty of the people was thus thought of simply as a moment in the constitution of sovereignty. To show this in more detail, we need to examine the arguments that support this non-actuality of the sovereignty of the people in theoreticians of sovereignty before Rousseau: Grotius, Hobbes and Burlamaqui. If I have chosen these three authors, it is because their arguments are different, and will allow us to grasp different figures of the non-actualization of the sovereignty of the people.

1.1 Grotius

Grotius defines sovereignty in the following terms in Chapter iii of Book i of *De jure belli ac pacis:*

> That is what civil power (*potestas civilis*) consists in. It is called sovereign (*summa potestas*) when its acts are independent of any other, superior power, so that they cannot be annulled by any other human will. I say by any *other* human will, as the sovereign himself must be excepted; he is free to change his will, as well as the one who succeeds to all his rights and consequently has the same power, not another power.[1]

Sovereignty (*summa potestas*) is defined by three properties: 1) it is a civil power whose acts are independent of any other, superior power; 2) its acts cannot be annulled by any other human will; 3) it follows that only the sovereign himself, or his successor with the same power, holds the liberty to change his acts.

---

[1] *De jure belli ac pacis* (1993: i, iii, vii, 1, 100); translation by Jean Barbeyrac, *Le droit de la guerre et de la paix,* Amsterdam, 1724 (1984: 120). All translations into English are by the translator of this article.

This all obviously has its origins in Bodin. However, Grotius distinguishes two subjects of sovereignty: a common subject (*subjectum commune*) which is the state (*civitas*) and a proper subject (*subjectum proprium*) which is the single or multiple person of the sovereign. Grotius obviously did not invent this distinction, but he draws the following conclusion from it: it is false to think that power belongs always and without exception to the people, such that the people would have the right to curb and punish kings every time they abuse their authority. A people disposes of the right to choose the form of government which seems to it to be the best; it therefore disposes of the right to submit to one or several persons, by a total (not partial) transfer of the right to govern. But the constituted power cannot then be called into question by the constituting power. Grotius advances this thesis against those of the Monarchomachs, to deny the existence of a right of resistance by the people or the lower magistrates. The difference made between the *subjectum commune* and the *subjectum proprium* is obviously the difference in the procedures which de-actualizes the sovereignty of the people or, if you will, only actualizes it with the notion of *subjectum proprium*, i.e. in the act by which it is alienated. Rousseau's sarcasm against Grotius's positions is well-known: "Grotius, a refugee in France, discontented with his fatherland, wanting to court Louis XIII to whom his book is dedicated, spares no effort to strip peoples of all their rights, and clothe kings in them, with all possible art."[2]

1.2 Hobbes

The second way of neutralizing the sovereignty of the people is that achieved by Hobbes. The notion of "sovereignty of the people" is employed several times by Hobbes, in particular in the *Elements of Law* at the beginning of the second chapter of Part ii.[3] But his political theory's object is precisely to refute the idea of any actual or effective sovereignty of the people. This refutation is carried out by a process of neutralization: attributing sovereignty to the people is theoretically conceivable, but it is by all necessity politically non-actual. The act by

---

2 *Contrat social* (*CS*), book ii, ch. ii (*OC* 3: 370).
3 "Out of the same democracy, the institution of a political monarch proceedeth in the same manner, as did the institution of the aristocracy (viz.) by a decree of the sovereign people, to pass the sovereignty to one man named, and approved by plurality of suffrage." (1969: part ii, ch. ii [xxi], §9); "And here as before in elected kings, the question is to be made, whether in the electing of such a sovereign, they reserved to themselves a right of assembling at times and places limited and known, or not; if not, then is the sovereignty of the people dissolved [...]" (§10).

which sovereignty is instituted, the act which gives birth to the civil person, installs a relationship between the represented (individuals) and a representative (a man or an assembly, at least in the version given in *Leviathan*). Now this assembly can be made up of a small number of men (aristocracy) or the totality of the represented (democracy). So there is no obstacle on the theoretical level to conceiving the people itself as sovereign. As the sovereign and the people are instituted at the same time, the people is sovereign when the represented institute themselves in totality as the representative. No argument in law forbids the conceivability of democracy, i.e. the sovereignty of the people, even if the word is not employed:

> The difference of Commonwealths, consisteth in the difference of the Sovereign, or the Person representative of all and every one of the Multitude. And because the Sovereignty is either in one Man, or in an Assembly of more than one; and into that Assembly either Every man hath right to enter, or not every one, but Certain men distinguished from the rest; it is manifest, there can be but Three kinds of Commonwealth.[4]

These three kinds, obviously, are monarchy, aristocracy and democracy. Hobbes envisages quite clearly that sovereignty can be exercised by the people over the people, and this is what he calls *Democracy* or *Popular Commonwealth*. However, what is not impossible in law is absolutely impossible in fact. "The difference between these three kinds of Commonwealth, consisteth not in the difference of Power; but in the difference of Convenience, or Aptitude to produce the Peace, and Security of the people; for which end they were instituted" (241). It is on the level of facts, then, that Hobbes intends to show the unviable character of democracies. The principle is this: there is an ineffectiveness of the sovereign will when it is attributed to the people, that is, to the *Generall Assembly of Subjects* (245). This ineffectiveness comes from the inoperability of the act of authorization, which is unable to constitute a difference between the instance that commands and the one that obeys. The popular commonwealth is always non-actual. From its institution it is destined either to collapse into disharmony (the state of nature), or to change into an aristocracy, then into a monarchy. On the political level the sovereignty of the people is non-actual and will always remain so.

In *Elements of Law* (1640), using an argument he did not take up in *Leviathan*, Hobbes showed that, chronologically, democracy is the first of the three forms of government:

> The first in order of time of these three sorts is democracy, and it must be so of necessity, because an aristocracy and a monarchy, require nomination of persons agreed upon; which

---

[4] *Leviathan* (abridged as *Lev.*), xix (1968: 239).

agreement in a great multitude of men must consist in the consent of the major part; and where the votes of the major part involve the votes of the rest, there is actually a democracy. (*Elements of Law*, part ii, ch. ii, §1, 118)

Already in this work, however, Hobbes showed that democracy is essentially unstable: politically, it cannot last. Indeed, it is where demagogy and ambition flourish, "insomuch, that a democracy, in effect, is no more than an aristocracy of orators, interrupted sometimes with the temporary monarchy of one orator" (part ii, ch. ii, §5, 120–121).Democracy is not a viable political regime, which is why it turns into an aristocracy, and aristocracy into monarchy. Sovereignty of the people, then, is not conceptually or juridically impossible for Hobbes, but it is radically non-actual on the political level. The people cannot be its own sovereign because it makes it impossible for the twofold structure of law/duty and command/obedience to stabilize.

1.3 Burlamaqui

The third form of neutralization of the sovereignty of the people is found in the *Principes du droit politique* by Jean-Jacques Burlamaqui. Here is the definition he gives of sovereignty in his *Principes:*

> As for sovereignty, it must be defined: the right of final command in civil society, which the members of that society have conferred on one and the same person so as to maintain order within and defense without, and in general to procure a veritable happiness under its protection and by its care, and above all to ensure the exercise of their liberty. (1984: II, i, ch. v, §i, 42])[5]

This definition is highly interesting for the elements it adds to seventeenth-century definitions of sovereignty, in particular the references to civil society, prosperity and happiness. As to the genesis of sovereignty, however, Burlamaqui remains very traditional: he underlines the fact that it consists in a convention of voluntary submission, by which "one can divest oneself, in favor of someone who accepts the renunciation, of the natural right one had to dispose fully of one's liberty and natural forces" (II, i, ch. vi, §v, 52). The interest of Burlamaqui's position, however, consists in the fact that the genesis of political sovereignty brings into play the term sovereignty of the people: "It must therefore be said that sovereignty resides originally in the people and in each individual in rela-

---

5 Roman numerals refer to book (or volume) in upper-case, to part or books within volumes in lower-case, to chapters and then sections in lower-case; Arabic numeral indicates pagination.

tion to himself, and it is the conveyance and reunion of all the rights of all individuals in the person of the sovereign which constitute him as such, and truly produce sovereignty" (II, i, ch. vi, §vi, 52).

In response to the objection that a multitude of free, independent individuals do not have sovereignty and therefore cannot confer it on the king, Burlamaqui shows that individuals possess sovereignty *virtually* in the form of sovereignty over themselves or the liberty to dispose of their own person.[6] Sovereignty is constructed on the basis of these seeds. But once it is constituted, one can no longer speak of a sovereignty of the people:

> Thus the distinction made by some politicians between a *real sovereignty* which always resides in the people and an *actual sovereignty* which belongs to the king is both absurd and dangerous; it is ridiculous to claim that even after a people has endowed a king with sovereign authority it yet remains in possession of that same authority, superior even to the King. (II, i, ch. vii, §xiii, 66)

The effectiveness of political sovereignty thus only exists here in the power instituted by the convention. The sovereignty of the people is only actualized in order to depose itself.

So we have studied three figures of the non-actualization of the sovereignty of the people. Rousseau's turning-point consists in moving to an exclusively actual conception of the sovereignty of the people.

2 Actuality of the sovereignty of the people

With Rousseau, the sovereignty of the people provides the sole legitimate, valid concept of sovereignty. This can be shown on two levels: the terms of the social contract and the concept of the general will.

Rousseau's intention is to modify both the problem of the social contract and the traditionally-given response. First, the problem: it means going back to the very first institution, that of the people. The people is at the center of

---

[6] The term "virtually" is explicitly employed by Burlamaqui: "The principal argument politicians employ to prove their opinion is that neither each individual among a large number of free, independent people, nor the entire multitude, as they in no way have the sovereign majesty, can confer it on the king. But this argument proves nothing: it is true that neither each member of society nor the multitude is *formally* invested with sovereign authority such as it is in the sovereign; but it is enough that they possess it *virtually*, that is to say that they have in themselves all that is needed to be able, by means of their wills and by their consent, to produce it in the sovereign." (1984: II, i, ch. vi, §xiv, 56; emphasis added).

the contractual operation, whose function until then had been to depose the people, taking away all possibility of being the effective subject of sovereignty. The social contract's object, then, is to show how the people is actualized as such: "Before examining the act by which a people elects a king, then, it would be good to examine the act by which a people is a people. For this act, being necessarily anterior to the other, is the true foundation of society" (*CS* 359). We cannot start with the distinction between instances that are external to one another – individuals, the sovereign, the people – in order to show that sovereignty is constituted by a transfer of rights from one to another. On the contrary, we have to account for the manner in which a multitude becomes a people: the people is not a moment in the constitution of political society, but its goal. The difficulty to be overcome is that of the constitution of a moral, collective body, superior to individuals (endowed with common force), but which yet does not transcend them (each individual remains as free as before): "To find a form of association which defends and protects the person and goods of each associate with all its common force, and by which each one, united to all, yet only obeys himself and remains as free as before" (360).

The contract's single clause, which is supposed to provide a response to this difficulty, only reproduces the antinomy between the moment of superiority – "the total alienation of each associate and all his rights to the whole community" (360) – and that of non-transcendence – "in giving himself to all, each one gives himself to no one" (361). The social contract has the air of a sleight of hand, by which the antinomy is affirmed to have been resolved simply by being displaced between other terms. The main part of the operation for Rousseau consists in substituting a distinction between points of view for the distinction between instances that are external to one another:

> This public person thus formed by the union of all the others formerly took the name of *City*, and now takes that of *Republic* or *body politic*; its members call it *State* when it is passive, *Sovereign* when it is active, *Power* when comparing it to its peers. With regard to its associates, they collectively take the name of *People*, and in particular call themselves *Citizens* as participants in the sovereign authority, and *Subjects* as being subjected to the laws of the state. (361–362)

The two terms between which the contract is realized are in fact the same, considered in two different ways: as a multitude of individuals on the one hand, and as a whole on the other. So it is not strictly speaking a juridical contract between two genuinely distinct instances, but the requalification of a single reality: individuals, who pass from the status of a disparate multitude to that of members of the whole: "Each one of us places his person and all his power in common, under the supreme direction of the general will; and we accept each member in the body as an indivisible part of the whole" (361). "We" is a requalification of "us."

The sovereignty of the people is the only actual, valid form of sovereignty because only the people can give a real content to the general will.

2.1 The generality of will

Generality is constitutive of the sovereign will. That will is indeed general, in its source, its object and its end. All its other properties – it is always equal, always just, necessarily seeks the public interest, etc. – are deduced from this formal characteristic of generality: "that the general will, to be truly such, must be so in its object as well as its essence; that it must arise from all in order to apply to all; and that it loses its natural rectitude when it tends towards some individual, determined object" (*CS* 373).

But what effective will can give real content to formal generality? What being can have a will that is general?

> When the whole people rules over the whole people, it considers only itself, and if a relation is thus formed, it is between the entire object from one point of view and the entire object from another point of view, without any division of the whole. So the matter which is ruled upon is general, like the will which rules. It is this act which I call a law. (379)

So the people is the subject of the general will, but also its object, and in that way is the real, actual subject of sovereignty: "As nature gives each man an absolute power over all his members, the social pact gives the body politic an absolute power over all its members, and it is this very power which, directed by the general will, as I have said bears the name of sovereignty" (372).

Generality is the formal condition on the basis of which both the content of the sovereign will and the moral being of the sovereign are determined. This passage from form to content is achieved by reducing every particularity which could affect the general will, and would immediately destroy it. In a first sense, for Rousseau it means purifying the general will from every particularity that could affect its source, its act or its object. This can easily be shown with regard to the law: "When I say that the object of laws is always general, I mean that the law considers subjects as a body and actions as abstract, never a man as an individual, nor a particular action" (379). So that, if generality is the formal condition of the content and subject of the sovereign will, it also determines its limit: "From this we see that the sovereign power, as absolute, sacred and inviolable as it is, does not and cannot pass the limits of general conventions" (375).

However this normativity of the formal condition of generality can only keep its immanence in relation to individual wills because it is presupposed in the heart of each of them. Without this presupposition it would be impossible to think of moral liberty in the civil state as Rousseau conceives it: "From what precedes one could add *moral liberty* to the acquisition of the civil state, liberty which alone makes man truly master of himself, for the impulse of appetite alone is slavery, and *obedience to the law one prescribes oneself is liberty*" (365, my emphasis). It is because everyone can hear the voice of the general will within that it is not simply a transcendent norm imposed on individuals from outside.

> How can it be that they obey and no one commands, they serve and have no master; so much more free in fact than under a visible subjection, no one losing any of his liberty save that which can harm another's? These prodigies are the work of the law. It is to the law alone that men owe justice and liberty. It is the salutary organ of the will of all, which restores in law the natural equality between men. It is the celestial voice which dictates to each citizen the precepts of public reason, and teaches him to act according to the maxims of his own judgment, and not to be in contradiction with himself.[7]

So it can be understood why the concept of general will is not only political, but also moral and even metaphysical. The general will can be conceived as a norm imposed on the individual, and as the expression of what is most proper to that individual: "Each individual, as a man, can have a particular will which is contrary or dissimilar *to the general will which he has as a Citizen*" (*CS* 363, my emphasis). The conflict is not only here between the individual's particular will which tends to the particular interest, and the general will of the sovereign's collective being which tends to the common interest; it is also internal to the individual himself, who hears both voices. This point enables the very famous affirmation: "whoever refuses to obey the general will shall be constrained to do so by the whole body: which means nothing other than that *he shall be forced to be free*" (364, my emphasis).

---

[7] *Discours sur l'économie politique* (*OC* 3: 248). Rousseau's paragraph begins like this: "The first and most important maxim of the legitimate or popular government, that is, the government whose object is the good of the people, is therefore, as I have said, to follow the general will in everything; but to follow it one must know it, and above all rightly distinguish it from individual will, starting with oneself; a distinction which is always most difficult to make, and for which only the most sublime virtue can provide sufficient enlightenment." (247–248).

2.2 The general will made absolute

Rousseau makes sovereignty absolute in a stronger way than his predecessors. The sovereign in Hobbes, for example, is much less absolute than Rousseau's general will, because he cannot reduce the right to resist to the power attached to the individual's very being.[8] "He shall be forced to be free" is an affirmation which is completely inconceivable in Hobbes. And in making sovereignty absolute, Rousseau also makes it sacred. Here we go beyond the language of morals and metaphysics, into that of theology: "The sovereign, solely in that he is," Rousseau writes, "is always what he ought to be" (CS 363). The being who is always what he ought to be is traditionally the divine being. And so the general will is indestructible, it can neither be annihilated nor corrupted: "it is always constant, inalterable and pure," even if it can be eluded (438). Sovereignty, defined by the legislative power which can only have as its subject the entire body of the people, is inalienable, indivisible, always upright – even though it can stray – and always has in view the common, sacred interest: "… the sovereign power, as absolute, sacred and inviolable as it is…"

Nowhere perhaps is the way Rousseau makes sovereignty sacred more powerfully apparent than in the chapter "Du droit de vie et de mort" in the *Contrat social*. To underline its scope we should recall that in Hobbes this right remains profoundly problematic: it cannot be founded on social convention, and thus appears as the return of an archaism at the very heart of the state (Zarka 1995: 228–250). Montesquieu, for his part, tends to consider the right of pardon, not that of life and death, as an attribute of sovereignty. In Rousseau on the contrary, no right of sovereignty is more assured than the right of life and death:

> Whoever wants to preserve his life at the expense of others must also give his life for them when it is needful. Now the citizen is no longer judge of the peril to which the law wants him to be exposed; and when the Prince has said to him: it is expedient for the state that you die, he must die; for it is only on that condition that he has heretofore lived in safety, and his life is no longer solely a benefit of nature, but a conditional gift of the state. (CS 376)

Making sovereignty sacred explains why any infraction of social law is considered a rebellion or a betrayal, which excludes the one committing it from membership of the social body. The criminal or ill-doer, whoever he may be, breaks the social treaty by his act: he is stripped of his quality as a moral person and can be exiled or put to death as a public enemy. The sacredness of the sovereignty of the people is conceived exactly on the model of that of the king's person,

---

[8] See Yves Charles Zarka (1995) on this, particularly chapter x "Du droit de punir" (228–250).

despite being affirmed *against* royal sovereignty and borrowing its attributes. Exile or death must strike the (as it were) impure being who offended against the sacred, and can never again become a member of the state. True, Rousseau himself underlines that the sovereign cannot pronounce a particular condemnation, but it is executed in his name: "But, it will be said, the condemnation of a criminal is a particular act. Granted; and so that condemnation does not belong to the Sovereign; it is a right he can confer without being able to exercise it himself." (*CS* 377) The result is obviously that the right of pardon hence becomes highly uncertain: "With regard to the right to pardon, or to exempt a guilty party from the penalty borne by the law and pronounced by the judge, it belongs only to one who is above the judge and the law; that is, the Sovereign. Even so, his right in this is not perfectly clear, and the cases for its use are very rare" (*CS* 377).

In case there is any need for a final confirmation of the way the secular is made sacred, it is to be found in the penultimate chapter of the *Contrat social*, "De la religion civile" (Of Civil Religion). Rousseau sets himself the task of showing that before Christianity there was no separation between the theological and the political – even concerning the Hebrews: "Each religion thus being uniquely attached to the laws of the state which prescribed it, there was no other way of converting a people than enslaving it, nor any other missionaries than conquerors, and as the obligation to change religion was the law of the conquered, one had to start by conquering before talking about it" (*CS* 461). So it is with Christianity that the theological and the political become separate, causing "the internal divisions which have never ceased to agitate Christian peoples" (462).[9] Rous-

---

[9] Rousseau's denunciation of the damaging political effects of Christianity seems to be inspired by Machiavelli's *Discorsi*. This is what Rousseau writes: "But I am mistaken in saying a Christian Republic; each of these two words excludes the other. Christianity only preaches servitude and dependency. Its spirit is too favorable to tyranny for tyranny not always to benefit from it. True Christians are made to be slaves; they know it and are hardly moved by it; this short life has too small a price in their eyes" (*CS* 467). We could compare this with the following passage from Machiavelli: "So if I am asked how it can be that in those ancient times peoples were more attached to liberty than they are today, I believe that it comes from the same cause which nowadays makes men less courageous. I believe it is the difference which exists between our education and that of the Ancients, which comes from the difference between our religion and Ancient religion. Having shown us the truth and the right path, our religion has led us to accord less esteem to the honor of the world. The pagans, esteeming it highly and placing in it the supreme good, were more determined in their actions. This can be observed in many of their institutions, beginning with the magnificence of their sacrifices compared with the humbleness of our own, where the pomp is more delicate and magnificent but nothing is ferocious or violent. Neither pomp nor magnificence was lacking in their ceremonies, but there was also bloody, horrible sacrifice, as numerous animals were killed. This terrible spectacle made men the same as itself. Be-

seau draws two conclusions. The first consists in saying that finally it is Hobbes who correctly saw both the evil and its remedy, proposing to unite the theological and the political under the aegis of the latter. This point should be underlined, as it is one of the only places where Hobbes is not only not condemned, but approved: "Of all the Christian authors, Hobbes is the only one to have correctly seen the evil and its remedy, who dared to propose uniting the eagle's two heads, bringing everything under political unity, without which no state nor government will ever be well constituted" (CS 463). The second consists for Rousseau in defining a civil religion whose object would be to lead each citizen to "love his duties"; the political sovereign would fix "the articles, not precisely as dogmas of religion, but as feelings of sociability, without which it is impossible to be either a good citizen or a loyal subject" (CS 468). When we examine the content of this civil religion we find that some of its articles of faith are properly theological (the existence of the divinity, the life to come, the happiness of the just and the punishment of evildoers) and others theologico-political: the holiness of the contract. In this way the sanctification of the secular, which we have encountered at different constitutive moments in the sovereignty of the people, is finally realized. Henceforth not only the social contract, but also the state's legislation, is sanctified in "a sort of catechism of the citizen."[10]

---

yond that, Ancient religion only rewarded men covered with earthly glory, such as generals and heads of state. Our religion glorifies humble, contemplative men more than men of action. Further, it has placed the supreme good in humility, submission and disdain for human things. The other placed it in greatness of soul, strength of body and all other things fitted for making men strong. If our religion requires that one has strength, it wants him to be more fitted for suffering than for strong things. So this way of living seems to have enfeebled the world and given it as prey to the wicked. They can dominate it in security, as they have seen that, in order to reach heaven, men in general think more of enduring blows than avenging them. Although it would seem that the world has been made effeminate, and Heaven disarmed, that no doubt comes more from the cowardice of those who have interpreted our religion in terms of idleness and not in terms of energy" (*Discorsi sopra la prima deca di Tito Livio* 1992: 149–150).

10 The expression comes from Robert Derathé in the notes to his edition of the *Contrat social* (CS 1504). But Derathé seems to consider this integration of the political in the domain of the sacred as a sort of accident: "We should be tempted to see it as a strange confusion of the profane and the sacred." On the contrary, I believe this to be a central point of Rousseau's political philosophy.

2.3 The composition of law and of virtue

In his theory of sovereignty Rousseau associates the juridical categories developed by theoreticians of natural law since Hobbes, and a theory of civic virtues which refers to the Roman republic and Machiavelli. He owes his notions of the state of nature and the social contract to natural law theory, even if he modifies their meaning. He owes his usage of the notions of virtue and fatherland to the republican tradition. So the general will is not only the source of the state's laws, it is itself rooted in the virtue of the citizens. We find a patriotism and an appeal to civic virtue which are highly consonant with Machiavelli.[11] Like Machiavelli, Rousseau associates love of fatherland and love of liberty.[12] Regarding virtue, he states in the *Social Contract*:

> A celebrated author [Montesquieu] has given the Republic virtue as its principle; for all these conditions cannot survive without virtue: but for want of making the necessary distinctions, this fine genius has often lacked exactness and sometimes clarity, and has not seen that, as sovereign authority is the same everywhere, the same principle must take place in every well-constituted state, more or less, it is true, according to the form of government. (*CS* 405)

Regarding the fatherland:

> Such is the condition which, giving each citizen to the fatherland, guarantees him from all personal dependence; a condition which makes for all the artifice and play of the political machine, and which alone makes civil engagements legitimate, for without it they would be absurd, tyrannical and subject to the most enormous abuses. (364)

---

11 It is well-known that Rousseau cites Machiavelli several times in the *Contrat social* and praises him highly: "In feigning to give lessons to kings, he taught great things to peoples. Machiavelli's *The Prince* is the book of republicans" (*CS* iii, ch. vi, 409). Rousseau also establishes a very strong relation between civic virtue and love of the fatherland in his *Fragments politiques*: "The love of humanity gives many virtues, such as gentleness, equity, moderation, charity, indulgence, but does not inspire courage, nor firmness, etc.: and does not give them that energy which they receive from love of the fatherland and which raises them to the point of heroism" (*OC* 3: 536). In the fragments concerning the comparison between the two republics of Sparta and Rome, Rousseau sounds very Machiavellian: "Always ready to die for his country, a Spartan loved the fatherland so tenderly that he would have sacrificed liberty itself to save it. But the Romans never imagined that the fatherland could outlive liberty, or even glory" (543). Machiavelli writes, for example: "Where one decides as to the salvation of the fatherland, *della salute della patria*, one must have no consideration of justice or injustice, pity or cruelty, glory or ignominy. Much more, neglecting every other consideration, one must in all things follow the party which saves it and preserves its liberty" (*Discorsi sopra la prima deca di Tito Livio* 2001: 249).
12 See the note on Calvin, *Contrat social*, book ii, ch. vii (*OC* 3: 382). For an examination of "Love of the fatherland in Machiavelli," see Zarka (2001: 13–26).

> All have to fight at need for the country, it is true; but also no one ever has to fight for himself. Do we not yet gain by running, for that which makes for our safety, a part of the risks we would have to run for ourselves as soon as it was taken away? (375)

Rousseau's concept of the sovereignty of the people, then, is set in place through the norm of generality; by making the contract and legislation absolute and sacred; and by the composition of law and virtue. However, the conditions just examined are so strong that they make historical realization of that sovereignty impossible in its original purity and holiness. In a certain way Rousseau makes sovereignty of the people the only actual form of sovereignty, but also makes that figure of sovereignty quite simply inapplicable in history: the French Revolution was to be the experience of precisely that impossibility.

Made absolute in this way, the sovereignty of the people cannot define real democracy. To become historical, democracy was to require emancipation from the absolute and the sacred to which Rousseau subjected it. That task will be achieved by liberal thinkers, in particular Benjamin Constant and Alexis de Tocqueville.

Translation by Edward Hughes, Université Paris-Sorbonne

Works Cited

Burlamaqui, Jean-Jacques. *Principes du droit politique*. Amsterdam: Chatelain, 1751. Reprint. Bibliothèque de Philosophie politique et juridique, Université de Caen, 1984.

Grotius, Hugo. *De Iure Bello Ac Pacis Libri Tres in Quibis Ius Naturae Et Gentium Item Iuris Publici Praecipua Explicantur*. Eds. B. J. A. De Kanter-van Hettinga Tromp, Robert Feenstra, and C E Persenaire. Aalen: Scientia Verlag, 1993.

Grotius, Hugo. *Le droit de la guerre et de la paix*. Trans. Jean Barbeyrac, Amsterdam, 1724. Reprint. Bibliothèque de Philosophie politique et juridique, Université de Caen, 1984.

Hobbes, Thomas. *The Elements of Law, Natural and Politic*. Ed. Ferdinand Tönnies. London: Cass, 1969.

Hobbes, Thomas. *Leviathan*. Ed. C. B. Macpherson. Harmondsworth: Penguin, 1968.

Machiavelli, Niccolò. *Discorsi Sopra La Prima Deca Di Tito Livio*. Ed. Francesco Bausi. Roma: Salerno, 2001.

Machiavelli, Niccolò. *Tutte Le Opere*. Ed. Mario Martelli. Firenze: Sansoni, 1992.

Rousseau, Jean-Jacques. *Œuvres complètes*. Gen. Eds. Bernard Gagnebin and Marcel Raymond. 5 vols. Paris: Gallimard, "Bibliothèque de la Pléiade," 1959–1995.

Zarka, Yves Charles. *Hobbes et la pensée politique moderne*. Paris: PUF, 1995

Zarka, Yves Charles. *Figures du pouvoir : études de philosophie politique de Machiavel à Foucault*. Paris: PUF, 2001

III **The Philosophical Novel: Culture as Nature's Supplement**

Christophe Martin
Nature and Supplementation in *Julie ou La Nouvelle Héloïse*

"Nature loves to hide." Heraclitus's enigmatic aphorism, as Pierre Hadot (2004: 30) reminds us, probably signifies that what is born ("nature") tends to disappear ("to hide") or to die.[1] From the beginning of the Christian era, however, Heraclitus's sentence was interpreted in a vastly different way. It was an allusion to the secrets of a nature that likes to shroud itself in mystery, and that men can only represent beneath a veil that calls for an unveiling. In the face of the secrets of nature, Hadot distinguishes two fundamental attitudes in western thought: the first, which he calls *Promethean*, appears in Antiquity. It encourages resorting to ruse, technology, and to a form of violence to seize nature's secrets from it and elucidate its mysteries. Encouraged by the Christian tradition, this attitude blossoms thanks to Francis Bacon and the scientific revolution of the seventeenth century, which aims to render man "the master and possessor of nature," as per Descartes's famous sentence derived from *Genesis*. The second attitude, which Hardot defines as *Orphic*, imagines, on the contrary, a state of immersion in nature leading to a kind of knowledge that is empathetic or merely contemplative, and that, respecting its veil, refrains from any violence against nature – the natural order of things being beyond our comprehension.

The eighteenth century seems to be a moment of extreme polarization between these two attitudes, with on the one side an encyclopedic movement that appears to actualize the scientific revolution initiated by Bacon and Descartes, aiming to make man "the master and possessor of nature" – consider for example d'Alembert's article "Expérimental": observation "is limited to the facts it has before its eyes, to seeing well and to detailing all the types of phenomena that *the spectacle of Nature* presents: it seeks on the contrary to *penetrate it more deeply*, [...] it does not limit itself to listening to Nature, but interrogates it and pressures it" (1756: 298) –, and, on the other, an "orphic" movement whose power cannot be understated, judging particularly by the success of abbé Pluche's work, which sanctified nature and invited readers to be content with simply respecting its secrets and admiring its spectacle – "*To fathom the very depths of Nature*, [...] is an arduous endeavor, the success of which is very uncertain, [...] *it is not necessary that the inner workings of the machine be open to us* [...]" (Pluche 1732: ix–x).

---

[1] See also Renaut's 1976 article, "La nature aime se cacher."

Where should we place Rousseau in this bipolarization? If he seems the most eloquent apologist, in the eighteenth century, of this orphic attitude towards nature, we will show that this orphic aspiration is far from excluding a Promethean one, and that his thought bears witness to his unique effort to apply schemas of action to nature. These schemas certainly do not come under a demiurgic kind of prometheism, but seek to understand the mechanisms of nature, to fathom its mysteries, even if it means (and therein lies the paradox) exerting a type of violence onto nature. We draw from *La Nouvelle Héloïse*, and in particular on two of Julie's practices: her horticultural activity, and her pedagogical activity. That is, the creation of the Elysée on the one hand, and the education of her children on the other. In both cases, the idea of compensating for nature appears as a paradoxical necessity, but whose deeper logic could be that of forming a compromise between the orphic interdict forbidding any violence against nature, and the yearning to observe nature in even its smallest details, even to manipulate it according to one's needs, as long as it is by following its rules.

1 Fatal secrets

At first glance, Rousseau clearly incarnates, in the eighteenth century, the model for an orphic attitude regarding nature.[2] A brief summary of some of Rousseau's statements on the subject will permit us to measure the paradoxical dimensions of some of the expressions appearing in *La Nouvelle Héloïse*.

The third letter to Malesherbes is particularly eloquent. Describing to Malesherbes his ecstasies in Montmorency Forest, Rousseau remarks: "I believe that if I had unveiled all of the mysteries of nature, I would have felt myself to be in a less delightful situation than that stupefying ecstasy."[3] Isn't that clearly saying that "the ecstasy of Being takes the place of impossible knowledge of the world," to use Starobinski's words, and that "subjective awareness of totality supplants objective discovery of nature and its laws?" (1971: 78). We should nevertheless note that the unveiling of the mysteries of nature is not for all that disqualified since it serves as a measure of the supreme pleasure that constitutes the ecstasy of being.

Such is also, we know, the principle behind the great rift between Rousseau and Diderot and the *Encyclopédistes*. Jacques Berchtold has fittingly noted that

---

[2] It is primarily as such that he is portrayed in Pierre Hadot's book.
[3] Rousseau, *Lettres à Malesherbes* (*OC* 1: 1141; 26 January 1762).

beyond the controversy on theatre, the attack against d'Alembert in the *Letter to M. d'Alembert on Spectacles* was also directed at the leader of "a cyclopean enterprise whose *gaze seeks to encompass everything* [...], *that makes science visible*; the spectacle offered [by the *Encyclopedia*] is that of the cogs and the machinery left after analysis" (2006: 286).

And yet it is even more important to respect the veil of nature given that, for Rousseau, the violence exerted on nature in order to wrench its veil is precisely what places men outside of nature and brings about catastrophe. It is not for lack of having received, from nature, the clearest providential warnings, dissuading men from using violence in their dealings with her and from committing this fatal mistake:

> The heavy veil with which she covered all her operations seemed to warn us adequately that she did not destine us for vain studies. Is there even one of her lessons from which we have known how to profit, or which we have neglected with impunity? Peoples, know once and for all that nature wanted to keep you from being harmed by sciences just as a mother wrests a dangerous weapon from her child's hands; that all secrets she hides from you are so many evils from which she protects you, and that the difficulty you find in educating yourselves is not the least of her benefits. (*DSA, OC* 3: 15 [*CW* 2: 11])

How not to deplore the "man's blindness, which, [...] makes him run avidly after all the miseries of which he is susceptible, and which beneficent Nature had taken care to keep from him?"[4] By what strange fatality were men not satisfied by the fruits that nature had deliberately scattered on the surface of the earth, such that they felt the need to reach into its entrails and laboriously extract the ore from them? For "it is even harder to attribute this discovery to some accidental fire, because mines are formed only in arid spots, stripped of both trees and plants; so that one would say that Nature had taken precautions to hide this deadly secret from us" (49). Much later, in the *Rêveries*, Rousseau returns to this mystery once more:

> In itself, the mineral realm has nothing lovely or attractive. Its riches, sealed up within the bosom of the earth, seem to have been removed from the sight of man so as not to tempt his cupidity. They are there, as though in reserve, to serve one day as a *supplement* to the genuine riches more within his reach and for which he loses taste to the extent that he becomes corrupted. Thus he must call on industry, labor, and toil to relieve his misery. He digs in the bowels of the earth. He goes to its center, at the risk of his life and the expense of his health, to seek imaginary goods in place of the real goods it freely offered him when

---

4 Rousseau, *Discours sur l'origine et les fondements de l'inégalité* (*OC* 1: 202 [*CW* 3: 74])

he knew how to enjoy them. He flees the sun and the day which he is no longer worthy to see.[5]

The "supplement" to the true riches of nature is here identified with perversion. Such is the righteous punishment that man inflicted upon himself when, instead of living in immediate proximity to Mother Nature, man sought to penetrate her entrails and take away its fatal secrets:

> He buries himself alive and does well, no longer deserving to live in the light of day. There, quarries, pits, forges, furnaces, an apparatus of anvils, hammers, smoke, and fire replace the gentle images of pastoral occupations. The wan faces of the wretches who languish in the foul fumes of the mines, of grimy ironsmiths, of hideous Cyclopes are the spectacle the apparatus of the mines *substitutes*, in the bosom of the earth, for that of greenery and flowers, of azure sky, of amorous shepherds, and of robust plowmen on its surface. (*R* 1066–1067 [62])

Substitution, a supplement for the beauties of nature, definitively points to corruption. In denying oneself the spectacle of nature by replacing it by the hideous spectacle of mines, man has not only disfigured nature, but inflicts on her the violence that, as Jacques Derrida noted, is at the very origin of society (1967: 212–213).[6] This perfectly orphic and anti-Promethean attitude is not Rousseau's last word in his work, which is, as we know, entirely irreducible to any rigid form of dualism.

2 L'Elysée

When in the fourth part of *La Nouvelle Héloïse* Julie shows Saint-Preux the garden which she calls her Elysée, she evokes the process by which men disfigure nature, suggesting in turn the image of a golden age in which nature freely unveiled its charms:

> Moreover, *nature seems to want to veil from men's eyes her true attractions*, to which they are too insensible, and which they *disfigure* when they can get their hands on them: she flees much-frequented places; it is on the tops of mountains, deep in the forests, on desert Islands that she deploys her most stirring charms.[7]

---

[5] *Rêveries du promeneur solitaire*, VIIe Promenade (*OC* 1: 1066–1067 [*CW* 8: 62]), my emphasis.
[6] See also Kofman's comments (1982: 140–141).
[7] *Julie ou La Nouvelle Héloïse*, iv, 11 (*OC* 2: 479–480 [*CW* 6: 394]), my emphasis. The pagination will refer to the English edition of *CW*.

Initially, Julie's discourse seems aligned with that of Rousseau's in the first *Discourse*. And yet a closer reading reveals a reversal in the function of the veil: what nature hides is no longer its secret "operations," as these have already been brought to light for man's misfortune, but its "true attractions," as though to put them out of reach and prevent their disfiguration. In other words the veil no longer constitutes a secret barrier. It is rather that which hones desire in lovers of nature.

In the following part of Julie's discourse, one sees more clearly the erotic and Promethean undertone at the heart of the orphic discourse: "Those who love [nature] and cannot go so far to find her are reduced to doing her violence, forcing her in a way to come and live with them" (*Julie* 394). The expression is at the very least paradoxical when written by Rousseau: unable to "catch nature in the act" as Fontenelle put it, Julie is "reduced" (the term is rather indicative of the tension exerted in this moment upon an action that is in theory contrary to the principles of Rousseauist philosophy) to experimentally reconstruct a piece of nature. However the entire rest of the visit will aim to show that this violence is not in fact one, or rather that this violence is not contrary to nature.

It is well known what key principle presided during the elaboration of this garden and that Julie formulates within herself: "nature did it all, but under my direction, and there is nothing here that I have not designed" (*Julie* 388). In this inversion of the Baconian axiom ("we cannot command Nature except by obeying her"), Julie is formulating the rules of an art of the natural, admittedly refusing any subjection to nature, but forcing her nevertheless to reside in a protected space and creating the conditions that will constrain nature to freely deploy its charms. Saint-Preux's error is believing that Julie's work is nothing other than "a passive abandon to the great productivity of nature" (Marin 122): "My goodness, it has cost you nothing but neglect [...] you closed the gate [...] nature alone did the rest, and you yourself could never have managed to do so well" (*Julie* 388).

It is a question neither of exploitation nor denaturing, but of healing, maintaining, and protecting a nature that is growing and developing: the birds are not prisoners of the garden, nor are they its guest, "it is we who are theirs" says Julie (*Julie* 391). While Wolmar's work in Clarens, wisely construed though it may be, comes from a rational exploitation of the wealth of nature, Julie's is removed from any relationship of domination, as Louis Marin noted: "[Julie's] direction, her order is less a commandment, the imposition of a plan or of a schema rigorously faithful to natural substance, than a connivance, a complicity of nature with *Natura naturans*" (Marin 1976: 122).

Rather than creating a model to serve as a norm for her actions, Julie focuses her attention on the course of things, seeking to find their coherence and profit from their evolution. In this way, the model she proposes for a scheme of action on nature shares some links with models of effective action and the "silent transformations" that François Jullien describes when he writes about Chinese wisdom. Instead of constructing an ideal form that is then projected onto things, the idea is to focus on identifying the favorable factors at the heart of their configuration (Jullien 1997: 32).[8] This schema of action seems to come less from the acting subject itself than from the object. As such, it is profoundly different from the one that transforms nature into culture, as is the case for Clarens's agricultural property: the Elysée's economy is parasitic rather than exploitative. An emblem of Julie's garden are these "creeping, parasitic plants that, trained upon the tree trunks, surround their crowns in the thickest foliage and their feet in shade and coolness" that affect Saint-Preux so prodigiously (*Julie* 389).

In l'Elysée, nature and culture intertwine and transform each other. Julie's garden thus appears to be the art of metamorphosis. Is this project excluded from any Prometheism? Likely not, if one considers the role played in it by ruse, artifice, and illusion: Julie arranges it so that one can no longer see "*anywhere the slightest trace of culture*"; "all this cannot be done without a modicum of illusion" (*Julie* 394). And yet, as Hadot reminded us, the Greek's *mēkhanē*, in other words ruse, is central to the Promethean ambition: technique cunningly works with the mechanisms of nature so that it submits to the needs of men. This discrete art of transformation, under the direction of Julie, is a manipulation. "The garden is a lie because it is the height of artifice that nature is reduced to imitating: in this inverted mimesis, traces of culture have been carefully erased, grass has hidden the vestiges of work and the irregularities of nature are none other than the simulations of art." In this perspective, Julie's work is also one of fiction, "a fiction whose components are violence and illusion" (Marin 130).

3 Julie's negative education

And yet, this art of being natural – which represents both the ultimate height of artifice and also the fortuitous discovery of Nature as an artist who knows how to give shape to its subject – is not reserved for Julie's Elysée. The entire pedagogical doctrine of a "negative education" that is at the heart of *Emile*, and whose essential principles have already been developed by Julie and Wolmar in the fifth part of *La Nouvelle Heloise*, is also based upon the refusal to "correct na-

---

8 See also Jullien, *Les Transformations silencieuses* (2009).

ture," that is, on the refusal to exert any type of violence on her. If, in many other respects, Rousseau's debt to Locke is considerable (despite his frequent criticisms of him), the originality of his pedagogical thought here is striking.[9] Locke demands that the pedagogue keep the child's nature in highest consideration so as to avoid a frontal attack on his native propensities. He nevertheless encourages the teacher to correct them "with art [that] they may be much mended, and turned to good purpose."[10] In *La Nouvelle Héloïse*, Rousseau expresses through Wolmar's words (in the form of a reply to one of Saint-Preux's statements), all of the indignation that this idea of wanting to correct nature arouses in him. The draft of Wolmar's answer is even more explicit than its final version:

> Correcting nature! said Wolmar interrupting me, isn't that changing it? What instruments will you use that do not belong to nature, and by what strange contradiction can you claim to make it stronger than it is itself? Are you going to combine the mind and sentiments like those disorganized bodies, or grafting men like trees to make them bear other fruits? (*Julie* 462)[11]

The idea at play here is indeed the Lockean notion of education as a "reparation" or a "correction" of nature. The concept of negative education is not yet theorized in *La Nouvelle Héloïse*, but its role is already mapped out since it defines itself as the art of managing the conditions that allow nature to blossom unfettered. Furthermore, the concept of negative education includes a collaboration between nature and man, the latter taking care to release nature's force and sustain the conditions that allow it to continue its progress free of inauspicious deviations.

Hence the double need to which the principle of negative education responds. On the one hand, a need for protection: much like within the gates of l'Elysée, it is necessary to preserve the "process of nature" to be careful not to trouble it – "do nothing and let nothing be done"[12] or according to Wolmar's terms, "forever abstain from doing anything at all, rather than act unadvisedly" (*Julie* 464). On the other hand, and this need is almost inseparable from the first, a *dilatory* need: one must not act prematurely, and must abstain from any inopportune intervention. "Leave nature to act for a long time before you get involved with acting in its place, lest you impede its operations" (*E* 242).

---

9 Regarding Rousseau's debt to Locke, see Schøsler.
10 Locke, *Quelques pensées sur l'éducation* (1904, § 102).
11 Variant of the text: "Correcting nature! said Wolmar interrupting me; that's a fine word; but before using it, you should have answered to what Julie just said" (*OC* 4: 564 [*CW* 6: 462]).
12 *Émile* ii (*OC* 4: 322 [*CW* 13: 226]). Page numbers will further refer to *CW*.

As in the case of the garden, this surrender to nature is but an appearance: like in the Elysée, nature does everything, but under the direction of the Wolmar couple. Concerning the first principle, the need for protection, Julie and Wolmar do not benefit from the same privileges as does Emile's tutor, who is guaranteed by the theoretical principle of the work a complete mastery of the child's environment. But they do benefit from an extraordinary combination of circumstances, as Julie herself remarks:

> [T]he success of my ministrations depended upon a combination of circumstances that has perhaps never been seen anywhere but here. It required the understanding of an enlightened father to sort out amidst established prejudices the genuine art of governing children from their birth; it required all his patience to lend himself to its execution, without ever giving the lie to his lessons by his conduct; it required children well born in whom nature had done enough so that we could love its handiwork alone; it required having around us only intelligent and well-intentioned domestics, who never tire of entering into their masters' views; a single brutal or flattering servant would have been enough to spoil everything. In truth, when one considers how many foreign causes can set back the best designs and overturn the best-laid schemes, one has to thank fortune for all the good things one does in life, and say that proper behavior depends on a great deal on happiness. (*Julie* 479)

Julie and Wolmar were thus able to tame fate by turning Clarens into a protected islet. It is because the community of Clarens removed itself from the rest of the world by turning in onto itself that the parents could allow their children to develop naturally without fearing that their character be depraved or constrained: "To protect them from vices that are not in them, they have [...] a prophylactic more powerful than speeches they would not understand, or of which they would soon tire. It is the example of the morals of all those about them..." (478).

The second requirement of the inactive method demands multiplying the *dilatory* strategies. It is imperative to ban any corrupted social customs from inopportune intrusion in an education based on nature: "Leave nature to act for a long time before you get involved with acting in its place, lest you impede its operations" (*E* 242). However, allowing nature to act does not mean leaving children to their own devices, any more than the work on l'Elysée consisted in closing the gates and allowing it to grow freely. Just as in the case of Julie's garden, it falls upon Saint-Preux to represent the bad reader, or perhaps Julie's foil, the one who confuses her patient work, as well as Wolmar's, by abandoning children to the forces of nature:

> That all would seem to me very fine, said I, if I did not see in it a disadvantage which greatly countervenes the advantages you expect from this method; it is to allow children to acquire a thousand bad habits that can only be prevented by good ones. Look at those who are left to themselves; they soon contract all the shortcomings they see exemplified, be-

cause those examples are convenient to follow, and never imitate the good, which is harder to practice. Accustomed to obtaining everything, to working in every circumstance their indiscreet will, they become rebellious, headstrong, uncontrollable... (*Julie* 465)

Negative education is anything but laissez-faire.[13] It is essentially the art of not perturbing nature's temporality, according to Alain Grosrichard: "If one wants to imagine the mechanisms of perversion in general terms, one can simply say it is a lack of recognition of nature's temporality. [...] Man is the one who forewarns nature and forces it to cover itself up" (1978: 52). It is an art skillfully practiced by Julie, in her garden as with her children. "Nature [...] would have it that children are children before they are men. If we want to pervert that order, we will produce precocious fruits lacking both maturity and savor, which will soon rot" (*Julie* 461). It is particularly important not to seek to develop knowledge in the child before having sought to ensure the development of the instruments of knowledge, meaning the education of the body and of the senses: "Reason begins to take shape only after several years, and when the body has assumed a certain consistency. Nature's intention is then that the body be strengthened before the mind comes into play" (*Julie* 461). Wolmar repeats the precept later on: "In any event, let the body mature, until reason begins to bud: Then is the moment to cultivate it" (465).

This art that relies on the perfect effacement of the educator as well as his omnipresence also consists in selecting the most efficient *stimuli*. This art is so essential for Rousseau that it is the only passage in the letter on education of *La Nouvelle Héloïse* that he copies almost word for word from *Emile*:

> All that surrounds him is the book in which, without thinking about it, he continually enriches his memory while waiting for his judgment to be able to profit from it. It is in *the choice of these objects*, it is in the care with which one constantly presents him the objects he can know, and hides from him those he ought not to know, that the true art of cultivating in him this first faculty consists; and it is in this way that one must try to form in him a storehouse of knowledge which serves his education during his youth and his conduct at all times. (*E* 248)[14]

The art of educating thus consists in large part in choosing not only the right objects, but more importantly the right moment for experiences.[15] The educator

---

[13] "If one had only to listen to the inclinations and follow where they lead, the job would soon be done" (*E* 485).
[14] *Émile*, ii (*OC* 4: 351), emphasis added. See also *Julie*, v, 3 (*OC* 2: 580–581 [*CW* 6: 475]).
[15] "If there is a favorable moment in life for this study, it is the one I have chosen for Emile" (*Émile* 399).

manages the rate of learning. He must know how to recognize propitious moments and the ideal frequency of the experiences. It is crucial to be able to seize the moment, the occasion (Rousseau often underscores the irreversibility of certain processes). This art should not however be confused with Aristotelian *Kairos*. Rousseau sketches out an entirely different notion of "occasion"; not as the opportune moment that comes up, by lucky chance, to incite action and favor its success; but as "the most opportune moment to intervene in the course of a process in action" (Jullien 2002: 87).

If Julie and Wolmar as pedagogues are not to be taken as demiurges, they remain guides that redirect circumstances or control the setting of experiences. Hence the intertwinement of a vocabulary of non-intervention and that of labor and shaping. Thus for Julie, the child "will always [have the time] to learn, but there is not a moment to lose for shaping a good natural disposition in him" (*Julie* 581). Wolmar's explanations are an even clearer evidence of this interweaving: "Once again the question is not to change the character and bend the natural disposition, but on the contrary to push it as far as it can go, to cultivate it and keep it from degenerating; for it is thus that a man becomes all he can be, and that nature's work is culminated in him by education" (*Julie* 464).

Even if education must supplement nature as late as possible in order to respect its particular rhythms, there is no education, whether it be natural or not, without supplementation or supplement.[16] And the educator is the indisputable presence of this supplementation. That is to say that there is in negative education, just as in l'Elysée, an art of the natural, a collaboration between nature and man in which man is in charge of releasing the power in nature and manage the conditions that allow nature to continue its progress free of unwanted deviation.[17] The concept of negative education as it is proposed by Rousseau tends towards a negative art: the educator's task "is only to let it arrange its work" (*E* 370). But in reality "one must use a great deal of art to prevent social man from being totally artificial" (*E* 485).[18] The work of the educator is to be found at the intersection of nature and culture, controlling a power that already

---

[16] "Without childhood, no supplement would ever appear in nature. Yet the supplement is here both humanity's good fortune and the origin of its perversion" (Derrida 1969: 211).

[17] The "systematic portion" of *Émile* is nothing other than the "course of nature" (*E*, preface, *OC* 4: 242).

[18] "It is through the perfection of culture (and thus by pushing "denaturation") that harmony with nature can be regained, and this second nature, resulting from art, no longer defines itself as an obscure and distinct equilibrium: it is illuminated by reason and supported by moral sentiment, unknown to the primitive brute." (Starobinski 1969: 25).

exists, and inserting himself into a pre-existing process in order to better complete it.

It is not surprising that Rousseau carefully avoids the artisanal metaphors found in Locke's pedagogical texts. The Rousseauist governor is nothing like a craftsman who adjusts machines or winds up springs, he is not a tinkerer who creates things from nature. It is not a question of composing and recomposing matter but of forming a living being, and Rousseau's technical metaphors belong to the language register of culture and gardening: "Plants are shaped by cultivation, and men by education" (*E* 162).[19] The art of cultivation mentioned here does not of course refer to a rationalized and passive exploitation of nature's gifts, nor to artificial grafting which is only capable of producing monsters, and even less the murderous cultivation that insists on "fashion[ing man] in keeping with his fancy like a tree in his garden" (*E* 161), but rather ultimately to the same art that allowed Julie to create her Elysée.[20] It is in this light that one can understand Rousseau's choice to raise Emile in the countryside, in a small village, in other words at the heart of a nature that is already cultivated, among men that culture has not yet monstrously denatured.

Rousseau's attitude, seemingly orphic, does therefore not exclude all Promethean aims: you do not always find in Rousseau a reluctance to exhibit the "Opera's machines" or to want to "penetrate the depths of nature" to use abbé Pluche's words. Thus, visiting the Elysée constitutes also, and above all, and invitation to demystify Julie's persistence in unveiling the hidden side of the garden. The secrets of its creation have some similarities with the opening of *Entretiens sur la pluralité des mondes*, as Jean-Philippe Grosperrin noted (1995: 29). As to the pedagogical project, it is indissociable from an anthropological examination that implies both observation and experimentation – an essential convergence manifested even more openly in Julie's words than in those of Emile's author. Rather troubling indeed, is the manner in which the tender mother, Mme de Wolmar, admits to listening to her children with more attention than they know, and keeping an "exact record" of their slightest movements. Julie explains that she has engineered a pedagogical method corresponding "exactly to the two objectives she had in mind, that is, *letting the children's natural disposition develop,*

---

[19] "A vicious phrase in their mouth is a foreign plant whose seed the wind brought in; if I cut it off with a reprimand, it will soon sprout again: instead I quietly look for its root, and take care to pull it. I am, she said to me with a laugh, merely the Gardener's servant; I weed the garden, I remove the bad seed, it is for him to cultivate the good" (*Julie* 478).
[20] On horticultural metaphors in *Emile*, see Grosrichard (1985: 98–100). Generally speaking, gardening metaphors are very common in the pedagogical discourses of the eighteenth century. See Simone Gougeaud-Arnaudeau (2000: 20 [ff.]).

and studying it" (*Julie* 477–478). This statement really helps to understand the dual nature of Emile's project, which is pedagogical and anthropological. For there is absolutely no doubt as to the exact nature of this study on which Julie embarks. Clarens is indeed, in its own way, a laboratory of origins providing access to Nature's best kept secrets: "so it is that the character [of children] develops daily before our eyes without restriction, and we *can study the impulses of nature in their most secret principles*" (478, emphasis added). Enough to compel us to see negative education as a series of compromises between the prohibition against exerting violence upon Nature and the desire to observe her in even the most minute of details.[21]

Thus, between the Promethean yearning to manipulate nature by fostering a relationship of control and domination, and the orphic yearning that seeks to restrain itself to a contemplative approach and denies itself the act of unveiling, Rousseau seems to indicate the possibility of a third path. Between the Baconian, who manipulates nature, controls and dominates her, and he who, like abbé Pluche, contemplates without touching, Julie incarnates another way that consists in working with Nature, in other words, to live in society with her. Julie's garden, like her pedagogy, is not Promethean, and neither are conceived as a subjection of nature, as the product of tyranny of knowledge and of the action exerted on a nature that "loves to hide," according to Heraclitus's aphorism. But neither are exactly orphic either: they respect the veil of nature, and entice her to deploy her charms. Seduction is halfway between violence and gentleness. Julie's garden, and her pedagogy, point to the possibility of a harmonious seduction of nature that in the end offers the ideal image of a complete (and simultaneous) metamorphosis of both nature and culture.

Translated by Karen Santos Da Silva

Works Cited

D'Alembert, Jean L. R. "Expérimental." *Encyclopédie*. 1756. Vol. 6.
Berchtold, Jacques. "*Le Spectacle de la nature* chez Jean-Jacques Rousseau." *Ecrire la nature au 18ᵉ siècle. Autour de l'abbé Pluche*. Eds. Françoise Gevrey, Julie Boch et Jean-Louis Haquette. Paris: PUPS, 2006.
Derrida, Jacques. *De la grammatologie*. Paris: Minuit, 1969.
Gougeaud-Arnaudeau, Simone. *Entre gouvernants et gouvernés: le pédagogue au xviiiᵉ siècle*. Villeneuve-d'Ascq: PU du Septentrion, 2000.

---

21 On this, see Martin 2012.

Grosperrin, Jean-Philippe. "Les lieux où règne Armide : jardins d'opéra dans le roman du XVIIIe siècle." *Les Voix de l'écrivain. Mélanges offerts à Guy Sagnes*. Eds. Jean-Louis Cabanès and Guy Sagnes, Toulouse: Presses de l'Université du Mirail, 1995.

Grosrichard, Alain. "Gravité de Rousseau." *Cahiers pour l'Analyse* 8 (1978): 43–64.

Grosrichard, Alain. "Jardins d'enfants ou les leçons d'*Émile*." *Le Temps de la réflexion* 6 (1985): 107–126.

Hadot, Pierre. *Le Voile d'Isis: essai sur l'histoire de l'idée de Nature*. Paris: Gallimard, 2004.

Jullien, François. *Traité de l'efficacité*. Paris: Grasset, 1997.

    Jullien, François. *Les Transformations silencieuses*. Paris: Grasset, 2009.

Kofman, Sarah. *Le Respect des femmes (Kant et Rousseau)*. Paris: Galilée, 1982.

Locke, John. *Quelques pensées sur l'éducation*. Trans. Gabriel Compayré. Paris: Hachette, 1909.

Marin, Louis. "L'effet Sharawadgi ou le jardin de Julie; notes sur un jardin et un texte (lettre xi, 4e partie, *La Nouvelle Héloïse*)." *Traverses* 5–6 (August 1976): 114–131.

Martin, Christophe. "'Faire violence à la nature?' Éducation négative et tentation expérimentale dans l'*Émile*. *Éduquer selon la nature. Seize études sur L'Émile de Rousseau*. Ed. Claude Habib. Paris: Desjonquères, 2012. 203–215.

Pluche, Noël A. *Le Spectacle de la nature ou Entretiens sur les particularités de l'histoire naturelle*. Paris: Chez la veuve Estienne… & Jean Desaint, 1732.

Renaut, Alain. "La nature aime se cacher." *Revue de Métaphysique et de morale* 1 (1976): 62–111.

Rousseau, Jean-Jacques. *Œuvres complètes*. Gen. Eds. Bernard Gagnebin and Marcel Raymond. 5 vols. Paris: Gallimard, "Bibliothèque de la Pléiade," 1959–1995.

Rousseau, Jean-Jacques. *The Collected Writings of Rousseau*. Gen. Eds. Roger D. Masters and Christopher Kelly. 13 vols. Hanover: UP of New England, 1990–2010.

Schøsler, Jørn. "Rousseau, disciple de Locke?" *Études Jean-Jacques Rousseau* 12 (2001): 215–226.

Starobinski, Jean. *Transparency and Obstruction*. Trans. Arthur Goldhammer. Chicago: The U of Chicago P, 1971.

Starobinski, Jean. "Introduction à Rousseau." *Discours sur l'origine de l'inégalité parmi les hommes*. Rousseau, *OC* 3: xlv–lxx.

Lucien Nouis
Recomposing the Diffracted Text: Rousseau and the Metaphor of the Book of Nature

The second book of *Émile* contains a scene of reading, whose symbolic potential is rendered all the more powerful by the fact that it is expressed through the simplicity of a pantomime. Such a scene could very well serve as a summary of all of Rousseau's ideas on the vulnerability of man in civil society:

> I see a man, fresh, gay, vigorous, healthy, his presence inspires joy, his eyes proclaim contentment, well-being; he brings with him the image of happiness. A letter comes in the post; the happy man looks at it; it is addressed to him; he opens it, reads it. Instantly his aspect changes. He becomes pale and faints. Coming to, he weeps, writhes, moans, tears his hair, makes the air resound with his cries, seems to have a frightful fit of convulsions. Senseless man, what ill has this piece of paper done to you then? Of what limb has it deprived you? What crime has it made you commit? Altogether, what has it changed in you yourself to put you in the state in which I see you?[1]

Here is for Rousseau the truth at the heart of every act of reading. Writing summons the subject to society, or rather to a *multiplicity* of relations, and by making him capable of being everywhere, through the virtuality of a voice that can be perceived at a distance, forces him to stand nowhere. Rousseau concludes: "We no longer exist where we are, we only exist where we are not" (*E* 214). Through a subtle displacement between "being" and "existing," the philosopher seems to suggest the beginning of an analysis of the experience of the virtual, of information sent and received from afar, thereby announcing more modern meditations on the anxiogenic properties of globalization and instantaneous communication, or on the progressive occupation of societies by simulacra and simulations.[2] Writing pushes the self outside of its limits (*hors de soi*). No longer perfectly contained, mentally and physically inhabiting one place, the recipient of the letter is taken hostage by a sort of unhappy ubiquity. Arguably, this passage is not only about letters, or writings addressed directly to oneself. Philosophy and fiction also have the power to fluidify and blur the limits of the subject. How can one exist in one place, when one is inhabited by the thoughts of others?

---

[1] Rousseau, *Émile, or on Education* (2010, *CW* 13: 214). All subsequent quotes in English refer to this edition.
[2] On this topic, see Michel Delon: "Cesser de vivre avant de cesser d'exister."

Jacques Derrida is right to underscore the fact that Rousseau distinguishes between "[...] a good and a bad writing: the good and natural is the divine inscription in the heart and the soul; the perverse and artful is technique, exiled in the exteriority of the body" (1997: 17). The first one, it is worth remembering, can be said to be "writing" only in the metaphorical sense. The "book of nature" or the "book of God," a book encompassing the entirety of the world, is always intimately understood, whereas the books of men, aphoristic and fragmentary, reliant on words, veil and interrupt access to this otherwise contradiction-free totality. In order regain access to it, one must follow the example of the Savoyard vicar: "I therefore closed all the books. There is only one open to all eyes: it is the book of nature. It is in this great and sublime book that I learn to serve and worship its divine author" (*E 473*). Several times in *Émile*, Rousseau insists on the idea that books can rob individuals of their own voices:

> I hate books. They only teach one to talk about what one does not know. It is said that Hermes engraved the elements of the sciences on columns in order to shelter his discoveries from a flood. If he had left a good imprint of them in man's head, they would have been preserved by tradition. Well-prepared minds are the surest monuments on which to engrave human knowledge. (*E 331*)

This declaration – fraught with the idea of the superiority of tradition (always oral, for Rousseau, and always lived) over bookish consigning – also speaks of books as prostheses that allow the reader to use words without investing them with any sort of intimate experience of the world, without taking in the ideas *"intus et in cute"* (inside and under the skin), to quote the famous epigraph of the *Confessions*. Reading gives the illusion of possessing knowledge, whereas in reality one is merely seduced by a superficial shimmering of words. Children, for example, are forced by their preceptors and parents to reproduce, like automatons, meaningless motions of the jaw:

> Apparent facility at learning is the cause of children's ruin. It is not seen that this very facility is the proof they learn nothing. Their brain, smooth and polished, returns, like a mirror, the objects presented to it. But nothing remains; nothing penetrates. The child retains the words; the ideas are reflected off of him. Those who hear him understand him; only he does not understand them. (*E 242*)

Rousseau signals a break within language: words are no longer used to express ideas and rather act as empty objects. This destructive pedagogy prevents children from using words as tools that refer to empirical and sensorial reality. They use them as if they only related to themselves, and were without any kind of meaningful connection with those who speak them or with the world around them. As a consequence, all the knowledge that words on a page are supposed to impart becomes lost: "In any study whatsoever, unless one has the ideas of the things represented, the representative signs are nothing" (*E* 245). Also, if books fail to teach children about things, it is because they often focus on the sciences "[that] one appears to know when one knows their terminology: heraldry, geography, chronology, languages, etc." (*E* 244). Words, here, become ends in themselves, and children naturally start to inhabit them rather than inhabiting the world. A child might even start to think that the latter has become the very sign that is presented to him:

> Thinking he is being taught a description of the earth, he learns only to know some maps. He is taught the names of cities, of countries, of rivers which he does not conceive as existing anywhere else but on the paper where he is showed them. I remember having seen somewhere a geography text which began thus: "What is the world? It is a cardboard globe." Such precisely is the geography of children. (*E* 245)

Something in these lines is reminiscent of the people imagined by Borges who, having developed a passion for cartography, end up hiding the thing under the sign by covering their realm with a map: "[...] the college of the Cartographers evolved a map of the Empire that was of the same Scale as the Empire and that coincided with it point for point" (Borges 1972: 141). In the same way, the cardboard globe becomes the only thing perceived by the child. For Rousseau such confusion between things and signs is symptomatic of a process of disorientation that is at work in society and language.

The exercise of repetition, the replacement of the individual voice with the text memorized through rote learning (a form of ventriloquism whereby the letter mimics the voice), becomes more and more insidious as the social imperative of conversation and representation grows more urgent. Whereas the child, when he merely repeated what he *did not* understand, only responded to the solicitations of parents and preceptors, the young adult who later performs his recitations is perfectly aware of their effects (he is fully conscious of the rhetoric he is using, and of the power his speech might have on others). For Rousseau, this kind of *learning* (radically different from *knowledge*) has no connection to the young man's own life and the place he lives in. It is remote, bookish, second-hand, without any value for the person herself. A pure imposture, one might add, in the sense, suggested by the etymology of the word, that something has been applied *over* the person: "Like Raymond Lulle's art, they are good for training fifteen-year-old Platos to philosophize in polite society and for informing a gathering about the practices in Egypt and India on the testimony of Paul Lucas or Tavernier" (*E* 641). It is worth mentioning here that the word "babil" is not only used by Rousseau in connection to children, but also refers to any kind of empty, parasitic, and superficial speech which is self-assured but devoid of any truth. Rousseau denounces the imposture of "This appalling multitude of philosophers whose babble confuses us."[3] He also dismisses Paris as "a city of chatter" which is not our "*centre*" (*E* 770) ["the place of us" (*E* 593)[4]]; a city where, again, all is merely "[...] babble, jargon, incoherent utterances."[5] Evil comes from the fact that people are incapable of reading for themselves, in order to live, but only to impress others:

> In this immense labyrinth of human reasoning you will learn to speak about happiness without knowing it, you will learn to speechify and not at all to live [...]. This method trains in speaking about everything, in shining in a social circle; it makes learned people, fine wits, talkers, arguers, happy people in the judgment of those who are listening, unfortunate people as soon as they are alone. (*Moral Letters* 180)

In the end, one might say that words, for Rousseau, have become the counterfeit money society relies on. The forms of learning he describes, even when they appear to be erudite and impressive, are worthless because they do not stem from experience – they come from the study of books and not of things:

> Vast erudition results less from a multitude of ideas than from a multitude of images. Dates, proper names, places, all objects isolated or devoid of ideas are retained solely by memory of signs; rarely does one recall *some* of these things without at the same time seeing the page on the right- or left-hand side where it was read of the form in which it was seen for the first time. (*E* 248)

This *interposition* of the page, of paper, is striking: instead of remembering something firsthand, the reader recalls the layout of the page where he first read an idea. Again, Rousseau sees the letter, the written sign, as a figure of substitution, threatening the singularity and unity of the self that experiences the world.

If the opposition between the book of nature and the books of men is a commonplace idea, there are times when it has greater currency. This, at least, is the thesis implicit in some of the remarks made by Ernst Robert Curtius in *European Literature and the Latin Middle Age*, when he credits the eighteenth century with having held a major role in the construction of the couple book of nature/books of men: "The catchy dictum that Nature is a book superior to all books found its way during the age of Rousseau into the theory of poetry too" (2013: 324). If Curtius does not pursue this line of inquiry much further, one can indeed find con-

---

3 Rousseau, *Moral Letters* (2007: 81).
4 It is worth noting here that the translation seems to have missed on the importance of the notion of "center": books, meaningless chatter, are precisely what take the individual away from his own center, and lead him, as it were, outside of himself.
5 Rousseau, *Julie* (1997, 6: 209).

firmation of this theory in a wide array of authors.⁶ Painters, playwrights, poets should all borrow their models from life itself, and observe moving flesh instead of merely painting from pictures and writing from books.

This way of understanding the formula "nature is a book that is superior to all books," albeit very central to Rousseau, might lead his readers to overlook a second level of opposition. The hypothesis I would like to propose here is that in the affirmation of the alleged superiority of the book of nature over the books of men, of the *singularity* of nature over the *plurality* of human production, is also at stake *a desire and a project to reduce the multiplicity of the human library to a single book, or to a coherent unity.* To speak of the book of nature, unique and singular, is also to be speaking of the evil that comes with the plurality of discourses and the sheer abundance of conflicting opinions. In other words, beyond the idea of nature as the *other* of books, one must underscore the fact that Rousseau, through his use of this opposition, is clearly inviting us to meditate *on books themselves, and on the new regimes of writing that should govern them.*

Before we come back to Rousseau, a digression on Diderot seems necessary, which will shed further light on the new opposition at hand. In the *Encyclopédie*, the philosopher indeed proposes that the mission of the Enlightenment should be to reduce the infinite plurality of books to a single book – that is, to rethink the written production of humanity on the model of the book of nature, which is singular, coherent, and devoid of errors. For Diderot, the books that occupy the shelves of libraries, the cabinets of philosophers and scientists, or are stored in the salons of academies, are full of mistakes. They compose a mess of aggregated pages each day thicker and more impossible to navigate. Readers cannot find *the Truth*, buried as it is in mountains of useless inscriptions: mud and gold, wood and marble are mixed together and have become inseparable. The confusion is such, Diderot states, that it is soon going to become more difficult to read the books of men than to go directly to nature itself: "As centuries pass by, the mass of works grows endlessly, and one can foresee a time when it will be almost as difficult to educate oneself in a library, as in the universe, and almost as fast to seek a truth subsisting in nature, as lost among an immense number of books." One encounters the very same idea in the article on the "Book," where Diderot accuses the latter of leading readers through endless loops: "[...] the errors, fables, follies they are filled with, their too great number, the little certainty one gets from them, are such, it seems to be easier to discover truth in nature and the reason of things, than in the uncertainties and contradictions

---

6 For crucial developments on the idea of the book of nature, see Blumenberg.

of books."[7] Such is the paradox of mankind, which reads its own books instead of that of the world, and becomes lost in them: the library becomes a monstrous supplement to nature, and the books that are deposited in it, far from helping understand nature, prevent their readers from grasping it in any clear way. They are merely *heaps* of material, *sedimentations*, all the more difficult to read that, contrary to the layers of minerals geologists find in nature, they are not the products of constant laws, but of the imaginations of the human mind. Philosophers like to point out, irreverently, that what is in appearance matter, fullness, or profusion, hides in fact a fundamental deficiency, a void, a lack of substance: a mass of paper and ink does not make a multiplicity of riches.

Precisely because it has become an obstacle to the legibility of the world, and to human development, this saturation of printed matter renders necessary the project of the *Encyclopédie*. Indeed, Diderot describes the latter as a major turn in the history of the progress of the human mind: a way of putting accumulated knowledge through the riddle of reason, of separating the wheat from the chaff, and of liberating mankind from the weight of its own productions. The *Encyclopédie* will make it possible to go from a confusing multiplicity to the rational singularity of a purged archive. To create a new Book of all books is the responsibility of the generations of the Enlightenment, who must spare posterity a task that will become more and more difficult as time passes: "We have therefore undertaken today for the good of letters, and out of interest for the human race, a work which our descendants would have had to undertake, but under much less favorable circumstances: when the overabundance of books would have made its execution extremely laborious." Paradoxically, the *Encyclopédie* offers posterity a negative transmission: the future will inherit an open space, a cleared forest, an open field in which to make its own inscriptions. For Diderot, the eighteenth century is a turning point between two approaches to the writing and consignation of human knowledge. What had been until then the general regime of writing only admitted two activities: composition and transcription, both aimed at preserving the archive. With the encyclopedic age, Diderot imagines a new separation: on the one hand, there will be those who invent, who come up with new materials, on the other, there will be an army of abbreviators, whose task will be to reduce books to a few lines, or even to nothing if it should turn out they are devoid of substance. The mission of this new philosophy, eclectic in the true sense of the term, is to assign to each idea its place in this new Book of books that would be a successful universal encyclopedia.

---

[7] My translation.

How the opposition between the book of nature and the books of men works is quite clear and obvious. If Diderot claims that the direct observation of nature is a shortcut to truth and knowledge, as opposed to the labyrinth of human libraries, it is in fact, before anything else, to invite his contemporaries to reproduce the unity and singularity of nature by purging the human archive of its errors. What is imagined here is a rational archive, inscribed in a single place, coherently written and managed by a dedicated army of men of letters and scientists. What Diderot seems thus to be retaining from the classical opposition between the book of nature and the books of men, is the necessity of accomplishing a passage from the multiple to the singular, from an intricate, diffracted archive, to a fluid and unified one. Here, the book of nature is inseparable form the second term represented by the books of men: the first one serves to inflect the second; it is its horizon, its vanishing point, which makes it possible to envisage the rational rewriting of the totality of human productions. In sum, the books of men have to become a single book, in order to approach nature – or rather, the Encyclopaedists must strive to come up with the very book nature would give if it could write in the languages of men.

What can be said, then, of Rousseau's interpretation of the opposition between the book of nature and the book of men? As we have already seen, the idea that nature rather than books, is what one must read, is everywhere present in his thought. Émile, for example, is only allowed one book, *Robinson Crusoe*; and in the *Nouvelle Héloïse*, Wolmar refuses Milord Edouard's proposition to send him books from Geneva: "I thank you for your books; but I no longer read those I understand, and it is too late to learn to read those I don't. I am nonetheless less ignorant than you accuse me of being. For me, the true book of nature is men's hearts, and the proof that I know how to read it is in my friendship for you" (*Julie* 540). But with Rousseau, just as with Diderot, there is also a desire to stem the discordant multiplication of discourses and to bring it all back to the singular: referring to the book of nature, here as well, is a way of transforming how books are thought, written, and read.

The main difference, perhaps, between Rousseau and the Encyclopaedists on this particular point, is that the passage from the discordant plurality of books to the unified singularity of the Book of all books, according to Rousseau, cannot be accomplished through the work of an army of readers and abridgers, but through the affirmation of a subjective consciousness. It is within the subject himself that the purge must be actuated. It is he, through his own judgment, who must find again the unity lost in the sea of opinions. The book of nature, according to Rousseau, can only be read through the exercise of an isolated consciousness, protected from the parasitical intrusions of civil society – that is, from the distortions that necessarily come from other people's books and discourses.

In order to make more explicit what could otherwise seem too abstract, a few examples should be taken here, which will serve to show how Rousseau articulates the tension between the singular and the plural within a reflection on the book. The first one comes from Rousseau's second letter to Malesherbes, where he recounts the famous "Illumination" on the road to Vincennes. What I will retain here from this very rich scene, which has been read from a variety of angles – from Augustinian intertextuality to the psychopathology of messianism – is the way in which Rousseau describes being summoned by the vision of his books to come. What is indeed remarkable is that his vision is not fragmented, nor multiple, but perfectly unified:

> Oh Sir, if I had ever been able to write a quarter of what I saw and felt under that tree, how clearly I would have made all the contradictions of the social system seen, with what strength I would have exposed all the abuses of our institutions, with what simplicity I would have demonstrated that man is actually good and that it is from these institutions alone that men become wicked. (*CW* 5: 575)

And he adds: "Everything that I was able to retain from these crowds of great truths which illuminated me under that tree in a quarter of an hour has been weakly scattered about in my three principal writings, namely the first discourse, the one on inequality, and the treatise on education, which three works are inseparable and form the same whole" (5: 575). One recognizes here the double movement of total understanding and of subsequent diffraction and disjoining – a movement that appears with remarkable consistency all throughout Rousseau's writings. As often, the true text, perfectly clear, cannot maintain itself in its initial coherence. As soon as Rousseau tries to grasp his vision, it becomes multiple and falls into pieces. From the book (singular) we arrive at books (plural), ideas become lost, holes and tears appear in the fabric of the text, what was clear becomes obscure, spaces and blanks untie connections that at first seemed evident: writing becomes fragmentary, incomplete, and imperfect.

Thinking the same movement, but in the reverse, from plurality to singularity, one can turn to the passage of the *Confessions* in which Rousseau recounts his second education, the one that intervenes under the auspices of Mme de Warens. Rousseau first explains how, desirous to read everything, he became lost in an ocean of words and ideas. With each book, with each page, he found himself being led to so many other books that a human life would not have sufficed to read them all:

> The false idea I had of things persuaded me that in order to read a book fruitfully it was necessary to have all the knowledge it assumed [...]. With this mad idea I stopped at every instant, forced to run ceaselessly from one book to another, and sometimes I

would have had to exhaust libraries before reaching the tenth page of the book I wanted to study. (*C* 196)

The impossibility of achieving this dream of exhaustivity thus forces him to change methods. This time conscious of the fact that everything is linked together, that the sciences "attract, help, mutually clarify each other" (196), Rousseau sets about to explore the encyclopedia (here, the totality of human knowledge) by going, according to the famous metaphor of the tree, from the trunk to the extremities: "First taking the encyclopedia I had been proceeding by dividing it into its branches" (196). But this method, he finds, also leads from the singular to the multiple. Again Rousseau is confronted with a multiplicity of complications and new ideas that make him lose his direction. In the end, instead of going in the direction of division and greater complexity, he chooses to follow the exact same path, but in reverse, and to go from the multiple to the singular, that is to take the branches of the tree "each of them separately, and pursue each separately up to the point where they rejoined each other" (196). In a way, what Rousseau describes here reproduces the passage of the multiple and confused, to the unique and coherent that is for Diderot the ideal horizon of the project of the *Encyclopédie*.

The last example I would like to evoke is taken from the first of the *Letters from the Mountain*, where Rousseau accuses his critics and persecutors of having artificially created contradictions in a work that should instead have been grasped in a complete and continuous act of reading. The philosopher thus deplores that all the coherence, the consistency and the strength of his writing is being reduced to nothing by those who read it with the aim of breaking it into fragments, and of destroying its internal logic and movement:

> How often have defamed authors and the indignant public not protested against this odious manner of hacking up a work, disfiguring all its parts, judging it by shreds picked from here and there at the whim of an unfaithful accuser who produces the evil himself by detaching it from the good that corrects and explains it, by twisting the true meaning throughout?[8]

Rousseau asks his readers if there should exist "a single book in the world, however true, however good, however excellent it may be, that could escape this infamous inquisition" (*CW* 1997: 151)? The answer is a resounding no: "No, Sir, there is not one, not a single one, not even the Gospel. For they would know now to place in it the evil that is not there by their unfaithful excerpts, by

---

8 Rousseau, *Letters Written from the Mountain* (1997: 150).

their false interpretations" (150). Even the Book of books, and with it the book of nature, inscribed in the heart of man, are threatened by ulterior fragmentations, denatured and dismantled by the works of theologians, pamphleteers, journalists.

Conscience, or the mind tuned to itself in an act of *prosoché* (attention to the self), logically becomes the sole means by which the dismantled individual can reconstruct the fragmented book of nature of which, by virtue of being human, he is the bearer.[9] Only this unity, this internal coherence, cannot ultimately be controlled outside of the self. Not only, as we have seen, can reading disrupt and disorient the self, but others, by reading Rousseau, can deconstruct his texts and make them say the exact opposite of what they were meant to say. Reading and writing become for the philosopher exercises in the affirmation of the self. Robert Damien, when he summarizes the arguments of those who are against the powers of libraries, asks a question that Rousseau could very well have formulated himself: "Why scatter the judgment of one's conscience in the conflicting and fragmentary knowledge of others, which alter it without providing answers (1997: 17)[10]?"

What, then, to conclude from the use Rousseau makes of the opposition between the book of nature and the books of men? Even though all this would need to be further developed, it appears clearly that what is at stake is not as much an opposition between books and the world, as between what philosophers judge to be good and bad books, ideas that need to be kept and others that should be dismissed. Rousseau, in this regard, is not far from Diderot. For both of them, it seems, the book of nature serves as the ideal model of a clear and coherent text. For Diderot, the *Encyclopédie* must strive to resemble such a text: it must create unity out of the confusion of the archive. Rousseau, for his part, imagines the possibility of a natural voice that would be immune to the babble of writing, and that, by virtue of remaining whole, coherent, would necessarily be truthful. Thus, the classical opposition between the two books – the natural one and the artificial one – must be understood differently: nature, here, is not really nature, the irreducible other of books, but rather a concept that allows the two philosophers to think about the book and to create a tension inside the archive. Rousseau, even when he is referring to the book of nature, is still meditating on writing and reading: it is a metaphor for the pure writing of the self, untouched by the confusing multiplicity of concurring voices.

---

9 On the concept of *prosoché*, see Hadot (1995: 84).
10 My translation.

Works Cited

Blumenberg, Hans. *Die Lesbarkeit der Welt*. Frankfurt-am-Main: Suhrkamp Verlag, 1981.

Borges, Jorge Luis. *A Universal History of Infamy*. Trans. Norman Thomas di Giovanni. New York: E. P. Dutton, 1972.

Curtius, Ernst Robert. *European Literature and the Latin Middle Ages*. Princeton: Princeton UP, 2013.

Damien, Robert. *Bibliothèque et État: Naissance d'une raison politique dans la France du xviie siècle*. Paris: PUF, 1995.

Delon, Michel. "Cesser de vivre avant de cesser d'exister. L'opposition entre *vivre* et *exister* chez Rousseau et ses successeurs." *Études Jean-Jacques Rousseau* 2 (1988): 67–85.

Derrida, Jacques. *On Grammatology*. Trans. Gayatari Chakravorty Spivak. Baltimore and London: The Johns Hopkins UP, 1997.

Diderot, Denis, and Jean Le Rond d'Alembert. *The Encyclopedia of Diderot & d'Alembert Collaborative Translation Project*. Translated by Philip Stewart. Ann Arbor: Michigan Publishing, University of Michigan Library, 2002. Web. 12 Oct. 2013. <http://hdl.handle.net/2027/spo.did2222.0000.004>. Trans. of "Encyclopédie." *Encyclopédie ou Dictionnaire raisonné des sciences, des arts et des métiers*. Vol. 5. Paris, 1755.

Hadot, Pierre. *Philosophy as a Way of Life: Spiritual Exercises from Socrates to Foucault*. Oxford: Blackwell Publishing, 1995.

Rousseau, Jean-Jacques. *Œuvres complètes*. Gen. Eds. Bernard Gagnebin and Marcel Raymond. 5 vols. Paris: Gallimard, "Bibliothèque de la Pléiade," 1959–1995.

Rousseau, Jean-Jacques. *The Collected Writings of Rousseau*. Gen. Eds. Roger D. Masters and Christopher Kelly. 13 vols. Hanover: UP of New England, 1990–2010.

Tanguy L'Aminot
Nature, Culture, and the Social Contract: Emile's point of view

In a book paying tribute to the philosophers that had influenced his thought, Edgar Morin wrote:

> Rousseau brought us the fundamental idea that nature is to be conceived of as a living, vital whole with which man must seek harmony and reconciliation. This idea of recovering our lost umbilical relationship to nature, while at the same time rediscovering our own nature, is incredibly new and modern. It did not exist among his contemporaries, the *Philosophes*. And I must say that a book like *The Lost Paradigm* was written in the spirit of *The Discourse on the Origins of Inequality*, for in it I sought, through the most recent discoveries in anthropology, prehistory, and ethnology, to grasp the "lost paradigm" of human nature. By that I mean the bond that links, within man, inseparably and contradictorily, nature and culture. This link had become invisible in a system of knowledge in which fields of knowledge were compartmentalized and without mutual communication: biological sciences on one side, social sciences on the other. Rousseau, however, is one of the rare thinkers able to understand human uniduality, composed of culture and nature, man being 100% nature and 100% culture. (Morin 2011: 62)

Nature is indeed an idea of the utmost complexity in Rousseau as it has multiple meanings that often intersect and further complicate our understanding of his thought. It refers all at once to human nature, the state of nature, the Golden Age, or the countryside, and likely has still more meanings. As though this complexity were not enough, philosophers have added their own in their commentaries of Rousseau's work. Victor Goldschmidt, for example, starts from the premise that Rousseau designates the despotism appearing as a logical result of the pact of the impostor in *The Discourse on the Origins of Inequality*, as "a second state of nature" in order to invert Rousseau's discourse and say that the state of nature is nothing but a state of war. He writes:

> The state of war, which is the extreme moment in the state of nature that immediately precedes the conclusion of a pact of association, is the one most comparable to the state defined as despotism. But this form of government brings us back to the state of nature, in its totality, and as this state, it is now thought of in terms of two traits and two traits only, given the slow progress that brought us to the state of war from our primitive state. These two traits are the dissolution of the governmental pact, and the right of the strongest, and it is in this that, according to Rousseau, it coincides with despotism. (Goldschmidt 1974: 753–754)

For Goldschmidt, the right of the strongest is at the very heart of the state of nature throughout the *Second Discourse*, and he rejects those commentaries that give it an idyllic interpretation. The state of nature acquires in his words a Hobbesian hue that aligns itself with those who question the libertarian nature of Rousseau's thought, a challenge that appeared in the mid-70s and gathered strength at the time of the bicentennial of Rousseau's death in 1978. Louis Althusser had furthermore initiated this tendency as early as 1967, since in his famous article on the *Social Contract* and its discrepancies he asserted that Rousseau was Hobbesian.

For Goldschmidt, this interpretation is the result of another one that equally contributes to the confusion of the diverse stages of the origins of societies as described by Rousseau in *The Discourse on the Origins of Inequality*. Against Halbwachs, Derathé, and Starobinski, he asserts that the pact of the impostor is just as valid as the social contract described in 1762 by the Genevan philosopher since, he claims, Rousseau was enough of a jurist to be familiar with the question already treated by Pufendorf and Hobbes, and admit to it. It follows then that:

> the contract of the "impostor" is thus perfectly valid (otherwise it could not create the "social order" that is a "sacred right") and it produces, as concerns wealth inequality, the same juridical effect as the *Social Contract:* "change usurpation into a true right" and here: establish the laws that, "out of a skillful usurpation made an irrevocable right." (Goldschmidt 579)

If Goldschmidt admits that one can nonetheless see, between these two contracts, "a displacement of emphasis and diverging appreciation, the object of the two treatises being different" (579), he does not find the difference to be decisive. The scholars who have since taken up this idea in fact no longer see any at all. Presenting things in this way means eliminating the last thirty pages that follow the pact of the impostor in the *Second Discourse* and the first four chapters of Book I of *The Social Contract*, in other words, the pages that show that the society of the false social contract is based solely on force and violence. Only from this simplification can we with ease, the way Goldschmidt and his successors have done, connect the two contracts, turning it into a single one that is thus validated as though by magic.

The topic is not without consequences and the confusion is likely far from innocent. It concerns not only the moment when the social contract is formed, giving this moment a kind of retroactive feeling of imposture, but it also allows us to justify "rousseausistly" the state of present-day societies. Indeed, if everything is interchangeable, if the true and the false social pacts are one and the same, today's individuals live not in a city-state defined by usurpation, but in a society validated by Rousseau himself. The citizen of today who votes becomes the same that Rousseau defined, and we cannot fail to see how the citizen, of whom Rousseau painted an exacting and passionate picture, becomes in the words of these recent commentators someone who settles for participating in public life by voting on the day that the authorities authorize him to. We should not be surprised to read in a recent magazine article that democracy, as Rousseau saw it, is reserved for a people made of gods, and thus impossible. What of the "true" thought of the philosopher as it is applicable to our modern societies, the one that leads to practice? Jean-Paul Jouary, ex-Marxist and author of *Rousseau, Citizen of the Future*, can thus write in 2012:

> In practice, Rousseau opts for an elective "aristocracy," meaning that rulers are elected not to "represent" and guide the people, but to obey them. The real problem no longer becomes that of forms of government, but that of the population itself, and its civic capabilities. However, many are the obstacles that must be overcome on the way to this collective freedom: citizens, for the most part, have access neither to the concepts necessary to a just juridical structure, nor to the abstract thought required to gain access to the "general will;" they have interiorized the prejudices and customs of existing unjust societies; they are much too eager to also benefit from privileges, and thus from the injustices that surround them, not to fear a just society. In this way, Rousseau's political philosophy, known for its reflections on natural right, on the State and on institutions, in fact leads to an appeal to the average humans' indignation, to their political formation, their education, and to the development of their civic customs. (Jouary 2012: 72)

This is a sleight of hand: Rousseau's citizen was in actuality an "indignant"[1] and today's indignant is thus the best disciple and agent of Rousseau's thought. An elective aristocracy that in other times was referred to as the proletariat's avant-garde, or for the upholders of High Culture, a spiritual elite, will take care of him and show him the true "general will" since he is too stupid to see it for himself. Exit chapter 1 of Book IV of *The Social Contract* in which it is written that "the general will is indestructible," that it remains "constant, unchanging and pure" in each of us. Exit also Robert Derathé who said that no one had ever been more resolutely, more sincerely democratic as Rousseau, "and this at a time when the most liberal effortlessly made the best of 'limited monarchy' or even 'enlightened despotism'" (Derathé 1970: 51). Now in 2012 he is promoted to aristocrat and father of the indignant. There is nothing to make us believe

---

[1] The notion of the indignant came out of Stephane Hessel's 2010 extremely successful book *Indignez-vous!*, which became an inspiration for the Occupy Wall Street movement in the United States.

in progress here, but rather it decries today's scholarship which thus transforms Rousseau into a simplistic and easily digestible slop.

The debate is important, as is the confusion when it comes to the state of nature and the beginning of societies, given that Rousseau's work forms a coherent whole. The moment at which men pass from the state of nature to that of society is the one in which they pass from nature to culture, and to thus cloud the issue incriminates the entirety of Rousseau's thought. Our modern commentators perform shifts in meaning that allows for reading Rousseau's work not as a text that contests modern societies and condemns their subterfuge, but one that justifies them and leads us to believe that we can use Rousseau to justify a reinforcement of laws and of the republican State; not a work that warns individuals against power, but a work that provides them with the civic dimension of obedience and submission.

Rousseau explains quite well in the *Second Discourse* how men passed from the state of nature to that of society, and he even defines that moment as being the best for mankind, the moment of a nascent society in which "although men had come to have less endurance and although natural pity had already undergone some alteration" they maintained a "golden mean between the indolence of the primitive state and the petulant activity of our amour-propre" (*OC* 3: 171 [*CW* 3: 48]). He also describes this moment in the *Essay on the Origin of Language*, a time of pastoral tribes, and of the birth of love, language, and morality. This stage of human societies was superior to the state of nature and beneficial to human beings, and if one must make comparisons, one could liken it to that period when men come together to form the social contract. They too come out on top when they leave the state of nature (despotism) to form a new world. Is that to say we can thus superimpose Rousseau's texts and declare, for example, that the men who subscribe to the social pact are the savages of the first part of *The Discourse on the Origin of Inequality?* That has been said, but it is an absurdity. Is that to say also that Emile, who receives a natural education destined to turn him in some ways into a new man of nature as well as a savage made to inhabit the cities, can here be superimposed onto the natural man of the *Second Discourse*, or onto the man entering into a contract in *The Social Contract?* This has also been said by scholars that have all too easily seen in the treatise on education a predominantly anthropological approach, a description by Rousseau of the passage from nature to culture within man. This is also, in my view, a simplistic and erroneous view, for Emile does not pass from nature to culture, from a primitive state to society. Nowhere in Rousseau's treatises is there a world in which the individual would be asocial – nature – and a world where he would be social – culture – with the education to allow him to pass from one to the other. There is no need to socialize Emile for he is already in society, and more specifically in the society based on the false social contract in which we also exist. It is in this way that Rousseau's book is useful to his contemporaries, and to us today as well since nothing would lead us to believe that the society of the social contract has come to an end.

Emile, the culmination of Rousseau's philosophical thought, can indeed help to understand this move from nature to culture. This text lends a much different meaning to *The Social Contract*, given that it contains in Book V an exposition of its basic principles, though we would be wrong to deem them identical. Numerous commentators have forgotten that the philosopher had firmly declared at the start of his treatise on education that it was impossible to form both a man and a citizen in modern societies, societies in which there was no longer homeland, city-state, nor father and family. A choice had to be made and Rousseau, as for him, decided to make a man. Scholars then look upon the citizen as the perfect form of man and resolve what they believe is a paradox, or yet another contradiction in the work of an author who himself admitted was not free of such contradictions. If they read Rousseau more carefully they would find in this fragment of the *Letter to Christophe de Beaumont* a passage that illuminates Rousseau's position and the meaning he gives to his own thought:

> I penetrated the secret of governments, I revealed it to peoples not so that they might shake off the yoke, which is not possible for them, but so that they might become men again in their slavery, and, enslaved to their masters, they might not also be enslaved to their vices. If they can no longer be Citizens, they can still be wise men. The slave Epictetus was one. Whoever acknowledges only the laws of virtue and those of necessity is no longer enslaved to men. That one alone knows how to be free and good in chains. (*OC* 4: 1019 [*CW* 9: 92])

If there is such an overwhelming tendency to resolve the contradiction raised by Rousseau at the start of *Emile*, it is perhaps also because the notion of citizen has become rather tractable. Rousseau maintained, from the first *Discourse* to *Emile*, that city-states and citizens no longer exist, and that individuals live in a society built on a false social contract. We have no reason to believe that the city-state of the real social contract has arrived, nor that any country today is governed according to the principles defined by the Genevan philosopher. In order to successfully adapt the ideas I have exposed, and to strengthen, thanks to Rousseau, a current modern idea of "citizenship," perhaps one must modernize the notion of the citizen itself. Our scholars are equally invested in this endeavor. The jurist Georges Burdeau declared during the Dijon Colloque of 1962 that "being a citizen means participating": the citizen is a member of the sovereignty as well as an individual that participates in it "to the extent that he identifies with the group"(1962: 223–224). Bruno Bernardi wrote more recently that for Rousseau "being a citizen means being a member of the sovereign" and, noticing the formal and almost tautological nature of this statement, added that it acquires no real meaning unless "one says in what consists the exercise of sovereignty and how the citizen participates in it" (2006: 215). He extends and even repeats, fifty years later, Burdeau's comment, when stating in a recent article that "the more men have the feeling of exercising power in society, the more they are attached to it; conversely, reducing them to passivity is turning them into enemies. Participating in a common power that steers society is the strongest factor that determines social cohesion" (Bernardi 2010: 67). Reframing the question as such could likely provoke thought and action in today's government, for the government must rely on jurists and philosophers to give meaning to their administrative decisions which are so often made on a day to day and ad hoc basis. Yet this reframing offers only a weak, watered-down version of what a citizen is in Rousseau's work. Bernardi certainly does not betray Rousseau's thought, but he does not go beyond immediate proof and he avoids essential questions such as that of knowing for what reason the "citizen" of today participates poorly or not at all in the world that governments and other interested parties offer him. Rousseau had nonetheless provided the ingredients for an answer in his *Social Contract* but, as we say, it is better to avoid questions that will rock the boat. The fact remains that this superficial analysis of the notion of citizen leads to the same results as that of the critics mentioned above, and offers a Rousseau ready for consumption by the users of the twenty-first century, those people in the position to award positions and medals, and whom Rousseau had condemned in his time.

A deeper and more compelling analysis than Bernardi's is Philip Knee's in his book *Penser l'appartenance* [*Thinking Belonging*]. Knee does not want to ignore the contradiction Rousseau brings up in *Emile* and the dangers inherent in "seeking to shape at the same time a man and a citizen by confusing the demands of nature with those of the city-state." He shows how patriotism, citizenship, and belonging are interconnected in Rousseau and asserts that for him "a citizenship without passion is unthinkable:"

> This is why any civic education goes hand in hand with a national education that brings together all of the passions inherent in a love for one's nation. But on the other hand, citizenship does not only come from feelings of belonging. It requires a drive for coherence and clarity so as to create laws and ensure their proper functioning. Once these laws have been formed, if the feeling of patriotism is strong, laws can themselves become the object of spontaneous love. Patriotism can then become enriched by citizenship, intermingling the subjective and the objective. But if patriotism and citizenship can provide their own similar justifications in the public good and thus complement each other, their respective motives – sentimental and rational – remain similarly at stake: on the one hand belonging to a community while participating in its creation by one's own will, and on the other linking one's most intimate feelings to a public and shared reality; in other words, belonging to a reality all the while ensuring that this reality is ours. (Knee 1995: 138)

Rousseau gives a perfect illustration of what a citizen is in the first Book of *Emile*, an illustration that corresponds much better to what Knee admirably expresses than to weak definitions of the citizen as someone who either deliberates or participates. Little attention has, in my view, been paid to those pages in which Rousseau looks back on his century and formulates a few important principles on which to base his pedagogical choices. The examples he gives have been taken to merely be part of the philosophical backdrop of the Enlightenment, referring tritely to a world that any thinker of that time is bound to reference. They appear in a paragraph whose opening lines have the authority and the style of a mathematical axiom on the subject: "Natural man is entirely for himself: He is numerical unity, the absolute whole which is relative only to itself or its kind. Civil man is only a fractional unity dependent on the denominator; his value is determined by his relation to the whole, which is the social body" (*E* 4: 249 [13: 164]). The assertion is quickly followed by its result, which, as it happens, is a social law: "Good social institutions are those that best know how to denature man, to take his absolute existence from him in order to give him a relative one and transport the *I* into the common unity, with the result that each individual believes himself no longer one but part of a unity and no longer feels except within the whole" (*E*, *CW* 13: 164).

The reader recognizes here the ideas of *The Social Contract* and, feeling in familiar territory, pays less attention to the three examples that follow to illustrate these words:

> A Citizen of Rome was neither Caius nor Lucius; he was a Roman. He even loved the country exclusive of himself. Regulus claimed he was a Carthaginian on the grounds that he had become the property of his masters. In his status of foreigner he refused to sit in the Roman Senate; a Carthaginian had to order him to do so. He was indignant that they wanted to save his life. He conquered and returned triumphant to die by torture. This had little relation, it seems to me, to the men we know.
>
> The Lacedaemonian Pedaretus runs for the council of three hundred. He is defeated. He goes home delighted that there were three hundred men worthier than he to be found in Sparta. I take this display to be sincere, and there is reason to believe that it was. Behold the Citizen.
>
> A Spartan woman had five sons in the army and was awaiting news of the battle. A Helot arrives; trembling, she asks him for news. "Your five sons were killed." "Base slave, did I ask you that?" "We won the victory." The mother runs to the temple and gives thanks to the Gods. Behold the Female Citizen. (*E*, *CW* 13: 164)

These three examples merit pause for they offer an image of the citizen, and we know that Rousseau thinks in images more than in ideas.

The first references the Roman general and consul Regulus, defeated by the Carthaginians during the first Punic war. The Carthaginians gave him the option of returning to Rome in order to obtain a cessation of combat from the Senate, but instead he encouraged the Romans to pursue their offense. Upon returning to Carthage as he had promised, he was executed. The second example is that of Paedaretus whose story Rousseau found in Plutarque's *Apophtegmata Laconica:* "Paedaretus. Someone told Paedaretus that his enemies were numerous. 'Good, he said, we will kill more of them, and in this way we will acquire more glory.' Seeing a certain man who was effeminate by nature, but was commended by the citizens for his moderation, he said, 'People should not praise men who are like women nor women who are like men, unless some necessity overtakes the woman.' When he was not chosen as one of the three hundred, which was rated as the highest honor in the State, he went away cheerful and smiling; but when the Ephors called him back, and asked why he was laughing, he said, 'Because I congratulate the State for having three hundred citizens better than myself.'" We should note that Rousseau left out the first two parts to give more force and coherence to his portrait of the citizen. From here on out we can consider the citizen to be a man of honor, respectful of both his word and of collective decisions, who shows pride and courage, and who is willing to go so far as to sacrifice himself. He lives in another plane and all of these sentiments are greatly respected even if they are seldom practiced. The final example Rousseau gives is, however, more difficult to accept for the reader. It is an example of Rousseau's technique that consists in brutalizing the reader in order to destabilize him and make him think. Some would say that this example is incongruous, but I believe on the contrary that it is essential and fundamental – in the same way as the previous examples in fact – to our understanding of what Rousseau develops in *Emile*. Rousseau is placing, in these ancient tales belonging to a lost world, the principles that define his current choices and positions. These example function much like the *Second Discourse*, which also describes a world that no longer exists but is nevertheless fundamental for understanding Rousseau's philosophical and political work. Avoiding taking them into consideration, as has been done until now, allows for the shifts in interpretation that I mentioned above, slippages that somehow allow Rousseau's citizen to coincide with the citizen created by today's liberal societies.

This third example is indeed difficult to tolerate, and the scholars who mention it sometimes speak of the inhuman nature of this mother who thinks above all about the victory of her people, which she puts before the death of her own sons. Rousseau nevertheless adds: she is a citizen! This last image allows us to define the two previous ones and understand that the citizen is not only this being full of noble sentiments, but above all the man or woman in which the nation lives. What these three figures represent are neither idle remarks nor moral lessons, even less an absurd kind of inhumanity; they show the general will of a nation that inhabits them and in which they have their place. This general will lives in them because the public being and the individual being coincide. It is the same coincidence that Rousseau attempts to methodically recreate in *The Social Contract*, but it no longer existed in the eighteenth century and even less today. Antiquity, Sparta and Rome produced citizens, but the world of the false social contract, of inequality, luxury, profit, and consumerism produces only lures and slaves, as well as all of those talking heads busy fooling others and themselves. The world is rather empty since the Romans and the passion for the City-state, as is noted by Knee, has disappeared.

Emile can therefore not be a citizen and his education is not geared towards citizenship, as those notions belong to a world as irreversibly lost as that of the dinosaurs.

Emile is educated for society. He has spent his childhood and adolescence in a village, in the countryside, not exactly outside of the world, but in a world adapted to his dimensions, as for any child or adolescent. His relationships were with the other children with whom he played, the adults of his neighborhood whom he saw in passing, his tutor, and the servants who took care of him. At times, the outside world came to him in the form of a street entertainer, but he did not leave the narrow sphere of this universe. Education does not consist, for Rousseau, in a learned sociability that would lead to an education on citizenship. This kind of interpretation is an echo of current scholarly, governmental, and social discourses from which it borrows its terms, rather than an echo of Rousseau himself who uses them nowhere in his *Emile*. The young student is not a being who must be socialized – in other words normalized[2] – in Rousseau's mind for he is part of society from the first day of his life. He must, however, be educated into society, understand it and discover it alongside his tutor, in the same way that he has understood the world of things and of necessities. From Book IV on, Rousseau describes a new direction for education, complementary to the former, and in many stages that sometimes resembles an initiation into a world whose meaning and codes the grown child must know.

---

[2] Rousseau constantly insists in *Emile* on what separates his student from other students raised according to traditional methods. It is out of the question for Rousseau to format Emile in order to shape him for integration into the world – quite on the contrary. What is important in Emile's education is that his judgment will be more just and lucid than that of his peers, who are used to obedience and not used to thinking, in response to the demands of political and economic systems. Emile is never the docile student who becomes the good citizen of societies of the false contract.

The first stage of this passage to adulthood, and of the encounter with others that comes from it, is given by the profession of faith of the Savoyard vicar. Though it is addressed to another young man and not to Emile, the discourse is Rousseau's opportunity to explain the place that the individual occupies in the cosmos. It is an opening into a world that is vaster and less limited by childish preoccupations, or by the present moment. It is a preparation to what will follow, and this sequel in fact requires caution and explanations between the young man and his master, between Rousseau and his reader. The renewal of the pact that unites Emile and the governor is necessary to the quest that is about to come, and Rousseau minutely describes the quest's complexities and stakes (*E, CW* 13: 493). It is a serious and important moment that shows the boundary between two universes: the one where we were dealing with a child and now we are dealing with a man; it is the one where it is important to "[get] a good grasp of social practices" (*E* 497). The education that Emile has received will guarantee future conduct. The tutor can ask without worry if there is a young man "on the entire earth who is better armed than Emile against everything that can attack his moral, his sentiments, or his principles[.] Whether there is one better prepared to resist the torrent" (*E* 501).

The encounter with society is presented in the form of a voyage. One leaves the protected world of childhood and village life to go to other places, and Books IV and V will narrate Emile's progress from one place to the next: from salons of Paris in which he is introduced, to the whorehouses where his tutor accompanies him. Emile discovers the world of his social caste and analyzes its state, its mediocrity. Book IV ends on his departure from the capital, in search of a more essential adventure: the search for the woman who will form, with Emile, the perfect couple. I have said elsewhere how Rousseau takes up, in Book V, the tone of chivalry novels from the Middle Ages, to show how the young man is initiated in an almost magical way to his lady.[3] I will not dwell on it here, even if each step of his love quest fits in with the education to society that I focus on here. Passing through various circles such as the forest, the village and Sophie's house to meet her in her garden, has symbolic value in the same way as does rain, getting lost, or the meal during which Emile hears the voice of the woman he already likes, recognizing her. Society is as present in this love story and often, it comes between the two lovers with its needs, its conventions, and the pain it brings about.

Each of the two young people must welcome the other and single-handedly be the society in which the other evolves. Emile must understand that he cannot move in with Sophie without compromising her; Sophie must accept that he

---

[3] On this, see T. L'Aminot (1997: 113–139).

works as a carpenter and is not free to devote to her the time she wishes. More serious problems are brought up, such as the inequalities between social states. Emile must accept that Sophie does not want to depend on him; he must accept her coquetry and take her pride into consideration much like she must accept not to model him only according to her desires. Society appears with increasing influence in the text, and always in the form of an obstacle to be overcome. The wounded peasant that Emile and his tutor meet one night while going to Sophie's is a nice example. He creates anxiety in the young girl who is waiting for them and does not see them coming. He forces her to take the exterior world into consideration. All of these novelistic/quixotic elements are not placed into the narrative out of pure fancy: they have as much philosophical worth as the discourses on the love of travel that are inserted at very precise moments and are woven into Rousseau's demonstration, which remains essentially philosophical.

The departure for foreign lands that leads to an exposition of the theses in *The Social Contract* is the most important initiatory stage. Up to this point, each obstacle has been surmounted. Rousseau takes care to stage the kisses and embraces that have shown the young couple coming closer together, initiated one to the other, one through the other. But neither of them, as rich in personality and as perfectly educated as they may be, can claim to replace society. Chrétien de Troyes had dealt with this idea in *Erec and Enide*. The young man must tour around Europe, (and probably the Mediterranean Basin and the Middle East), according to custom. Rousseau takes the opportunity to call up his theoretical conception of the political, and in so doing he points to a particular way in which to read and use *The Social Contract*. Emile receives the book as though it were a key permitting him to appreciate and gage the various types of governments and societies he will encounter. He can understand their functioning and thus see their faults and their consequences according to the criteria that Rousseau's theory offers. The text appears here in an abridged form in contrast to the book that the philosopher was publishing at the same time as *Emile*, and Yves Vargas is surprised that Rousseau did not choose to include it into his narration in its totality. He further notes the differences between the two and sees a "conservative orientation" from *The Social Contract* to *Emile* (Vargas 1995: 264).[4] This is where the interweaving of the novel and the theoretical treatise acquires meaning. Rousseau presents a version of the *Contract* adapted to the character he has created. Emile does not, indeed, need the last chapters of the text that address methods

---

4 For more on the difference between the two texts, see Vargas's excellent analysis (1995: 25 – 265).

of slowing down the decadence of the Republic (*la Cité*), or methods of maintaining social cohesion, such as the chapter on civic religion. No need for the latter since there is no Republic and he will not be a leader: the Savoyard Vicar's profession of faith is enough. Emile furthermore does not need those parts from *The Social Contract* that deal with the right to revolt or with possible revisions of the social pact. All of the differences between the two texts that Y. Vargas has correctly pointed to, and to which I refer the reader, become meaningful if one takes into consideration the character of Emile as envisioned by Rousseau. He needs to understand how states and societies function, not to oppose or overthrow them, but to find the one that will allow him to lead a peaceful and rustic life. Rousseau's additions in this last book also have meaning, as they show that man lives in a situation governed by rights with respect to his co-citizens, but not with respect to other populations. They confirm that *Emile* does not position itself as participating in a philosophical debate about rights, but rather as pertaining to its use in the context of everyday life, of a given situation of which Emile will here give an example. Rousseau behaves with his character much in the same way he behaved with the Corsican and the Polish who came to ask for a constitution for their people. The version of *The Social Contract* contained in *Emile* is thus perfectly adapted to Rousseau's intentions, to the novel's intrigue and therefore is wanted by its author. Novel and philosophy are here perfectly complementary.

The Social Contract is thus even less the scathing revolutionary attack that it has been denounced as being by so many commentators, nor is it a user's guide that would permit the governments that apply it to better dominate men and force them to be free. It is a treatise on the functioning of government, a clear explanation of legitimate power and the missteps that must inevitably happen, since there is for Rousseau no perfect society, no ideal State. Even the Republic of *The Social Contract* is destined to decadence and perversion: the time when public good and individual good coexist is always limited, and the passionate bond between sovereign and subject always ends up breaking. Rousseau is constantly weary of the ascendency that any State can have over the individual: social ties can be negative and often alienating.[5]

Thus Emile is not destined to be the citizen of a perfect Republic, nor even of an imperfect one. The Republic exists no more in Book V than it did in Book I. He is neither a Roman nor a Spartan, but only a decadent created for a decadent society.[6] But does this reading given to us in Book V exclude all other readings?

---

5 See T. L'Aminot (2013: 127–144).
6 On this point, see T. L'Aminot (2006: 41–47).

Perhaps not, and in this way the revolutions begotten by *The Social Contract* constitute the life of the work itself, and the study of their reception enriches the teaching and the understanding of Rousseau's text.[7] Neglecting them, as philosophers, teachers, and scholars often do in order to keep to Rousseau's text alone, is also the sign of criticism's blindness and limits. Furthermore, the application of the *Social Contract* that Rousseau gave in his *Constitution Project for Corsica* and his *Considerations on the Government of Poland*, are also examples of readings. With *Emile*, nonetheless, Rousseau gives the model that is the most generally adapted to societies built on a false contract, such as the ones we are in now.

Having returned from their journey, Emile and the tutor consider the future and the place they will hold among men. The latter had already established the context for their research before their departure:

> [...] if there is any legitimate and sure means of subsisting without intrigue, without involvements, and without dependence, it is to live by cultivating one's own land with the labor of one's own hands. But where is the State where a man can say to himself, 'The land I tread is mine'? Before choosing this happy land, be well assured that you will find there the peace you seek. Be careful that a violent government, a persecuting religion, or perverse morals do not come to disturb you there. Shelter yourself from boundless taxes that would devour the fruit of your efforts and from endless litigation that would consume your estate. Arrange it so that, in living justly, you do not have to pay court to Administrators, their deputies, judges, priests, powerful neighbors, and rascals of every kind, who are always ready to torment you if you neglect them. Above all, shelter yourself from vexation by the noble and the rich. (*E, CW* 13: 648)

The knowledge of social mechanisms and other nations was merely destined to help Emile find shelter, and be fully aware of the advantages and dangers of living in such or such a country. Is there room for citizenship at this stage? It is what numerous commentators proclaim with force, forgetting here the choice between the man and the citizen formulated by Rousseau in Book I. Rousseau does not avoid the question, and the tutor mentions it in his discussion with the young man:

> If I were speaking to you of the duties of the Citizen, you would perhaps ask me where the fatherland is, and you would believe you had confounded me. But you would be mistaken,

---

[7] Wang Xiaoling's book *Rousseau in China* in this regard is exemplary. His analysis of *The Social Contract* by way of the discourses of Chinese revolutionary intellectuals at the beginning of the twentieth century, underscores the importance of political concepts in a much more profound way than the analyses of so many current philosophers. The passion that Rousseau inspired in China, much like he had done during the French Revolution, breathed new life into the Citizen.

dear Emile, for he who does not have a fatherland at least has a country. In any event, he has lived tranquilly under a government and the simulacra of laws. What difference does it make that the social contract has not been observed, if individual interest protected him as the general will would have done, if public violence guaranteed him against individual violence, if the evil he saw done made him love what is good, and if our institutions themselves have made him know and hate their own iniquities? O Emile, where is the good man who owes nothing to his country? Whatever country it is, he owes it what is most precious to man – the morality of his actions and the love of virtue. (*E*, *CW* 13: 667)

It is with "the good man" that the discourse ends, and not with the Citizen. Rousseau also exposes here the same doubts as to the existence of the latter as before. Emile was not educated for sociability, but for humanity according to the wish formulated by Rousseau: "Men, be human, it is your first duty; be human for all states, for all ages, for anything that is not foreign to man." Rousseau, who definitely does not master the art of equivocating the way today's philosophers do, also places these remarks in the mouth of the tutor. In the very last pages of his book, he evokes the happiness that awaits the young couple:

It seems to be already reborn around Sophie's dwelling. You will do no more than complete together what her worthy parents have begun. But, dear Emile, do not let so sweet a life make you regard painful duties with disgust, if such duties are ever imposed on you. Remember that the Romans went from the plow to the Consulate. If the Prince or the State calls you to the service of the fatherland, leave everything to go to fulfill the honorable function of Citizen in the post assigned to you. If this function is onerous to you, there is a decent and sure means to free yourself from it – to fulfill it with enough integrity so that it will not be left to you for long. Besides, you need have little fear of being burdened with such a responsibility. As long as there are men who belong to the present age, you are not the man who will be sought out to serve the State. (*E*, *CW* 13: 668–669)

The tutor is indeed thinking here about the possibility of a social and moral change (even more than a political one), but if he does raise the hope that the citizen may be reborn, the end of his discourse undoes it. Rousseau stays absolutely pessimistic on that point. Eighteenth-century society, the one of the false contract, will not see the rebirth of the citizen, nor even of the taste for the public good. In *Confessions*, Rousseau explains that at the time that he was writing *Emile*, in 1759, her learns of M. de Silhouette's misfortune. He writes a letter to the controller general of finances praising his administration and his rigor with the financiers, for which he was quickly thanked.[8]

We can now appreciate the true value of the interpretation Ghislain Waterlot subjects this passage to, an interpretation that confirms what I have said at the

---

[8] Rousseau, *Confessions* (*OC* 1: 531–532 [*CW* 5: 445]).

beginning of this essay, that is to say that critics want to make us believe that Rousseau's citizen and the citizen of our modern societies are one and the same. Waterlot has the further merit of citing the same excerpt that I used regarding the Spartan woman, but to then add: "What Rousseau meant to say, in the beginning of *Emile*, is that there is henceforth no citizenship possible on the model of Antiquity, that men can no longer be galvanized to that degree by their political communities, for the true religion is already much too diffuse" (2004: 93). Nothing, however, alludes to religion in the excerpt, and this interpretation is more Waterlot's than that of Rousseau, who eliminates the possibility of a civic education. On the contrary, Waterlot's manipulation here gives him the opportunity to reign Rousseau back onto the side of the citizen and to say that "Emile's work is cut out for him:"

> One must show how a particular education, the one that Emile's tutor represents, can respect natural man and allow him to naturally and progressively (meaning at the end of his youth) reach the understanding of a reasoned natural law that leaves him fit to be integrated, as man and as citizen, in the human societies already constituted, without being a depraved education. For even though the country where he lives is but a shadow of a republic, "he who does not have a fatherland at least has a country. In any event, he has lived tranquilly under a government and the simulacra of laws. [...]. Where is the good man who owes nothing to his country? [...] If the Prince or the State calls you to the service of the fatherland, leave everything to go to fulfill the honorable function of Citizen in the post assigned to you." (Waterlot 93)

The reader can appreciate how the commentator silences Rousseau by interrupting him in the very spot that upsets this nice fabrication of the citizen, since the Genevan philosopher continues after this remark: "If this function is onerous to you, there is a decent and sure means to free yourself from it – to fulfill it with enough integrity so that it will not be left to you for long. Besides, you need have little fear of being burdened with such a responsibility. As long as there are men who belong to the present age, you are not the man who will be sought out to serve the State." Waterlot also cuts a passage in which Rousseau says that it is of no matter that "the social contract was not observed," as though it were necessary to flatten Rousseau's thought to ensure that it corresponds to present-day constructions.

Rousseau does not believe in the possibility of the citizen, but he still believes in the possibility of the good man. D. H. Lawrence, the author of *Lady Chatterley's Lover*, had, however, published a study on the subject that shows that this good man, "born out of the tortuous folds of the brains of men like Rousseau or Diderot, out of the very site of their emotions," has himself become a robot in the twentieth century. The good man succeeds in this robotic *tour de force* that consists in isolating himself entirely from the great passions. He substitutes the passion for life with reasonable social virtues. Be honest in your material affairs, be good to the poor, experience "sentiments" for your peers and for nature. *Nature, yes, but with wealth.* There is nothing to venerate in it. Any veneration is out of place. But it is ok to "feel." To experience these "sentiments" in the appropriate way, it is of course important to be "free," that nobody comes to hinder your path. And to be "free," one must be an enemy to no-one, one must be "good." And when we are all "good" and "free," we will experience all of the best "sentiments" towards everything (Lawrence 2004: 285).

The good man, along with the citizen, are the right people to incarnate the figures that today's conformism apparently needs. Is this the ideal to which Rousseau aspired, or is this the construct given to us by some Rousseau criticism, and more generally by dominant liberal and mercantile ideology? Rousseau has become in this way a very politically correct thinker whose claws have all been filed down in order to adapt him to current philosophical consumption. He purrs and exudes boredom, and the philosopher Axel Honneth can henceforth bring in his concept of recognition and thus join the philosophical concert in vogue, join the collective submission.

For me, it is hardly important that Rousseau did not choose the path of the citizen. Quite to the contrary, since the concept allows for any manipulation and serves to crush the individual in contemporary societies. What pleases me in Emile is his lucidity, for if he is not a citizen, Emile is a lucid man. His education taught him to observe and make just judgments, and it is useful for him at the stage where he will choose the country and the regime under which he will live. He does not participate; he is not a citizen; he resembles the Anarch as represented by Ernst Jünger in his novel *Eumeswil:* a man who lives in alienating and oppressive societies who shelters himself as much as possible and who stays outside of the trends that steer the herd. He remains skeptical as to the enthusiasm generated by societies and rulers, whether they be civil or democratic, well-meaning, or hostile to any social group.[9] He is "determined to go along with nothing, ultimately taking nothing seriously – at least not nihilistically, but rather as a border guard in no man's land, who sharpens his eyes and ears between tides" (Jünger 1998: 119).[10]

---

[9] See T. L'Aminot (2010).

[10] The position of the Anarch is more complex than it might seem. *Eumeswil*'s narrator declares that though he may be convinced of the imperfection and the vanity of any effort, in a world "in which all great ideas have been eroded by repetition," and where they would no longer motivate anyone to lift a finger, he is not a conservative in the way Chateaubriand is. If he considers with humor his professorial palavers "in front of an audience that now only bites at the most trivial

The end of *Emile* that Rousseau left us and that we know under the title of *Émile et Sophie, ou les Solitaires* [*Emile and Sophie; or the Solitaries*], is indeed unfinished, but the fragments that extend the two known letters confirm the summary left by Bernardin de Saint-Pierre. *Emile et Sophie* confirms that Emile is an Anarch, since after having lost Sophie and his children, he already had these words: "I am alone, I have lost everything, but I have myself left, and despair has not annihilated me" (E, *CW* 13: 685). Also, when he finds himself captured by the Barbarians and reduced to slavery, he incites a passive rebellion against the warden who mistreats them (him and his fellow captives). Raymond Trousson correctly writes:

> It is not a revolutionary action: always recognizing the law of necessity, he challenges neither the principle of slavery, nor the authority of the master, but only the barbarism of the treatment that threatens to deprive the master of his capital. In a society of slaves such as *The Discourse on the Origins of Inequality*, only the pact of constraint exists, not the pact of association that would create a real social contract. Emile thus speaks to the master in the language of his interest. Recognizing his capacities, the master names Emile warden. Word of his merit reaches Dey, the severe but just sovereign for whom Emile becomes councilor and right-hand man. (Trousson 293)

Emile does not become any more of a powerful man in Algiers than he was a citizen or a person of note after having been married. He leaves Africa and finds in the island of Lampedusa a young Spanish woman with whom he isolates himself away from men and renews his past adventures. He even becomes bigamous when Sophie finds him and lives with the young couple. Emile is thus in some way an Anarch before its time, made to live in the imperfect and more or less despotic societies of his time. He is certainly not the disciplined and well-educated citizen for the city-State of *The Social Contract* that numerous Rousseau scholars still imagine.

Translated by Karen Santos Da Silva

---

baits of passing days," he stays serious in appearance: "Thus I take my duties seriously within an overall context that I reject for its mediocrity. The important thing is that my rejection actually refers to the totality and does not take up within it a stance that can be defined as conservative, reactionary, liberal, ironic or in any way social. One should avoid changing one's work shift in the ever-increasing corvée of the civil war./ On this premise, I can, to be sure, take seriously what I do here. I know that the subsoil moves, perhaps like a landslide or an avalanche – and that is precisely why relationships remain undisturbed in their details. I lie aslant on a slanting plane. The distances between people do not change. I actually see them more sharply against the deceptive background. Their standing so close to the abyss also arouses my sympathy" (Jünger 1998: 137–138).

Works Cited

"Lire le Contrat social." *Le Nouvel Observateur*. Special issue: *Rousseau, le génie de la modernité* 76 (juillet–août 2010).
Derathé, Robert. *Jean-Jacques Rousseau et la science politique de son temps*. Paris: Vrin, 1979.
Bernardi, Bruno. *La Fabrique des concepts: recherche sur l'invention conceptuelle chez Rousseau*. Paris: Honoré Champion, 2006.
Burdeau, George. "Le citoyen selon Rousseau." *Etudes sur* Le Contrat social *de Jean-Jacques Rousseau. Actes des journées organisées à Dijon pour la commémoration du 200ᵉ anniversaire du Contrat social*. Paris: Les Belles Lettres, 1964.
Goldschmidt, Victor. *Anthropologie et politique: les principes du système de Rousseau*. Paris: J. Vrin, 1974.
Jouary, J. P. "*Contrat social* et démocratie." *Le Point Références: Les Textes Fondamentaux*. Paris. *Voltaire contre Rousseau* (mai-juin 2012).
Jünger, Ernst. *Eumeswil*. Paris: Folio, 1998.
Knee, Philippe. *Penser l'appartenance: enjeux des Lumières en France*. Montréal: Presses de l'Université du Québec, 1995.
L'Aminot Tanguy. "La fée et l'initiatrice: Sophie." *Études J.-J. Rousseau* 9 (1997): 113–139.
L'Aminot Tanguy. "Rousseau contre l'État." *Réfractions* 30 (Spring 2013): 127–144.
L'Aminot Tanguy. "Émile, un décadent au sein de la décadence." *Études sur le XVIIIᵉ siècle* 34 (2006): 41–47.
L'Aminot Tanguy. "Max Stirner et Rousseau dans *Eumeswil* de Ernst Jünger." *Rousseau et l'Allemagne à l'époque contemporaine: de Cassirer à Jünger et Hentig: Actes du colloque international de l'Université de Greifswald, 23–25 Avril 2009*. Eds. Reinhard Bach, T. L'Aminot and Catherine Labro. Montmorency: Société internationale des amis du Musée J.-J. Rousseau, 2010.
Lawrence, D. H. *De la rébellion à la réaction*. Trans. Béatrice Dunner. Monaco: Éditions du Rocher, 2004.
Morin, Edgar. *Mes philosophes*. Meaux: Germina, 2011.
Rousseau, Jean-Jacques. *Œuvres complètes*. Gen. Eds. Bernard Gagnebin and Marcel Raymond. 5 vols. Paris: Gallimard, "Bibliothèque de la Pléiade," 1959–1995.
Rousseau, Jean-Jacques. *The Collected Writings of Rousseau*. Gen. Eds. Roger D. Masters and Christopher Kelly. 13 vols. Hanover: UP of New England, 1990–2010.
Rousseau, Jean-Jacques. *Emile or On Education*. Trans. & Ed. Christopher Kelly and Allan Bloom. *Collected Writings*, vol. 13. 2010.
Trousson, Raymond. "Emile et Sophie, ou les solitaires." *Dictionnaire de Jean-Jacques Rousseau*. Eds. Raymond Trousson and Frédéric Eigeldinger. Paris: Champion, 1996.
Vargas, Yves. *Introduction à l'Émile de Rousseau*. Paris: PUF, 1995.
Waterlot, Ghislain. *Rousseau: Religion et politique*. Paris: PUF, 2004.

Contributors

Paul Audi graduated from the École Normale Supérieure (Paris, France) and is Doctor and Professor of Philosophy. He is the author of about fifteen books on the relation between ethics and aesthetics, including *L'Empire de la compassion* (Paris, 2011). He dealt with the political philosophy of Jean-Jacques Rousseau in his two books, *Rousseau, une philosophie de l'âme* (Paris, 2008) and *De la véritable philosophie, Rousseau au commencement* (Paris, 1995).

Simon Critchley is Hans Jonas Professor at the New School for Social Research. His books include *Very Little... Almost Nothing*, *Infinitely Demanding*, *The Book of Dead Philosophers*, *The Faith of the Faithless*, *The Mattering of Matter, Documents from the Archive of the International Necronautical Society* (with Tom McCarthy) and *Stay, Illusion! The Hamlet Doctrine* (with Jamieson Webster). An experimental new work, *Memory Theatre*, and a book called *Bowie* were both published in 2014 and a book on suicide is forthcoming. He is moderator of "The Stone," a philosophy column in The New York Times, to which he is a frequent contributor.

Anne Deneys-Tunney is Professor of French at New York University. Her specialty is the Enlightenment and its relation to contemporary literature and philosophy. Her latest publications include *Un Autre Jean-Jacques Rousseau : le paradoxe de la technique* (Paris, 2010) and the edited volume *Philippe Sollers ou l'impatience de la pensée* (Paris, 2011).

Pierre Guenancia is Professor of History of modern philosophy at University of Burgundy (Dijon, France). He has published various books and articles on Descartes, Pascal, and also on representation, identity and cosmopolitanism.

Philip Knee is Professor of Philosophy at Université Laval, Québec. His recent publications include *L'expérience de la perte autour du moment 1800* (Oxford, 2014), and an edited collection of essays, *Rousseau et le romantisme* (Montmorency, 2011).

Tanguy L'Aminot is an honorary research fellow at the Centre National de la Recherche Scientifique, France. A specialist of the reception of Rousseau in the twentieth century, he serves as co-editor, with Catherine Labro, of the periodical *Rousseau Studies*; he published the *Bibliographie mondiale des écrits sur J.-J. Rousseau, XVIIIe–XXIe siècles*.

Stéphane Lojkine is Professor of French Literature at the Université Aix-Marseille, France, and Director of the Interdisciplinary Center for Studies in Literature in Aix-Marseille, where he leads the Utpictura18 program and database for text and image research. In 2013, he organized the exhibition Le Goût de Diderot in Montpellier, France, and Lausanne, Switzerland.

Christophe Martin is Professor of eighteenth-century French literature at Université Paris-Sorbonne. His areas of expertise include the works of Fontenelle, Marivaux, Montesquieu, Prévost, Diderot, Rousseau, the eighteenth-century French novel, and the relations between literature, philosophy, anthropology and pedagogy in the eighteenth century.

Mira Morgenstern is Full Professor of Political Science at the City College of New York. She is the author of *Rousseau and the Politics of Ambiguity: Self, Culture, and Society* (1996). Her recent book, *Conceiving a Nation: The Development of Political Discourse in the Hebrew Bible* (2009), discusses the role of biblical texts in the canon of political theory. She is currently working on a study of Rousseau's writings on the Bible.

Lucien Nouis is Associate Professor of French at New York University, where he teaches courses on eighteenth-century literature and philosophy. He is the author of *De l'infini des bibliothèques au livre unique: l'archive épurée au XVIIIe siècle* (Paris, 2013).

Pasquale Pasquino is Global Distinguished Professor in Politics at New York University. He published notably on political and constitutional history and theory; his current research project concerns the role of constitutional/supreme courts in stable democracies.

Karen Santos Da Silva is a Lecturer of French at Barnard College. She has published articles on the intersection between moral writings and the novel in the late seventeenth to early eighteenth centuries, and is currently working on a manuscript focusing on the works of Marie-Jeanne Riccoboni.

Masano Yamashita is Assistant Professor of French at the University of Colorado, Boulder. She has published articles on Rousseau and affect, rhetoric and democracy in the French Enlightenment and eighteenth-century materialist theater criticism.

Yves Charles Zarka is Professor at the Sorbonne, Université Paris Descartes, where he holds the Chair in political philosophy. He is the director of the journal *Cités* (PUF), and at Paris Descartes University he directs the PHILéPOL (Philosophy, Epistemology and Politics) team whose research deals with the "emerging world," i.e. the major mutations taking place in the contemporary world.

Index

Adorno, Theodor 62 f.
Althusser, Louis 112, 180
Animal 1, 4 f., 12, 24, 34, 48, 54, 60 f., 67–69, 73, 121, 147
Anti-Enlightenment 40
Aquinas, Thomas 45
Aristotle 48
Aron, Raymond 13
Artificial man 116
Artificial soul 116
Association 16, 58 f., 102, 111, 115–117, 143, 179, 195
Atheist fanaticism 30
Audi, Paul 85
Augustine 29
Authentic life 128
Authentic savage man 126
Authoritarianism 102
Authority 27–29, 33–39, 41 f., 85, 91, 111, 139, 142 f., 149, 185, 195
Authority of nature 30, 32, 35, 37 f., 42

Babbitt, Irving 69
Bacon, Francis 153
Bad citizen 130
Bearer of evil 28
Belonging 37, 42, 184
Berchtold, Jacques 154
Bergson, Henri 12
Bernardi, Bruno 183 f., 195
Biological science 3, 179
Blumenberg, Hans 171
Bodin, Jean 105, 139
Bonald, Louis Gabriel (de) 42
Borges, Jorge Luis 169
Bréhier, Émile 31
Bronner, Stephen Eric 63
Brown, Richard H. 134
Buffon 74
Burdeau, Georges 183 f.
Burlamaqui, Jean-Jacques 138, 141 f.

Caillois, Roger 23
Cajetanus, Thomas 45

Carondolet, Abbé de 91
Catechism of the citizen 111, 148
Categorization 122, 129 f., 133 f.
Celestial voice 34
Chateaubriand, François-René 40, 194
Christian tradition 29, 153
City-state 180, 183 f., 187, 195
Civil man 27, 46 f., 185
Civil religion 38, 111 f., 116 f., 147 f.
Clark, Rebecca 69
Classification 129, 135
Claudel, Paul 88
Collective life 16, 29
Collective will 30, 36
Collegiality 103
Commitment 20, 75, 130
Common good 37, 114
Common power 184
Common self 39
Commonwealth 116, 140
Communism 102
Complexity of language 120
Condition of possibility 20, 117
Conscience 30–36, 40, 42, 96, 115, 176
Consent 13, 15 f., 18 f., 27, 33, 36, 39–41, 141 f.
Constant, Benjamin 14, 20, 59, 72, 133, 135, 146, 150, 172, 181
Constituent Power 103, 107
Contradiction 58, 112, 120, 128 f., 145, 159, 168, 171, 174 f., 183 f.
Corrupted society 40
Counter-Enlightenment 42 f.
Critchley, Simon 111
Curtius, Ernest Robert 170
Customs 5, 33 f., 38, 160, 181

Daily life 71, 79, 134
d'Alembert, Jean-Baptiste le Rond 3, 37, 58, 135, 153, 155
Damien, Robert 176
Davy, Georges 16, 20
Death 3, 12, 27, 32, 54, 77, 127, 146 f., 180, 186

Index

Dehumanization 125
Delegated power 105 f.
Deleuze, Gilles 70
Delon, Michel 167
Deneys-Tunney, Anne 1, 57, 62, 112
Dependence 29, 39 f., 59, 62, 74, 111, 149, 191
Derathé, Robert 45, 101, 148, 180 f.
Derrida, Jacques 2, 6 f., 11, 20, 115, 156, 162, 168
Descartes, René 13, 22, 30 f., 74, 153
Desire 2, 29, 34, 37, 39, 46 f., 59, 76, 86–98, 123–125, 132 f., 157, 189
Despotic regime 102
Dictator 103, 105–108, 128
Dictatorial magistracy 103
Diderot, Denis 31, 49, 58, 67 f., 76, 80, 114, 154, 171–173, 175 f., 193
Disaster 2, 28
Dissimulation 30
Dissolution of the governmental pact 179
Divine instinct 30, 34, 43
Divine order 30, 36, 74
Divine will 29, 42, 114
Doctrine of emergency 106
Durkheim, Emile 11
Dynamics 75

Eidos 113
Emanation 87
Emergency power 107
Emergency situation 102
Enchanted world 30
Engagement 122, 132 f., 135, 149
Enjoyment 74, 87, 89, 95–97, 99
Enlightened despotism 181
Enlightenment 2 f., 14, 27, 29 f., 33 f., 36, 38, 42, 45, 57, 59, 62 f., 67, 69, 80, 96, 119, 145, 171 f., 185
Enlightenment ideal 41
Envy 28
Equal individuals 104
Essence of humanity 132
Estrangement 132
Ethical 39, 57, 62, 64, 69 f., 88, 90, 94
Ethical freedom 85

Evil 28 f., 32, 77, 115 f., 126, 128, 148, 155, 170 f., 175, 192
Evolution of desires 121
Executive power 105
Existence 4, 19, 28, 31, 39, 69–71, 76 f., 91–95, 111, 120–122, 126, 128, 130–133, 139, 148, 185, 192
Extraordinary events 102

Faith 25, 35, 45, 111, 148, 188, 190
Family 11, 15, 54, 71, 79, 127 f., 183
Fanaticism 35, 114, 116
Fellow creatures 121 f.
Fiction 116 f., 158, 167
Fictional Force 117
Fictive being 126
Foresight 124
Forms of government 140, 181
Foucault, Michel 58 f.
Franquières (de) 34, 86
Free association 117
Free will 122 f.
Freedom 2, 5, 29, 52–55, 57–59, 62, 64, 68, 74 f., 85, 90 f., 115, 119, 122, 134 f., 181
French Enlightenment 27
Freud, Sigmund 11, 79
Friedrich, Carl Joachim 106

General will 18, 37 f., 111, 114–117, 131–133, 142–146, 149, 181, 187, 192
Generality 23, 33, 93, 144 f., 150
Gildin, Hilail 133
Ginsborg, Paul 103
God being 29
Goldschmidt, Victor 45, 179 f.
Good 4, 14, 28, 30–34, 37–40, 54, 70, 77 f., 85, 91, 101, 103, 114 f., 128, 143, 145, 147 f., 155, 159–163, 168 f., 172, 174–176, 183–188, 190, 192, 194
Good man 192–194
Gougeaud-Arnaudeau, Simone 163
Gourevitch, Victor 112 f.
Grosperrin, Jean-Philippe 163
Grosrichard, Alain 161, 163
Grotius, Hugo 138 f.

Index

Guattari, Felix 70
Guenancia, Pierre 11

Habermas, Jürgen 58, 117
Hadot, Pierre 153f., 158, 176
Halbwachs, Maurice 180
Happiness 21, 27, 32, 37, 39, 52, 59, 70, 74, 76, 87f., 93, 96, 99, 115, 123f., 126f., 131, 141, 148, 160, 167, 170, 192
Harmony 35, 59, 70, 79, 115, 162, 179
Hegel 19, 63, 135
Heidegger, Martin 57
Helvétius 27, 31
Heraclitus 153, 164
Hobbes, Thomas 13, 24, 46, 113f., 116f., 123f., 138–141, 146, 148f., 180
Holy concupiscence 32
Homeland 55, 183
Honneth, Axel 194
Horkeimer, Max 62
Huet, Marie-Hélène 79f.
Hulliung, Mark 27
Human choice 135
Human creativity 133
Human developments 129
Human race 114, 172
Human recognition 122
Human uniduality 179
Human will 5, 85, 138
Humanity 5, 14, 18, 20f., 29, 42, 49, 60, 70, 72, 97f., 115–117, 122f., 128, 135, 149, 162, 171, 192
Humankind 114f.
Hume, David 117
Husserl, Edmund 85
Huts 124, 127

Ideal Polis 129 Ideal polity 128, 131, 133
Ignorance 22, 42, 59, 71, 102
Imaginary 37–40, 48, 52, 74, 76, 79, 155
Imaginary politics 40
Imaginary projection 39
Imperfect justice 40
Independent man 114
Indignant 175, 181, 185
Individual autonomy 42
Individual differences 121

Individual morality 30
Individual Power 124
Individualism 43, 113
Inequality 1f., 4, 6, 12f., 18, 20f., 28, 40, 59f., 68, 70, 72, 80, 112f., 116, 121–123, 125f., 128, 174, 179f., 182, 187, 195
Inflexibility of law 105
Inner delectation 31
Inner voice 30, 35, 115
Institutional 36, 103–106
Intellectual 33, 58, 71, 104, 122f., 129, 131, 191
Interests 5, 15, 18, 37, 88, 130f., 133
Intolerance 27, 30, 35

Jansen 45
Jealousy 28, 128
Jonas, Hans 62
Jouary, J. P 181
Jullien, François 158, 162
Jünger, Ernest 194f.
Justice 37, 39f., 114f., 145, 149

Kant 4, 16, 117
Kelsen, Hans 101
Knee, Philippe 27, 184f., 187
Knowledge 1, 11, 22, 27, 32, 47, 58–60, 62, 73, 96, 102, 115, 131, 153f., 161, 164, 168f., 172–176, 179, 191
Kofman, Sarah 156

La Mettrie, Julien Offray 67
Lacan, Jacques 121
L'Aminot, Tanguy 179, 188, 190, 194
Lane, Joseph H. Jr 69
Law 33, 38f., 41, 68, 74, 77, 92f., 105–107, 111–113, 115, 117, 128, 139–141, 143–147, 149f., 154, 172, 180, 182–185, 193, 195
Lawrence, David Herbert 193f.
Legislative power 105, 146
Legislator 37f., 42, 105, 107, 111, 117
Leopold, Stephen 57
Lévi-Strauss, Claude 2, 7, 11–25, 61, 120
Levinas, Emmanuel 90
Liberty 36, 39–42, 119, 122f., 132, 135, 138, 141f., 145, 147, 149

Limitation   73, 85, 92, 132, 134
Limited monarchy   181
Limits   15, 18, 51, 69, 87, 94, 97, 106, 116, 129, 145, 167, 191
Locke, John   30f., 41, 105, 107, 159, 163
Lojkine, Stéphane   45, 51
Love   5, 27, 31–33, 37, 41, 49, 52f., 55, 63, 80, 88, 99, 123, 125–129, 134, 148f., 153, 157, 160, 164, 182, 184, 188, 192f.
Löwenstein, Karl   106
Lucas, Paul   169
Lulle, Raymond   169

Machiavelli, Niccolo   101–106, 147, 149
Madison, James   104, 131f.
Magistracy   101, 103f., 108
Maistre, Joseph (de)   42
Malebranche, Nicolas   31f.
Manin, Daniele   103
Manipulation   38, 125, 127, 131, 158, 193f.
Marin, Louis   157f.
Maritain, Jacques   36
Martin, Christophe   153, 164
Marx, Karl   11, 14
Materialism   30f.
Maupertuis, Pierre Louis   67
Mauss, Marcel   20
McKenzie, Lionel A   102
Metaphysics of feeling   31
Miller, Donald F.   121
Mixed government   103f., 106f.
Mommsen, Theodor   103
Monadic individual   120
Monopolistic leadership   107
Monopoly   107
Montaigne, Michel   33f.
Montesquieu, Charles Louis de Secondat   27, 41, 119, 146, 149
Moral conscience   30
Moral inclination   33
Moral inequality   4, 40
Moral intuitions   111
Moral judgment   125
Moral rationalism   117
Moral thought   123
Morally good   32

Morgenstern, Mira   119, 121, 126–129, 131, 133f.
Morin, Edgar   179

Narcissistic   115
Natural feelings   32, 34, 40
Natural goodness   32
Natural justice   40
Natural man   1, 3f., 14, 29, 32, 47, 49, 60, 97, 122f., 125, 182, 185, 193
Nippel, Wilfried   103, 106
Norm   4, 29, 34, 36, 41, 145, 150, 157
Nouis, Lucien   167

Obedience   39–41, 75, 141, 145, 182, 187
Object of analysis   121
Offray de la Mettrie, Julien   67
Open deliberation   42
Ordini   105
Organ   94, 105, 145

Pascal, Blaise   27, 34, 39f., 80
Pasquino, Pasquale   101
Passions   1, 5, 27–29, 37, 46, 70, 77, 80, 86, 92, 95f., 117, 130f., 184, 194
Pastoral tribes   182
Patriotism   126, 149, 184
Pelagianism   27
Perfectibility   5, 28, 31, 60f.
Perrin, Jean-François   69, 78
Pharmakon   115
Pious fanaticism   30
Pity   5, 23f., 28, 32, 49, 60f., 72, 80, 121f., 126, 129, 149, 182
Plato   113f., 169
Pluche, Abbé   153, 163f.
Pluralistic   102–104
Pocock, J.G.A   104
Political authority   30, 38, 102
Political choice   123
Political education   40
Political imagination   30, 40
Political institutions   111–113, 137
Political legitimacy   41, 111
Political order   19, 39f., 106
Political sphere   123, 128, 131
Political transparency   41

Political world 39
Politics of Borders 128
Poppenberg, Gerhard 57
Popular sovereignty 36, 42, 111, 117
Positive religions 34, 36
Postigliola, Alberto 101
Power 13, 15f., 18, 24, 37, 39, 54, 57–60, 64, 68, 70, 75, 77f., 85–95, 97f., 103–107, 116, 121, 124f., 135, 138–140, 142–144, 146, 153, 162, 167, 169, 176, 182, 184, 190
Power allocations 119
Power of desire 86
Power-relationships 40
Power to act 85, 91f., 94f., 97f.i
Practical reason 33, 117
Pre-governmental State 121
Pre-moral 32
Present pleasure 31
Pride 28, 32, 46, 52, 186, 189
Primitive feeling 31
Private interest 113f., 116
Pufendorf, Samuel von 180

Rationalism 27, 30, 36, 117
Reconciliation 179
Religious symbols 37
Renaut, Alain 153
Republicanism 102, 104
Resistance 22, 70, 86, 103, 139
Rohault, Jacques 68
Roman Republic 102, 104, 149
Romantic love 124, 126, 128
Rousseau, Jean-Jacques 1–7, 11–17, 19–25, 27–42, 45–50, 52–54, 57–62, 64, 67–80, 85–98, 101f., 104–107, 111–117, 119–135, 137–139, 142–150, 154–157, 159, 161–164, 167–171, 173–176, 179–195
Rules of conduct 115

Sacralization 117
Sacred right 180
Sage 87f.
Saint-Bonnet, François 101f.
Sampieri, Jean-Christophe 50
Sartre, Jean-Paul 12f., 17f., 24

Saussure, Ferdinand (de) 11
Savage state 31
Schiller, Friedrich 70
Schmitt, Carl 101–103, 106f.
Schøsler, Jørn 159
Schumpeter, Joseph 107f.
Seduction 27, 164
Self-authorizing 111
Self-esteem 28
Self-foundation 42
Self-government 131
Self-gratification 126
Self-knowledge 31, 73, 79, 98
Self-legislating capacity 41
Self-love 2, 28, 32, 52, 60, 80, 87–92, 95–97, 99
Self-manipulation 125
Self-other dialectic 128
Self-preservation 5, 97, 126, 129
Self-reflection 122
Self-serving point of view 131
Self-sufficiency 60, 62, 74, 76, 87, 92
Semi-learned 40, 42
Sense experience 31
Shklar, Judith N 120
Sickness 3, 27
Signs 39, 135, 169f.
Simulacra of law 192f.
Sin 18, 28f., 31f., 40
Skepticism 27, 33, 36, 42
Social cohesion 121, 184, 190
Social conditions 29
Social cooperation 122
Social dissonances 127
Social life 3, 14–17, 20, 28f., 39
Social ranks 104
Social spheres 122
Socialization 29, 32, 122
Socrates 116
Source of morality 30
Sovereign 3, 12, 38, 52, 74, 111, 138–149, 183, 190, 195
Sovereign dictatorship 107
Sovereign power 105f., 144, 146
Sovereign reason 33
Spinoza 93

Starobinski, Jean 46f., 53, 120, 154, 162, 180
State of war 113, 116, 128, 179
Strength 38, 40, 42, 78, 85–90, 92, 94–96, 98f., 122, 148, 174f., 180, 183
Suarez 46
Submission 27, 33, 70, 141, 148, 182, 194
Subordinated power 106
Suffering 18, 28, 32, 89, 92, 95f., 99, 148
Supreme inequality 128

Talmon, Jacob L 120
Taylor, Charles 69
The Authority of nature 27
Thomist tradition 33
Tocqueville, Alexis (de) 150
Transcendence of civil religion 117
Transcending nature 119
Transparency of hearts 30
Transparent 38, 42, 134
Trousson, Raymond 195
True self 31

Universal good 32

Vargas, Yves 189f.
Vaughan, C.E. 101
Virtue 32f., 40, 42, 59f., 70–72, 74, 76, 86, 88f., 94, 98, 115, 145, 149f., 176, 183, 192, 194
Voice of God 30
Voice of nature 6, 29f., 34
Voltaire 27f., 35, 74, 111

Waterlot, Ghislain 192f.
Weakness 17, 58, 86–89, 91f., 94, 96, 98
Wealth 18, 27, 54, 63, 71, 128, 157, 180, 194
Will 18, 27–30, 33f., 36–38, 42, 68, 78, 80, 85, 88–91, 93–98, 111, 114–117, 131f., 138, 140, 142, 144f., 161, 184, 194
Will of all 131f., 145

Xiaoling, Wang 191

Yamashita, Masano 67

Zarka, Yves Charles 1, 46, 137, 146, 149

www.ingramcontent.com/pod-product-compliance
Lightning Source LLC
Chambersburg PA
CBHW021726220426
43662CB00008B/728